Colgate Darden:
Conversations with Guy Friddell

Colgate Darden:
Conversations with Guy Friddell

University Press of Virginia

Charlottesville

THE UNIVERSITY PRESS OF VIRGINIA
Copyright ⁽ᶜ⁾ 1978 by the Rector and Visitors
of the University of Virginia

First published 1978

Frontispiece: Photograph by Robert Llewellyn.

Library of Congress Cataloging in Publication Data

Friddell, Guy.
  Colgate Darden: conversations with Guy Friddell.

  Includes index.
  1. Darden, Colgate Whitehead, 1897- 2. Virginia—
Governors—Biography. 3. College presidents—Virginia—
Biography. 4. Virginia. University—Presidents—Biography.
I. Darden, Colgate Whitehead, 1897- joint author.
F231.D27F74   975.5′04′0924   78-7026
ISBN 0-8139-0744-6

Printed in the United States of America

To Pierre

Contents

Preface

Virginians hold Colgate Darden, Jr., in special regard. On the morning of a recent election an elementary school teacher telephoned the Darden home to find when he was going to vote at the precinct in her school's auditorium. Then she lined her fourth-graders at the windows to watch the tall, white-haired former governor of Virginia go to the polls.

When Darden speaks to college youths, they listen spellbound to the flow of humor, historical and literary allusions, prophetic judgments—and rise, invariably, to applaud the sage.

But he is an exceedingly active elder statesman. In 1959, when he retired after twelve years as president of the University of Virginia, behind him also lay two terms in the Virginia House of Delegates, four terms in the House of Representatives, four years as Virginia's governor during World War II, and tours of duty on the national scene that included service as a delegate to the United Nations. He was, he said, going home to rest.

Scarcely had he reached Crab Creek on the Elizabeth River before Governor Almond summoned him to a seat on the State Board of Education. Then Governor Harrison drafted him to lead in reopening Prince Edward County's public schools, and Governor Godwin assigned him to the Commission to Revise the Virginia Constitution on which he promoted a constitutional mandate for quality education.

He always is projecting to improve Virginia—and all the while declaring that there is no such thing as progress. In addition to continuous public service, he and Mrs. Darden help in numerous private charities. Infrequently, long after the deed, word of it leaks. For instance, each year that he was president of the University of Virginia, he turned back his salary.

Talking with him almost daily, listening as he brought the wisdom of the ages to bear on current events, marveling at the candor with which he described himself and others in the rough and tumble of politics, enjoying his humor rooted in rural Virginia, I yearned to share his recollections. For years he brushed aside the idea.

Finally, on a Saturday in December 1974, with high expectations on my part and deep skepticism on his, we sat down with a tape recorder for the first conversation. As it turned out, he enjoyed revisiting the boyhood fields of Southampton County. Thereafter, weekend after weekend for two years, the two of us, joined occasionally by my wife, Gin, talked. The scenes of his life—the exuberant boardinghouse at the University of Virginia, his feelings under the guns of Verdun, golden days at Oxford, entry into political tumult as a foot soldier in Harry Flood Byrd's campaign for governor, and the adventures of public service—unfolded smoothly on the bolt of memory.

There came a day when the talk had to stop. We had to reduce more than sixty interviews to thirty and cut nearly every interview by half. Here, too, the Governor was instructive. Asked whether we should leave out a paragraph, a page, or even a chapter, his usual response was: "Pitch it out! Pitch it out!" But if the proposed deletion contained some remark that was less than flattering to him, he said, "That must stay!" It was a lesson in objectivity.

Indeed, reviewing the manuscript, Professor Louis D. Rubin, Jr., of the University of North Carolina remarked, "Of all the major figures in Virginia politics, even including Harry Byrd, Darden's personality is best suited for this kind of commentary for there was always a kind of objectivity and detachment about him that accompanied the partisan role, and so he will come right out with things that other figures of perhaps equal importance would never say or perhaps even think."

As Benjamin Muse, the Republican who opposed him for governor in 1941, pointed out, Colgate Darden was not afraid to walk alone: "It is no mean compliment, even from a critic of the Byrd Organization to say of those generally able men who have led—and misled—Virginia during the past quarter century that Darden is the noblest Roman of them all. He never hesitated to follow his convictions."

This, then, is a conversational self-portrait of a man who followed his convictions. For advice and encouragement in putting it together, the Governor and I are indebted to Dr. Rubin, to Walker Cowen and Susan Lee Foard of the University Press of Virginia, and to our secretary, Dorothy Keefe of Norfolk.

Under my questioning the Governor took some paths he might not otherwise have followed, and, of course, left out persons, places, and things that would have appeared in a more orthodox memoir. One other thing. Laughter, so much a part of his life, interspersed these conversations.

GUY FRIDDELL

Norfolk
January 23, 1978

Colgate Darden:
Conversations with Guy Friddell

MY MOTHER LIVED IN ARTHUR'S COURT

F. To begin, Governor, let's talk about your boyhood.

D. It's very simple, just growing up on a big farm about four miles west of Franklin on what is now Route 58. It had been my mother's home, Marle Hill. My father was a North Carolinian whose grandfather had been a Virginian. All the Dardens started out in Virginia in Isle of Wight County about 1635. Brothers came there from England. My father married Katherine Pretlow and moved back to Virginia, but he got to be a more violent North Carolinian the longer he lived, and he lived to be an old man.

He got so tired of the bragging around about Virginia he could not put up with it. It was enormously oppressive to him. In the latter part of his life when I'd go by to see him and say: "Dad, I went to a very interesting meeting the other day out in Southwest Virginia and they had 1,500 or 2,000 people there," then he'd say: "I know that was interesting. I remember a similar occasion as a boy in North Carolina except they had a lot more people there than the crowd that you saw."

There wasn't anything you could tell him about Virginia that he hadn't witnessed or been a part of in Carolina on a much larger scale when he grew up. And while I know he was pleased that I should be governor of Virginia, the one thing that would have fixed him was had I been governor of North Carolina. While he was happy that I should be president of the University of Virginia, if I had been president of Chapel Hill, it would have been perfect!

About all they had to talk about when I was a boy was the War Between the States. I had great difficulty figuring out how the South, having won every battle, could possibly have lost the war. In an argument, when my father got sufficiently worked up, he would declare, "North Carolina left more men dead on the field at Gettysburg than Virginia sent there."

My father grew up in Mapleton, North Carolina, about three miles from Murfreesboro on the Murfreesboro-Winton Road, where his father and grandfather had operated a small school, Elm Grove Academy. All the Dardens, as far as I can gather, were very much opposed to the established church. They had to go along and pay whatever the colonies exacted of them until Jefferson freed them with his Statute for Religious Liberty, and then they popped over into the Baptist church, the Fundamentalists.

In the first half of the last century North Carolina saw enormous growth of little private schools, seminaries and academies of one kind or another. Some people teaching at the little school also were interested in Chowan College in Murfreesboro and had something to do with the founding of it. About the time the Baptists got Chowan College going, Elm Grove Academy began to die away.

My father didn't go to college, nor did any of his half-dozen brothers. It was a large family, and they were just struck down, as was everybody else, by the war. They had a good deal of land, but it was not profitable enough to support the offspring. They found their way into other things. One brother joined the navy as a boy. He used to come and tell us monstrous stories about his travels. He went around the world with the fleet in 1907. Another uncle told us that he had been to a moving picture and seen a newsreel of the sailors marching in Tokyo and there was his brother strutting along.

F.   Why did your father come to Virginia?

D.   He found employment with the Albemarle Steam Navigation Company which ran boats from the railhead at Franklin to Edenton on the Albemarle Sound and to Murfreesboro on the Meherrin River. He and mother lived at Edenton when they were first married and later moved to the company headquarters at Franklin. The line was owned by my mother's cousins.

Mother was born at Beechwood, the place which we still own. Her father, a farmer, had served in the War Between the States. Other members of her family were Quakers, but he was an Episcopalian. He died just a year or two before she married my father.

On the side my father operated the farm with the help of a good manager. We raised peanuts, cotton, and corn. Cotton has now almost disappeared, but peanuts have always been a backbone crop. Cash was hard to come by, but we had a great vegetable garden and hogs and cattle. The population around there had more than ample food and needed only a little cash to buy clothes, sugar, and coffee.

F. Where did your mother go to school?

D. She and her three sisters were educated by a governess hired by her uncle Sam Pretlow for his three daughters. He was a Quaker, and the most prosperous of the brothers. My mother's father had gone off to the war and his affairs were in nothing like as good order. But Sam Pretlow was, I believe, one of the largest landowners in Southampton County. He lived some distance away, eight or ten miles, which was right much in those days. His three daughters, who were so good to me, went to live in a lovely home in Franklin after his death. After being taught with her Uncle Sam's children, my mother went to college at the Episcopal Female Institute in Winchester. Then she taught in public school.

After they married, my father continued for a time to work for the steamboat company and then he moved over to farming entirely. The coming of good roads disestablished the freight handling on the rivers into Carolina. The trucks took it over. When he was working on the ships, he'd sometime take me with him. The ship would put into a farmer's wharf and pick up some cotton or peanuts and then go along a few miles to another place and pick up some goods and put some off.

F. It sounds almost like colonial times.

D. It was the end of the colonial system in a way. In those days ships went out of Norfolk and traded up the Pagan River to Smithfield, up the James, up the York, and up the Rappahannock and other rivers. From Franklin they traded down to the Albemarle Sound. They were 230-foot boats, powered by coal-fired boilers, and built to carry freight of any description and a few passengers. Traffic flourished on the rivers for many years, and then it ended with the coming of the trucks.

My mother also was fearfully busy. Although she had servants to help her in the house, she ran the garden, supervised the preservation of the meat in the smokehouse, saw that the little dairy house was in order, and looked after the twelve or fifteen colored families that worked and lived on the place.

F. How were public schools in your youth?

D. Quite good, really, in Franklin. The high school was just coming into being then. The offerings were limited, but the teachers drilled you over and over in English, geography, history, and arithmetic. Many children didn't go to school and many didn't attend a full year. They were home working on the farms.

During this time an event of enormous consequence was the establishment of the RFD, the Rural Free Delivery, which was a revolutionary influence. It made just a totally different world. With the advent of the RFD, there also came a publication called *The Youth's Companion*. It was the greatest magazine ever published, in my opinion. I'd watch for that just like you'd watch for some unbelievable event. The postman would come by and stick it in the box a mile away, and I'd go fetch it. In the beginning my mother read it to me, and I think she enjoyed the stories as much as I did. Later we added another magazine, *American Boy*. As time went on, I reached the point that I read them by myself, but all of it went back to my mother's love of reading. She was never too busy to stop and read to me.

She lived, largely, in the world of Walter Scott and other romanticists. She loved to read Malory's *Morte d'Arthur*. She was as familiar with King Arthur's Court as you are with this living room. It was in Camelot that she lived, actually, although she was sitting out there on a farm in Southampton County. She knew Scott's *The Lady of the Lake* inside and out. She knew his novels, and she read many of them to me.

     F.   Did she read to you at any particular time?

     D.   Most any time. Any time we'd sit down. You have no idea how leisurely country life moved along in those days. It wasn't easy, by any means. There was a lot of work, but we were living out there in the country away from anybody or anything, and there were far fewer distractions. It would be like living in the Rocky Mountain foothills now. Occasionally somebody would come jogging past on the road but not very often. Sometimes hours would pass, and nobody would go by. You'd see them moving about the fields where they were working around on the farm, but the house was all to itself. It was left open at night. Nobody ever thought of locking any doors at night, just went to bed. Never occurred to you that anybody was going to be wandering around stealing. And if you were going into town, you'd be away most of the day, but even so you didn't lock up the house. You just left it. Can you imagine that now?

And in that solitude we read. We read Cooper's *Leatherstocking Tales* by the hour. Who was the great Indian leader . . . Deerfoot? Oh, my gracious! We used to wander through the woods up there in New York, the Mohawk Valley, where you'd jump if you heard the birds squeak in the tree, thinking that was right in the middle of an Indian entrapment of one kind or another. And my mother took full part in it. She wasn't just reading to me. She lived it.

I grew up with Uncle Remus. My mother knew the stories, and we'd read and reread Uncle Remus's carryings-on and refer to them around the house. She had Macaulay's *Essays* and she used to talk and read about Edmund Burke's condemnation of Hastings in Parliament at which the women who were attending the trial wept and fainted and fell about. His summation against the British rule in India and how terrible it had been are very moving lines. I couldn't repeat them to save my life although I have read them many times since. She just popped it right off.

She loved to recite. The selections that I remember best were from Scott and then the Death of Arthur. She could go till your blood just tingled, really, when she told of the return of Excalibur to the lake. What was the name of the fellow to whom Arthur handed the sword when he was dying? Bedivere! Arthur ordered him to hurl it into the lake. Twice Sir Bedivere went to the shore but couldn't bring himself to throw the sword in the water. Arthur was dying and each time he told him to go back and on the third time Bedivere hurled it out over the water in the frosty night and out of the lake came this arm, clothed in white samite, whatever samite is, and reached in the air and seized the sword by the hilt before it touched the water and drew it under.

F. I believe he flourished it and drew it under.

D. Yes, I think that's true. Yes, sure he did. You know mighty well Malory wouldn't have let him just pull it under. He had to have him flourish it around two or three times.

But the passage she loved more than anything else was in *The Lady of the Lake*. Roderick Dhu in disguise led his enemy, James Fitz-James, through his own lines. Then in a barren, rocky glen where nobody saw anybody, Dhu gave out a whistle and clansmen simply sprang out of the earth and he said, "These are Clan-Alpines' warriors true and Saxon—I am Roderick Dhu!" All the time Fitz-James had been telling him how he was going to catch Roderick Dhu and what he was going to do to him. Well, Mama could get herself worked up to a point of excitement that when she got to Roderick Dhu and he whistled, it was just every man for himself! Ah, Lord. Well, you know what it was when I can remember it after these seventy years.

F. Isn't it unusual that a woman should appreciate what was basically masculine poetry?

D. It is essentially the age of the romantics, don't you see? And I think women probably enjoy that more than men do.

F. Yes, sir, but I'm thinking about today's feminism and there's not much place for women in *The Lady of the Lake,* despite the title.

D. To understand its attraction you must know the times. We had a big farm and we were comfortable and with plenty to eat, but in the backwash of Reconstruction there was deep deprivation and poverty. It wasn't so noticeable because everybody was deprived. I think it's a matter of comparison in the world. If you live in an age in which everybody lives about the same, you don't notice it so much.

And my mother simply moved to another world. Roads were poor, but she transported herself to another age. She only occasionally got back home to look around Southampton County and worry about the trouble and illness among the people who lived on our farm and worked for us. Books took her through exceedingly hard years that were endured by all. She bought books in town, and she had another source of supply because her younger sister, Mary Denson Pretlow, had gone to New York as a girl to work in the public library. She'd buy books and send them down to Mother. In the last forty years of her life my aunt was a librarian in Norfolk. The Pretlow Library in Ocean View is named for her.

Occasionally my mother attended meetings of the Franklin Book Club. It was a get-together time. There were not enough of those occasions when I was a child. There are too many of them now.

F. How many children were in the family?

D. The ones that are here now. My sister Katherine, two years younger than I am, and my brother Pretlow, seven years younger. All of us are living within a half mile of each other in Norfolk.

F. So all that reading helped set your course?

D. It had a great deal to do with setting my course, and it added immeasurably to the pleasure of my life. In the olden days I could read for hours at a time. Nowadays, of course, Connie has to read to me a good deal because of my failing eyesight.

F. Your sister Katherine remembers reading Howard Pyle's version of Robin Hood to your brother Pretlow. When she reached the last chapter and said, "And now we come to tell the death of Robin Hood, and those little children who do not wish to read about it may end the story here," your brother went upstairs to his room. Pretlow, she said, used to dress up like Robin Hood.

D. I have no doubt that is true because that's somewhat like him. He is quite an emotional sort of fellow, and he could well imagine himself as Robin Hood.

F. He said he thought he was Robin Hood and called a little colored boy Little John.

D. That colored boy was named Shag. He and Pretlow were great friends. He lived on our place. And I remember Pretlow telling me a year or two ago that this nice looking colored person came up and spoke to him and said, "I'm Little John!" And then, when Pretlow looked puzzled, he said, "Don't you know me? This is Shag!"

F. Your sister remembers that your mother used to sit on the porch in the twilight and recite favorite passages.

D. She did. And she did something else which I think is even more interesting. She'd sit on the porch in the twilight and look at the tree line across the road in a large field in front of our house, an open field of about 100 acres; it is flat, deadly flat country, but my mother used to sit there and talk about that view. I never could see anything particularly spectacular in it, but she did.

F. She remembers your mother saying that the black people had learned something nobody else had ever learned before and that was how to live on nothing. Of all the duties your mother had, the ones that weighed the heaviest concerned the black people on the farm.

D. Oh, it was by all odds. She drove herself unbelievably. Occasionally when one was sick we could get a doctor from town, but in most cases she prepared the medicine and looked after them and went to their homes to see how they were getting along

and if they were getting enough food. She had a very great capacity
to appraise and counsel and advise and carry them along. In all of
her dealings she was steadfast in her convictions and temperate in
her judgments. For instance, she was a stout member of the WCTU,
but not a prohibitionist.

      F.   Was she a strongly religious person?

      D.   Oh, yes; but she wasn't a zealot. There wasn't
any fuzzy thinking about her in that.

      F.   Your sister's recollection is that after the war
the landed gentry didn't have the training or disposition to do anything but what it had been doing before the war.

      D.   What she's talking about there is the tremen-
dous cost of slavery. But for the importation of slave labor there
would have developed in the South a different type of life entirely.
Waves of North Europeans, arising out of the political disorders
of 1848, would have come to the South, but rather than compete
with slave labor they moved to the cities and westward.

In those days land was the basis of wealth in the South. I saw it
with my father. Land was almost like a drug to him. He'd rather
own a piece of land than anything else in the world. That was the
one thing that insured independence. He was always buying land
and frequently overextending himself.

What was happening in his lifetime and to a degree in the early
part of my lifetime was the transition of the South from an agrarian
to an industrial economy. It was all agrarian as he grew up. That's
the only living that people knew. They ordered their affairs on that
basis. The men cured the meat, and their wives canned vegetables
and fruits. Consequently, the great change, and I saw it in the full,
was a transition, with halting steps, it's true, but into an industrial
economy that gained ground rapidly with the First World War,
when Europe drew on us so heavily for supplies. Really what Franklin Roosevelt referred to as the arsenal of democracy during World
War II had taken place much earlier when the United States became not only an arsenal but also a granary for Europe. It was in
1914–18 that the page was turned.

      F.   Isn't it amazing that what amounts to the Old
Virginia of colonial times is as close to us as that?

      D.   It is not so close. That's seventy years ago we
are talking about. That isn't any time in the history of a nation but

after all very few now living remember those days. Most of them are gone.

It was the final transition. I remember I watched road building when I was a child. My father joined in with neighbors and they built a direct road into Franklin, a much shorter one than the old road that we'd used. And that brought another far-reaching change in our lives.

I saw the beginning of the transportation of school children and the building of central schools to get away from little one-roomers. Now I didn't go to the school that was built near us because my father thought that the school I was attending in Franklin was as good, or better, and he didn't want to change us to a new school although I think the school officials put considerable pressure on him to have me go. It would have been convenient because the children rode to and from school in what was called a kiddie car, an awkward, trucklike vehicle drawn by horses. It came close to our home, but my father maintained that the school in Franklin was to his liking.

We drove a little horse and buggy. I'd take my brother and sister back and forth with me, although frequently she stayed with relatives in Franklin, especially in bad weather. Before they were old enough to go to school, I rode horseback. The roads were none too good in winter. It was not anything like as easy as you'd think in driving because in Southampton there were a couple of red clay hills between my house and Franklin. It's hard to notice them now. They have been graded out for cement roads, and you pass over them hardly realizing that in the old days they were fierce.

What marked the schools was the teachers' insistence on thoroughness. It wasn't any question of "well, you'll figure this out for yourself." You did it with them. They drilled you day after day after day. And then, of course, back in those days they questioned you in class. Made you answer up in public. And you felt very stupid when you couldn't answer.

Our extracurricular activities were limited. We had a good deal of playing at recess time. We had what we called little recess at eleven o'clock and then at about noon a big break for dinner. Then we'd come back and stay until four o'clock in the afternoon, and it was dark in the wintertime driving home.

Five or six of us from the country didn't go home to lunch. We

had to eat what we'd brought in a little paper bag or a tin lunch
box that our mothers had fixed up for us. We'd assemble in one
room near a big stove. They kept the rooms overheated. We'd sit
around there and eat our lunch, which was a fairly quick operation, although the lunch was ample.

The one great thing I relied on was sweet potato. I always had a
full sweet potato my mother fixed for me. And then some other
things, a slice of ham and a biscuit perhaps; but always there was
a sweet potato because I counted on it heavily. As the winter went
on they were sweeter and sweeter as they cured in the sweet potato
hills at home. After lunch we'd go out and play, and I'd feed and
water Star, my horse, in a little stable on the school property that
formerly had been part of a female seminary. We'd have forty-five
minutes or more playing outside before the town children returned.

When the time came to go to college I was strongly aimed at going
to the College of William and Mary, largely because a friend of
mine, Will Shands, who lived a few miles away in Courtland, had
gone there and liked it very much. And then for some reason my
father decided in the fall of 1914 that he was going to send me to the
University of Virginia right off, and that was that!

He had a great many problems because of the collapse of the
cotton market during the war in Europe. Cotton declined to a point
you couldn't sell it. So throughout the United States there was a
move to buy a bale of cotton just in token of support of the southern
states that were crucified by what amounted to a German embargo,
with the merchant ships all afraid to move in the Atlantic. Cotton
lasts indefinitely after it's ginned, and people put a bale in store
windows to show they were helping to carry the load. A few years
later farmers had an era of comparative prosperity because of its
sale for gun cotton, uniforms, and other supplies, but when I went
to the university cotton was in a deep hollow.

   F. Was your father involved in politics?

   D. Yes, he was a red-hot politician. He was the
county registrar for some years until he failed of reappointment
owing to his rigid interpretation of the new State Constitution. He
was part of the old Martin organization. Its members believed
firmly, as did those in the Virginia Organization following them,
that unless you belonged to the order, you were not qualified to

govern. It was protecting the Commonwealth against the unquali-
fied, composed largely of people who disagreed with them. He had
strong opinions and was an avid daily newspaper reader. He had
to know the whole thing. He got his paper every day, and it was a
Norfolk paper.

He also supplemented his information by being a regular attend-
ant at court day. The courthouse was everything. The old court day
which came periodically in Virginia was a meeting time for everybody. We would gather up in Courtland and swap yarns and carry
on at a great rate and keep abreast of events.

      F. Your sister says your father encouraged you all
to think there was nothing you couldn't do.

      D. He was applying it to his own family, but he
believed that there was nothing that anybody couldn't do if he really
set himself to it; that if a person cried his holt and did his work, he
could accomplish anything.

      F. Did what, Governor?

      D. Just cried your holt. You are bound to have
known that as an old Virginia expression. You cried your holt when
you grabbed hold to something. That means you've really come to
grips with it like a terrapin that won't turn loose until it thunders.

      F. She remembers that your father didn't want
you hunting with anyone except himself.

      D. He wanted me hunting by myself or with him
because he was afraid that in the excitement some other boy would
shoot me or I'd shoot somebody. He was quite a hunter in certain
seasons. They were great days. We used black powder. You could
take a twelve-gauge shotgun and go down to a ridge in the woods
where there were hickory trees and, and course, in the early fall
squirrels were up there just thick. They were cutting out mast and
you would draw bead on a squirrel way up in a tree and fire and
then absolutely disappear in a swirl of black smoke. You could
not see five feet away from you, and you had to wait and listen to
hear if the squirrel fell out of the tree to know whether you had
killed him. You couldn't see up to him at all because the black
smoke had just wiped out everything.

      F. She said that you loved to take apart the family
car.

      D. I spent hours on that. Not to its profit and not

to mine, but I fancied myself as a mechanic of the first order. I worked on it no end, and I incurred the ill will of the rest of them because I had it down working on it when they wanted to go for a ride. So she would remember that well.

F. She said you would dismantle the entire motor, take it apart piece by piece, lay it all out on the grass, and then put it together again.

D. I never went that far, but I was fairly good for an amateur. I can assure you of that. I also developed a vulcanizing system for repairing tires that was really before its day. Yes, I did. That was the era in which you went for an automobile ride and you spent as much time patching tires on the road as you did riding in the car. You were an undoubted success if in a four-hour trip you didn't spend over half of the time patching tires.

F. She said that your father couldn't drive and that you drove him.

D. Never drove in his life, nor did he make any attempt to learn. He was absolutely unconcerned about it. But he was right sizable on direction. He could sit down there by you and tell you when, where, and how to go. Then, of course, back in those days we didn't go on many trips. Coming to Norfolk was a monumental thing. Be like going to the moon today. But he'd get a map and sit down beside you and he'd figure out everything and give you directions. I was just like a sailor down here steering a ship under the eye of a quartermaster, telling him exactly what to do. That's the way I maneuvered. I think probably we made one trip to Raleigh, which was almost unheard of.

F. You were very patient with him, she said.

D. I don't know about being patient with him, but I know he was in complete charge and authority. He drove vicariously and enjoyed it.

F. Did he go with you to Charlottesville?

D. He went with me because he was positive I couldn't get there by myself. I was just seventeen years old. I had been away from home only once or twice. I had gone to New York once. It was a monstrous journey with my aunt who came home on a vacation and took me up there for a visit. Oh, my God! I never saw such stuff. She and some other girls who worked in the library had an apartment down on Twenty-third Street. They'd leave me there with the maid when they went to work and then they'd take me to a show at night.

Then my other venture would be to go to Staunton. We'd move up from this malaria belt for a month in the summer and, as we called it, "go to the mountains." That's what people in Tidewater would talk about. And it apparently did some good. Although I was a victim of malaria and had a terrible time with it, I think even in my case it helped some. And that was the extent of my travels other than as a very little person when my father took me to Chattanooga with him on a business trip when he was a claim adjuster for the Albemarle Steam Navigation Company. He took me up on Lookout Mountain and I never forgot it because I looked down in the valley and saw the trains. I thought they were toy trains, the sort you got at Christmas that were propelled by a big spring. You'd wind up the engine and it would scoot along a track. And I was after him to buy me one so I could take it home from Chattanooga. Gave him no end of trouble about that. I went back a few years ago on top of the mountain and looked down in the valley and actually the trains do still look small.

And so I think he felt positive if he turned me loose that I would never get to the university in Charlottesville. I remember sitting in Norfolk waiting with him for the call of the C&O boat to take us to the train in Newport News. We'd come down from Franklin on the Seaboard or Southern to catch a little passenger steamer, the *Virginia*, built for the C&O. They advertised it as being the fastest little ship on the bay, and she was, in truth, a speedy little thing. The engines were powerful and the master knew her so well he could shoot her in and out and whip her around just as though she was a toy. It would go flashing across the Hampton Roads to Newport News.

And while we were waiting in Norfolk for the boat, a colored fellow would come through the station bawling out the stops. He'd call Newport News, Lee Hall, Williamsburg, Windsor Shades, Providence Forge—it's all been abandoned now—and finally Richmond. Then from Richmond he'd run up Mineral, Louisa, and Gordonsville, where you used to get chicken lunches, and, finally, Charlottesville. It was brought home to me years later. I was waiting in the airport in London on the way to an educational conference in India and this fellow came in and started bellowing out the stations. One of them was a short stop across the Channel into Brussels and the next stop was some place like Rome or Athens. Then he called Constantinople, Damascus, Karachi, and Delhi. Here that fellow had spanned at least 5,000 or 6,000 miles, calling out the stops of these planes, but it didn't impress me half so much as the 150 miles getting up to Charlottesville. It seemed to me we were going to the ends of the earth.

BILL JONES AND THE CHICKEN BONES

D. I think my father picked out my classes at the University of Virginia in 1914. He talked to the registrar. I know he picked my rooming house, for which I have always felt a deep debt. In shopping around among places to live, he landed me down with Miss Lelia Smith on Fourteenth Street. That was a low rent area, $2 or $3 a month lower than Madison Lane in the central part of the university. Those of us with Miss Lelia boarded at $13 or $14 a month.

She was one of the greatest people I've ever known. She was a chubby person, very mobile in her expression, and just as genial, generous, and kind as could be. She always took our side. Whatever we did, she understood. Twenty-five boys took their meals at her place. Many were living up in the university. As a matter of fact, I moved up on the Lawn after a year, but I continued to board with Miss Lelia.

Oh, it was grand! She gave us everything in the world to eat. She couldn't have made any money, even as cheap as food was in those days, because we were always hungry. As sure as there's a heaven, she's got a place there. There isn't any question in my mind about that. She's thoroughly ensconced, waiting for the rest of us to get over there, and I'm sure she is expecting we'll be there. She's probably going to be disappointed, but she won't rest until we're all there.

I kept in touch with her until she died. Last time I saw her, two or three weeks before I took office as governor, I spent the afternoon with her in the Confederate Home in Richmond where she was living in retirement. We laughed and talked about the university the whole afternoon. We had the time of our lives. She had that same spirit, she hadn't lost any of it.

She had a great collection on Fourteenth Street. There were Pat Callaway, a fine pitcher, Jack Davenport, Gilbert Campbell, and

Bill Jones. Bill was the son of Congressman William A. Jones, a leader in the old days of the political opposition to the Virginia Organization. Bill was champion wrestler in the university, and the thing that I remember best was a skill he developed at meals.

We sat at two long tables in the dining room and Bill sat about halfway down one table facing the wall. On the wall was a long picture of the Colosseum. It must have been six feet long and two feet high. Suspended by wires from a molding around the top of the room, it leaned out just a little with the bottom resting against the wall. Bill would sit there eating fried chicken, and instead of leaving the bones on his plate he'd flick them up and over behind the Colosseum. He did that with complete abandon and with great accuracy. He never missed! He was the envy of all of us. It went on for months, and then one day the thing gave way with a cascade of chicken bones all over the dining room floor. Those dry bones rattled and charged and recharged across the floor.

Not only had he picked the bones clean, but they had dried, you see, with the months that he had them on storage, building up his supply. The floor was highly waxed and they just cascaded across—zoom!—as though you turned loose a flood of water right out all over the floor.

Bill never said a word. He never admitted to any liability in reference to it and wondered along with the rest of us how in the world the bones ever got behind the picture. Listen, you'd think he didn't know how in the world the thing came about.

The second year I lived at 21 West Lawn next to Professor Charles Kent's pavilion. He was an austere professor of English and an awful good one, and very tolerant because God knows he put up with enough noise from us down the Lawn. But we never heard a peep from him.

        F.   Was there much extracurricular activity?

        D.   Yes. I loved sports—football, baseball, track, all of 'em—but I was not good at any of 'em. The school was just run over with fraternities. They dominated the life of the university. A few weeks after I arrived, I joined Phi Gamma Delta. My cousin had been a member. Not until much later did I sense the unfairness of a social situation in which the nonfraternity man was regarded as an outsider.

F.   Was there any particular professor you liked very much?

D.   Oh, there were a number that I liked. They differed in their methods, but all were very good. C. Alfonso Smith, we used to call him C. Alf, went later to the Naval Academy as a professor of English. I tell you, you are picking up old times!

There was Professor Thomas Fitzhugh who taught us Latin and who lived down the Lawn a little ways from me. Dr. Fitzhugh had a curious theory of Latin rhythm that he called the Sacred Tripudium. It was a beat of three. It didn't make any sense to any of us, but we fell into it very rapidly because we had sense enough to know that unless we agreed with it we would never graduate from the University of Virginia. You had to have Latin or Greek for your degree. If you elected Latin, you didn't become a graduate of the University of Virginia unless you were a Sacred Tripudium man. It was just that simple. We fell into it. Not one of us ever understood it.

I, for one—and I prize this very highly—lived long enough to hear him say it didn't amount to anything. The admission came about in this way. When I went to the University of Virginia as president, Dr. Fitzhugh was living in retirement and, sitting in an armchair, he would receive visitors in the afternoon. His wife Trudy, a gentle, nice person, was still living.

A. K. Davis, a professor of English and a classmate of mine back in Dr. Fitzhugh's time, said to me one day, "Let's go out and see Uncle Tom this afternoon." I said, "Fine, suits me." So we went out in the late afternoon, had a little drink of some kind, and A. K. said, "Uncle Tom, we were talking about the Sacred Tripudium."

"Yes," he said, "there was nothing to it, nothing but a fraud." He said, "I learned years later there wasn't anything to it."

So, going back to the university, I said to A. K., "Isn't any question about it, he's a very distinguished person, but it took him a number of years to discover what every one of us knew in the first two weeks we were in the class."

I had in physics one of the best teachers I ever saw in my life, Llewellyn Hoxton. His brother ran Episcopal High School for years. Dr. Hoxton's patience was inexhaustible in explaining physics. He saw that I was struggling mightily just to keep up because that was the big league for me. He had no end of little stories with which he'd illustrate his lecture. He'd go along for a while and then he'd tell us a story which would bring the class back to life. It kept us always interested and he was very mild and gentle.

Only once did I ever hear him get at all excited and that was much later. He and I were friends for years after that. A little before I went up to Charlottesville as president, a bill in the General Assembly for higher faculty salaries got bogged down, and I was sitting here in Norfolk one day and the phone rang and it was Dr. Hoxton. He said, "I'd like for you to go up to Richmond and talk to the governor and get this bill out for the university." I said, "Dr. Hoxton, I haven't got any authority up in Richmond. There isn't anything I can do up there. I just don't have the authority." He said, "Like hell you haven't!" He said, "You get on up there, and see him and get something done about it!" That's the only time I ever heard him lapse into that kind of positiveness. Otherwise he was very gentle.

      F.   He knew better, didn't he, when you said you couldn't help?

      D.   He knew there wasn't a damn word of truth to it.

Ellis Tucker taught me mathematics. He was very good. We always had a lot of fun with Ellis because he would go to the board to demonstrate something in mathematics and he'd say, "I'll draw you a picture of it." And he would draw a triangle or whatever it was. He wasn't a good drawer, but he'd make it out to where we could understand what he was talking about.

I joined the class in astronomy rather than take advanced mathematics. I wasn't much on mathematics, but the astronomy was enormously interesting because Professor S. A. Mitchell would take us out and let us peep into a small six-inch telescope set up on Dawson's Row. Then once or twice during the year he'd take us up to the big telescope on Observatory Mountain and let us lie down in the cradle and put our eyes up and peer into space. It just brought the heavens right down to us. I learned a lot about stars. I'm not in the league with Connie. She's got a far better idea of them than I ever had, but it's been fabulously interesting to me ever since I realized how inconsequential this planet of ours is in the whole hierarchy and galaxy.

Oh, life was very leisurely then. The world seemed to be absolutely established! Nobody dreamed that the British Empire would ever be impaired or that the Russian czars would ever change. It was a set, full world. The German war was a diversion, but it seemed that the Germans would be beaten in a little while. And then when Christmas came on and they had reached for Paris and the world settled into a grim understanding of what was going on, you saw the change start. The whole thing which we had grown up with and were so sure about we saw was insecure. We didn't see it was crumbling. We didn't see that far ahead. But I imagine it's the same feeling that people have when earth tremors take place, in that they have a growing uneasiness.

F.   You enjoyed college thoroughly, didn't you?

D.   Oh, I enjoyed it immensely, but I had a desperately hard time, largely because, as I look back on it, I really didn't know how to study effectively. I was the first fellow who had been there from our high school. How in the world I stayed is beyond me. I was just beyond my depths, floundering around. I figured once I had spent five hours every day on Latin.

I was at the university two full academic years. I went in the summer of '14, and then I left at the end of the school year in '16 and went with the American Field Service to drive ambulances with the French.

F.   What was the atmosphere at the university as the war in Europe intensified?

D.   An extraordinary one of crusading. We had a firm belief that we were going to end war. After we entered the war, the Germans were referred to as Huns. We were engaged in stopping an assault on Western civilization and in eliminating war as a means of settling human differences. We believed it. The country believed it. There were many songs and good ones that expressed this spirit. None of that appeared in the Second World War, as I remember it.

But when I went with the ambulances, we were going out of the American colleges as volunteers to pay what we conceived to be a debt to France for having pulled us out of the drink here at Yorktown. It was a period of great romanticism, really. It was a world that was created in considerable part by skillful propagandists, because the horror stories that were circulated about the Germans were blood chilling. They were later investigated by a high-level British commission. I saw the study while I was at Oxford with a son of a commission member. Not a single one of the charges made against the German army and its General Staff was substantiated. But the propaganda created in this country somewhat the same sentiment, I imagine, that launched the Crusades in Europe.

With us it was a mass enthusiasm for the right, in a way. We thought we were going to create heaven on earth. We were going to get away from despotism and from the oppression the German militarism represented. It was deeply inculcated in the American people, and it alleviated the hardship in the armed services. We believed that we were in the service of humanity and of God.

F.   It was poor history to call them Huns, wasn't it?

D.   That's right, but nobody paid any attention—as they frequently do not, even now, to the facts in a case. It set in with a soul-gripping enthusiasm, an unbelievable belief in the coming of the Golden Age.

F.   Why did you volunteer for ambulance service?

D.   A very simple thing, it was then. It seemed to me that this war was a final gamble by the Western Powers to check Germany in what was its determination to create a world empire. And then, too, it was by no means certain the United States was going to join in. Young people thought that this was a bid of the militarists and that if it could be put down we might move into a period of eternal peace. We were far too trusting.

F.   Was it so unrealistic? Suppose we had supported the League of Nations?

D.   Yes, the gesture was there, and I think it's probably something that we've got to come back to. The United Nations and the League of Nations have been bitterly disappointing, but I don't believe there is any way of undergirding world peace without concerted action by the great powers. And it has to be action by people genuinely devoted to peace, who are not trying to grab the instrumentality to advance their own selfish interests. Before World War II the League of Nations could have stopped Mussolini when he assaulted Ethiopia had it been willing to embargo oil. The Italians had none. Their army had been mechanized and it traveled on oil, but not one country dared touch them. The League passed pious resolutions opposing what the Italians were doing. You can imagine how effective that was with Mussolini and the crowd of army officers surrounding him. Haile Selassie warned the League that if he went down under the Fascist assault they would ultimately end the same way.

        F.   So you went to France in 1916 to save the world?

        D.   Three of us—Douglas Bolling, Clark "Plug" Lindsay, who later ran the Charlottesville *Progress,* and I—hit on the plan of joining the ambulance service with Bobby Gooch, a Rhodes Scholar at Oxford who had been driving with the French and was home on leave. We four set forth on the old *Chicago* and slipped out of the harbor of New York, no lights, off to this great adventure.

NEVER SUCH SLAUGHTER

D. From Bordeaux we went to Paris and after ten days to sections along the front, Plug Lindsay and I to Section One at Verdun, Gooch and Bolling to Four. When we arrived in July 1916, the horror of that front was unbelievable. The assault on Verdun had been scheduled to start on February 11, 1916, but a snowstorm delayed it for a week. It opened with a heavy shell that crashed in the yard of the Bishop's Palace at Verdun.

The Germans came in mass formation, a green tide that moved across the landscape, blown apart by the French 75s, and then the conflict settled down to trench warfare. The French held just in front of Verdun, and there the stalemate lasted. Attacks and counterattacks, usually at night, went on for months, the seizing of a small segment or a little salient. They couldn't get the dead out, and a sickening sweet smell of rotting bodies hung over the battlefield. The lines disappeared. There was nothing but shell holes, and the rains came, and filled them with water. On both sides, 1,100,000 disappeared, taken prisoner or killed, along those eighteen miles. There never has been such slaughter. It went on in savagery for ten months until the end of the year, when the Germans saw they couldn't break through. Then, too, pressure was mounting on another part of the front. The cost was just prohibitive. Both sides ground their armies to death there.

We arrived in July. Ambulance drivers for Section One were quartered at a lovely place called Château Billemont, headquarters of a large quarrying operation across the main highway. After some instruction we started driving. It consisted in going up that main highway over which the French supplied the troops at Verdun. It passed through Verdun and crawled a mile or two up a range of hills, beyond which were the Germans. That range was covered with French 75s, which is, I believe, the finest gun ever made. It fired almost like a revolver. It was extraordinarily accurate. It didn't jar itself out of place. The recoil mechanism was awfully good. The French fired it with great rapidity. At night the sides of the hills came alive with intermittent flashes as though electric switches were being thrown off and on. Areas on the hillsides would blaze up, go down dark, and blaze up again. The Germans were firing back trying to knock out the French batteries, and also knock out the road we used.

You couldn't drive on it in the daytime because the Germans had balloon observers high enough in the air so that they could look over behind our lines, just as the French were peeping over into their lines from balloons. The Germans blasted away at the road. Soon as night closed in, we started going up to get the wounded. Couldn't carry a light. There were no lights on the cars, ambulances, or trucks. The French ammunition trucks came helling down the road, not paying any attention to anybody, and you either got off or they'd run over you. Just feverish activity the night through until dawn. The day brought an eerie silence broken by occasional gunfire. The French put hundreds of prisoners to repairing the road under the fire of the German guns.

F. Tell me the story about the eccentric shell.

D. We were camped at Verdun, just back of the city but forward of heavy French guns that had been brought on rail cars from the fleet. They were firing over our heads at German positions around the forts of Douamont and Vaux. No end of crows were flying over the battlefield. Didn't make any difference how heavy the firing was or what. They went back and forth.

Several of us were standing looking at the heavy guns firing. If you stood in line and trained your eyes you could pick out the big shells as they arced over toward the Germans. I had picked out this shell and was following it along when the shell seemed to turn at a right angle—just flipped around and went off sharply. Most extraordinary thing!

For a second or two it baffled me. What had happened, the shell had picked up in its wake a crow that was flying across there, sucked it in, and turned it over two or three times. Didn't hit the crow, didn't kill it, but flipped it around two or three times. The crow righted itself and flew off at a right angle. For a short time it seemed to me that the impossible had happened—that this big shell had turned ninety degrees on its course.

In the fall of 1916 we went to a quieter area at La Grange aux Bois in the Argonne Forest. Not far away at Champagne, the French had been preparing for a major offensive. The Germans anticipated their plan and struck hard at the buildup and broke it up. Casualties were so heavy the French were afraid to move them through the country because of the effect on civilian morale; they simply piled up the wounded in hospitals near the front. The lines stabilized, and we were kept busy caring for the wounded from the artillery duel which continued along the front.

      F.   How would you characterize your companions?

      D.   They were college boys, generous and outgoing—idealists, romanticists maybe. There wasn't anything selfish about them. They believed deeply in another world that wasn't about to be born. The French appreciated our being there and after the service at Verdun cited our unit for bravery under fire.

We were attached to the Thirty-Second French Infantry and we were commanded by Lieutenant Robert de Kersauson, who had fought with the Boers in the South African War and of whom Jan Smuts had said if he'd had ten thousand De Kersausons, he would have been in London.

In the winter after we were settled at La Grange aux Bois, malaria popped out on me. The French sent me to the American Hospital at Neuilly, a suburb of Paris. At first the doctors couldn't find a trace of it, but after a second round of testing they reported that I had a deeper malarial infection than they'd ever encountered. I'd always been subject to it. They injected quinine in the bloodstream, a treatment they developed in the African colonies, and it stopped the malaria. I never had a touch of it again.

The doctors told me to go down to the Mediterranean and sit in the sunshine. I went in the spring of '17 and was there until almost the time the United States declared war in April. That day I was in Paris. They rounded up Americans from one service and another and mixed them with the British and marched us in a helter-skelter way down the Champs Elysées toward the Place de la Concorde. Of course, the parade thrilled the French. They thought the American army was out there.

From there I set out for home, and in the journey I encountered the most extraordinary performance of a bureaucracy in my life. When I had come into France to join the ambulance service, I had a box of cigars—I had reached the point at the University of Virginia where I could smoke a cigar, an awfully impressive thing. I don't know where I got this box of cigars. I suppose somebody gave them to me. But when I got to Bordeaux on the way in, the customs people pounced on it as a violation of the French tobacco monopoly.

A customs officer made me leave the box of cigars, but he gave me a receipt and said, "When you leave France you can get them back." I said to myself, that will never happen, because I'll never get back to Bordeaux.

But it turned out I was to sail from Bordeaux going home, and I had in my wallet the receipt for my cigars. So I presented the receipt to a customs officer and said, "I'd like the cigars."

He walked around to a cubbyhole, scrounged around, and, to my astonishment, pulled the cigars out and handed them to me. It had been about seven or eight months. I don't know how much stuff had passed through there meanwhile.

       F.   France was in a fight for survival!

       D.   That's right. Absolutely for survival. But not a flicker, not an eyelid had been raised when I presented the receipt. Just walked back, fumbled around, and produced my cigars.

I came home and joined the naval air force. I took the examination in Washington and went ninety days to ground school at the Massachusetts Institute of Technology. In January 1918 we went to the air station in Miami. The air station wasn't ready to do the training and the navy sent us to Pensacola as one of the first classes. There were canvas hangars. We'd fly the planes during the day and wash them off at night because the seawater would corrode the lacquer finish on the wings and fusilage.

We trained through the spring of 1918 and I was a naval pilot waiting for my commission at Pensacola when the marines decided to organize some land-based squadrons. The navy released a number of us to the marines, and we went to a landing field in the Everglades.

The mosquitoes back there were as big as robins and hungry as starving alligators. They were a torment to the officer of the day when he inspected the sentries at set times during the night. When my turn came, I hit upon an idea which I thought was very good. I decided that I would inspect the guard by using a motorcycle and a sidecar.

I had this boy who was running the motorcycle, shooting me around; and, of course, the motorcycle struggled mightily plowing through the sand and you could hear it for three or four miles. The idea didn't appeal to any of the higher command of the marines. As a matter of fact it shocked them beyond belief and almost terminated my service. As a marine officer said to me, "How in the hell could you check on whether the sentry was awake or asleep when you made enough noise to wake up the people in Miami?"

That, I told him, hadn't occurred to me; I was so pleased I'd found them all alert, attending to duty.

And I think then that he teetered on the very edge of ejecting me. All that saved me was that I was a naval pilot and the marines never did think the navy had sense enough to run an airfield anyway. They weren't surprised at anything that happened. But had I been from the beginning in the Marine Corps, had I been through the boot camp and pulled off a stunt of that kind, I'd have been home in Franklin in no time.

We trained in JN-4s with Hispano-Suiza motors. The Jenny was a very reliable biplane, but the flying field, laid out in the sand, was primitive. The motors had to struggle to pull the wheels out of the sand. Then the plane skimmed over the sand until it was airborne. From that land school I went back to France.

     F.   Had you had any feeling when you left France that you would go back?

     D.   I didn't have any such feeling because when I left the French hadn't told the troops that Russia had been knocked out of the war. The situation in Europe was far grimmer than I had realized.

     F.   What you had seen of the war didn't deter you from enlisting?

     D.   Not a bit. I was such a firm believer in the cause. I was too young and didn't have sense enough to be afraid. In France we were put next to British squadrons on the Channel coast between Dunkirk and Calais. The marines organized four squadrons of fighter-bombers each with fifteen or twenty pilots. I was in Number One. Our combat planes were British de Havillands with American Liberty motors. I did no active service in the lines because we had not received our equipment. A few pilots did some flying with the British. Ralph Talbot, a friend of mine from South Weymouth,

Massachusetts, was one of the boys flying sorties with the British. One day, just seventeen days before the armistice, he was going to test his plane, a DH-4, which had been repaired after being shot up in a dogfight. He asked me to fly with him. I sat down in the gunner's seat, a strap that dropped down in a revolving metal ring. I didn't bother to fasten the seat belt. At the end of the field a large pit had been dug for the storage of bombs. The dirt thrown up on the side made a sizable bank.

Trying to get off the field, the plane was laboring. After one unsuccessful attempt, Talbot started another run, and the plane managed to get a foot or two above the ground, but he must have forgotten about the bomb pit. I glanced over the side and saw the bank a tenth of a second before we hit.

It was like a fast runner being caught by the feet by a giant and slammed down. My head cracked against the metal ring. When the plane went on its nose, I was shot out like a rock off a catapult, so low that those who saw the accident didn't realize I'd been thrown clear. In dragging bombs back from the edge of the flaming wreckage, they stumbled on me in a wheat field beyond the runway. They placed me across the laps of two fellows in an open staff car.

I came to on the way to the British hospital at Calais. I didn't know that Talbot had been killed. I didn't remember fully what had happened, but the first words I blurted out were: "Hell, I ain't dead!"

One of them said, "No, no, they couldn't kill you!"

Then I lapsed into unconsciousness. My failure to fasten the seat belt had saved me. Hitting in the field dislocated my back which resulted in a temporary paralysis that immobilized me for a short time. Because I was recovering from a mild case of the flu, I was placed in the influenza ward. Many died during that fall's dreadful epidemic. The attendants would come in and set up a light screen around a patient's bed and then the next thing you knew the screen was gone and the bed was empty. The boy had died.

They bandaged a gash in my left leg, but they didn't put a cast on my back or attempt to set the bones in my face. The best cure, the doctor said, was for me to lie still. His estimate proved right. The bones knitted together. It did throw my face a little out of balance. The right side is not exactly like the left.

After about two weeks they sent me to London to an American

naval hospital in Hyde Park, a beautiful home that belonged to an Englishman engaged in the diamond trade in South Africa. During the German air raids on London we would go to the roof of the house and watch antiaircraft shells breaking over London and try to pick up the German planes that were flying very high. A morning came when there was very heavy firing and we climbed to the roof and looked around and there were no bursts in the air. The sky was clear. We realized the war was over, and they were firing the guns to celebrate.

We went out in town, and it was like a stunned place. There wasn't any noise except for a low murmur. Next day the celebration was building up. People were coming in from the country, and that night we went to Trafalgar Square where there was the wildest crowd I've ever seen. They drove taxicabs into the bonfire built at the base of Nelson's monument, and the flames touched Nelson's feet.

During the first week in December four of us started by train to Liverpool where we were to embark next day for home. In the compartment with us was a little Welsh girl—she couldn't have been over twelve or thirteen years old—and she was shiny and spick and span with a broad English face and not a touch of makeup.

She wore a kind of homemade stuff of a coarse material, very durable; but the thing that took you as it does so often with the British people is that she simply shone with soap and water. You could see that she was turned out in first-rate shape, especially because she was on the way home from work in London. She'd been coating canvas wings of airplanes with lacquer. The minute the war was over, the factories shut down, bought their help tickets, and sent them home.

Time came for lunch. She reached down and pulled out a little brown bag and opened up the most Spartan lunch and offered to share it with us. We just took a nibble. But we were so overwhelmed that we went to the passageway outside our compartment to talk it over. She was on her way to Wales and would have a layover in Liverpool of five or six hours.

"This child has been so kind to us, let's give her a supper," we said.

We reached Liverpool, and we took her to the Adelphi Hotel for tea. The waitress appeared and looked with utter disdain at the little girl.

"Teatime is over," she snapped. "We're not serving any more."

"Let us tell you now. We are going to have tea for this girl," we said. "Either you are going to get it, or we'll go out there in the kitchen and make it ourselves."

Two or three of us moved that way, and that threw them into such commotion that they agreed to bring some tea if we would sit down. The people sitting around didn't look on us too kindly. In the first place, I don't think they were overly partial to Americans, which is understandable. What really knocked them over was this little Welsh girl in the plainest kind of clothes.

We gave her tea, and a delegation went to Liverpool's plushest restaurant and reserved a table in the center of the dining room. Time came for supper, we marched in, sat her at the head of the table, and gave her a feast the like of which you've never heard. Along about 8:30 we gathered her up, took her to the station, put her on the train, and waved goodbye to her and off she went.

That girl, I'm sure, if she is still living, has never forgotten the dinner we gave her at the restaurant. I hadn't thought of it in years. It came back to me the other day. When the first part of December came around, I got to thinking about those old times. But I'll tell you, you realized how terrible was the drain on British manpower in the First World War when they had little children like that working.

Talbot received posthumously the Congressional Medal of Honor for the fight in which he had participated a few days before the crackup. Years later, in 1936, I went to the Boston Navy Yard for the commissioning of the *Ralph Talbot,* a destroyer named for a valiant young man.

THE SUN ACROSS THE QUAD

D. When we reached New York, we highballed off that ship, and in a little while we were scurrying all over the city, going home. I was hospitalized in naval hospitals in Florida and Washington, D.C. I was retired from the marines in the summer of 1919 and entered Columbia Law School that fall. After a semester a recurrence of trouble with my back forced me to drop out. I remained at home a year, during which I taught history in the high school in Franklin. I enjoyed it very much.

F. Did the veterans receive any government aid?

D. Oh, yes. The government had a program of help with books and other materials. The development of it was rooted in something fairly deep, and that is the growth of social responsibility by government. Before the war broke out, the government hardly touched the day-to-day lives of the people. Its fundamental concerns were foreign affairs, national defense, and interstate commerce. But the First World War brought a considerable change. The Veterans Act was the beginning of legislative programming which laid the groundwork for legislation of help for all classes during the depression. Also the selling of bonds through the various liberty loans laid the foundation for subsequent widespread sale of corporate securities to the public.

F. When you came home, did you get your B.A. degree at the university?

D. Yes, in 1922, and I welcomed help that in the long run was not good. We were given war credit on our degrees. Without that credit all of us who did go back probably would have finished anyway and thereby achieved a better basic education. The war did not substitute for the knowledge that we would have gained as students piecing out academic requirements for degrees.

I went to a series of summer schools at Charlottesville to finish work on my B.A. degree while I was going to law school at Columbia

University. Columbia allowed you to take extra work and night classes, which I did and earned a master's degree in public law.

F.   Then you were working on three different degrees at one time: a B.A. degree from Virginia and law and master's degrees from Columbia.

D.   Well, I was skirmishing around on three fronts, but you could do almost anything you wanted back in those days if you'd do the work. In the first place, the whole schedule wasn't anything like as complicated as it is now, just as life itself was simpler than it is now. Life has been greatly complicated in part by the growth of knowledge.

From Columbia, I went to Oxford in 1923. On my way I received notice aboard ship that I had been awarded a Carnegie Fellowship in International Law. That year at Oxford gave me an understanding of the problems that affected the United States and yet lay outside its borders. I also came to realize that international law did not rest upon a very secure ethical foundation. It turned on armed power. International law was what the great powers said it was in order to serve their own interests.

The year did show me that the organization of the world was extremely complex and that the advancement of world trade was of substantial importance to the general welfare of people. As you increase world trade, you lift, maybe slowly, but you lift peoples' standards of living. By interchanging their labor they can live better. For that reason the stay in Oxford was very beneficial.

It buttressed my theory that you had to have some world organization, some community of interest for the preservation of peace. You couldn't do it by a single dominant power. I was a great believer in Woodrow Wilson's theory of the League of Nations along with some other Americans and the English. A group of us used to go from Oxford on little speaking tours. It was a depressing pilgrimage because the British had been so terribly hurt by the war. The idea of a general cooperation with Germany and other powers wasn't easy to discuss. It didn't fall on very receptive ears. And yet, the more I thought and talked about international law, the more convinced I was that some agreement between the great powers was the only way in the world to substitute some system of law for war as a settler of differences.

We went to Scotland one time making speeches on the coming

brotherhood of mankind. Well, the British took a somewhat dimmer view because their sufferings had been so great. They knew, really, what they were up against, and we were over there telling them what they should do; but, anyway, we labored at it, and they received us courteously. I remember going up to Yarrow. The shipyards were down, and we'd speak to these little groups of people that obviously were hungry and desperate on the streets. They no more knew what we were talking about than if they had been listening to Sanskrit.

I was enrolled in Christ Church. I started living in the Meadows, but I was susceptible to colds, and I asked the authorities if they didn't have some room in a drier place. They gave me one in an attic. I moved there for the balance of the year; but, of course, I took lectures around the university.

I remember listening to the Russian jurist and professor, Sir Paul Vinogradoff, a great authority on international law, a giant of a man who lectured at All Souls. He must have been six feet five, weighed three hundred pounds. In the room was a small grate, a little coal fire flickering around, just to take the very edge off the rawness, not to make it warm. But Vinogradoff would come in wearing his black gown, stand in front of the fire and shut it off from everybody, and lecture to us in broken English. Not a one of us had the faintest idea of what he was talking about, and we were so dog-gone glad when it was over and he moved his bulk away so that we could get a touch of the fire before we went out into the raw weather.

The young Englishmen coming up to Oxford were fine people, and they had an assurance and certainty that they were rulers of the world. In later years the English sensed the shift in world power, but when they came back from the First World War, where they all suffered terribly—every family had made a contribution in dead or wounded—they did not seem to understand, nor did any of the rest of us, that the British Empire was not going to last forever.

At Oxford there were a fair number of Indians from the ruling houses in India, people who controlled a great deal of wealth even in that very poor country. But they didn't seem to be welcomed in England as dark brothers of the empire. They were more or less aloof, as were the English themselves. In that way the education of the Indians at Oxford was not particularly helpful to the British in holding together the empire. The graduates did not go back to

India as supporters of the empire. The revolutionaries who ended British rule were in many instances the products of the English universities.

Their isolation in school did not seem to be a matter of race. Many Canadians didn't think they were given enough attention. I think the British looked on the Canadians as colonials. They thought it was foolishness for anybody to think otherwise, and they held the Americans to be a much sorrier brand than their own colonials. But all of it has gone now, all of it slipped away. I went back to Oxford right after the Second World War. On every side were evidences of how terribly the English had suffered. Everything was changed except some remnants of class snobbery, which doesn't belong solely to the British. It really is something nourished by the more stupid of the human race without regard to color or nationality.

F. How long were you a student in Oxford?

D. I was there a year. Robert Gooch and I traveled a lot during the long vacation and on one trip we went to Athens. One pleasant thing about it, we disagreed on everything. I never encountered anything on which we agreed until recently. I was out to see him in Charlottesville the other day. I told his sister, Mary Stuart, "I'm a little worried about Robert because we fell into agreement on one or two things, and I know that's a bad sign."

I'd always known Oxford was a great university although I never expected I'd get there. It was a fascinating experience and so interesting in retrospect, as I told you, because there was no thought then that the British Empire was at a moment of crisis. The difference between the Americans and the English students was this: the Americans had come to the conclusion that they ruled the world, and they were bent on telling everybody about it, more certainly after they got a couple of beers. We'd go over to the American Club—which probably was a disaster; we'd been better off just filtering around in the British clubs—and get one or two beers and holler and shout about what we had done in the war, which did not please the British with their gigantic losses, to say nothing of the French with their terrible casualties. It had a further defect, that it was not true. Now the British assumed that they ruled the world, but it wasn't necessary to tell anybody, because anybody with any sense would know it.

Nobody realized how terribly the whole Western structure had been wounded in the First World War. You know, the First World War when you look back on it was a civil war in the West, a terrible bloodletting from which Western civilization never recovered. There's no better illustration of the utter futility of war than what happened in 1914. The Europeans, the French and Germans with their great armies and the British with a fleet that controlled the ocean, stood at the very peak. All they had to do was sit around a table and say: Now look here, don't let's throw the world away by quarreling among ourselves. Let's resolve our differences and go on with the development of our lands.

But they couldn't do that. The Germans were bent on getting more trade, and they plunged into an abyss from which nobody came out without horrible wounds. The impetus for self-rule that set in with added virulence after that brought on the dissolution of the colonial empires. It may be that the assertion of these masses— many of them illiterate—trying to run government will bring a society that is better, but it has not yet done it. Any more than a man could have said two or three hundred years after the Romans left England that living was better. It wasn't until probably 1700 that living in England as a whole for people was as easy as it was in the days of the Roman domination in the early part of the Christian era.

Some years ago I visited Ghana when Nkrumah ruled it. It had tremendous reserves in the coffers and he was wasting much of the money in monuments to himself instead of building schools and hospitals for his people. He was a demagogue of the first order, strutting and parading across the world scene.

There isn't any doubt that there was exploitation in the colonial system, but neither is there any question about the worth of, well, let's say the Indian civil service that was developed by the British, a priceless heritage to the new state. When the British retired, they left India and their other colonies with civil services that made the carrying on of the governments easier. Now India appears to be slipping back. Maybe their internal problems are so very great that the country is unmanageable. Nobody can do anything with it. The poverty and the setting up of the Moslem state in Pakistan and then the tearing off of the eastern section and setting up of Bangladesh— the seeds of all those events were sown in the First World War.

That conflict set in motion the dismemberment of the Western group that had dominated the world for several centuries. What you see now is the continuing unraveling and the inability to set in place again the apparatus of government that's required by the vastly enlarged administrative problems that have come to these new countries.

F.   You would think self-government could cope with the demands.

D.   What many observers wonder is whether self-government is viable. That is yet to be demonstrated in some countries. They make an effort to maintain the appearance of a free government, but the substance is not there.

F.   Does the fact that they hold on to the appearance indicate that the mass of the people desire self-government?

D.   Probably it does. The yearning to be free is the most powerful force in human existence.

F.   Have you been back to Oxford?

D.   Once, at about Christmas time. On my way to an educational conference in India in 1949, I stopped in London for a day or two. I said to a friend, "I'd like to see Oxford again. It's been a long time since I was a student."

He insisted on sending me in his car. So the driver took me to Oxford one brilliant December day. We drove along, chatting, and I noticed that Oxford has become industrialized; the Morris works of my day had been greatly enlarged. The town had grown out, and the old section was terribly crowded. You could look in the faces of those people and see what a dreadful time they had had.

We turned off and came to Christ Church and I got out of the car and walked through Tom Gate into the magnificent main quad built by Cardinal Wolsey, down to the Meadows where I lived until driven out by dampness, on over to Peck Quad, where I found dry lodgings in an attic; and on my way back, I peeped into the little cathedral which gives onto the main quad.

I came back to the car and said to the driver, "Let's go back to London."

He said, "You want to go back to London after you have been up here less than an hour?"

"Yes," I said. "I came up here for one thing. I wanted to see if the sun struck as brilliantly across the main quad as I remembered it when I was a student years and years ago. And it has been a perfect day. The sun was brilliant and the shadows were clear-cut and I know what it is now and I'm ready to go back. I haven't got anything else I want to see. Far as I'm concerned, this is Oxford."

STARTING OUT AS A
FILE CLOSER

D. After spending a year at Oxford, I went to work in the law office of State Senator Jim Barron, a political leader in Norfolk. One day in 1925 Harry Byrd came in to see Jim. Harry was campaigning for governor in the Democratic primary against Walter Mapp of Eastern Shore, also a member of the Virginia Senate.

It was the first time I ever laid eyes on Harry. He was young and he stayed in good shape working and walking in the apple orchards that he already was starting to accumulate. His father, Richard Evelyn Byrd, had been Speaker of the House of Delegates. His uncle, Hal Flood of Appomattox, was a prominent member of the House of Representatives and a close ally of Senator Tom Martin, a former railroad lawyer who ran the Organization.

I enlisted in Harry's cause because I shared his view that the state should try to raise by taxes the money that was needed to build roads; but much of the strength down this way, especially in my home county of Southampton, was for Mapp and the theory of bonding the state.

Mapp had teamed up with Methodist Bishop James Cannon, the boss of Virginia in the Prohibition era. Cannon ran it. And Harry set out on his own, and my going with him was like a foot soldier falling into line with a lot of other people. Jim Barron was an old Organization man and Harry's close friend and that, too, influenced me; but I was just a file closer, a private hurrying along, closing up the files in the rear ranks.

Then came the Smith-Hoover presidential fight of 1928, and I went around and spoke for Smith to very sparse audiences, because, to start with, mighty few were going to vote for Smith, he being wringing wet and on the top of that a Catholic. With Cannon and his preachers whipping up emotions over liquor and the Catholic church, it was just about as rough in Norfolk as it could be.

To show you the extremes to which our opponents went, they set up little kiosks on the sidewalks along Granby Street featuring terrible anti-Catholic pictures of the Spanish Inquisition. It was vicious and mendacious; my decision is one I've never regretted, because Al Smith was a superior person. Had we elected him president, he would have done much to cushion the terrible depression. He understood what had to be done for people in the mass. Herbert Hoover never did. It wasn't meanness on the part of Hoover. It was simply a lack of understanding.

F. Isn't it strange that a man who had done relief work for people abroad shouldn't have grasped—

D. I don't think so. I think he did it *for* them, never *with* them. I don't think Hoover ever realized the enormous power of people working together in the political system. Smith did. He knew it from the ground up. Hoover was a humanitarian, but he didn't understand politics. He did not realize the problems of government anything like as well as Al Smith did.

F. Byrd told me that he made twenty-four speeches in that campaign and that Smith lost by 24,000 votes, which led him to conclude that every time he made a speech Smith lost a thousand votes.

D. I tell you, Harry faced up to it. That was the acid test. In North Carolina, United States Senator Furnifold Simmons, a Democrat, went over with Hoover and the drys of North Carolina. In the next election Josiah Bailey, a dry and a distinguished lay leader of the Baptist church, whipped Furnifold and retired him to private life.

F. Byrd used to say that in the Democratic Convention of 1924 he got in a cab with Bishop Cannon and Cannon told him, "This is not your turn to run for governor!"

D. And Byrd told his father, who said, "Now you've got to run." Probably Harry made the last part up to bolster his decision.

Richard Evelyn Byrd appears to have been one of the most popular fellows we ever had around Virginia. He was not the hatchet man that Harry was on occasion. You know Harry had a vindictive streak in him as big as, well, as big as his body, practically. And he loved the scalping. He flourished under it. Harry's father said that Harry had the face of an angel but never to cross him.

F.   Because he had the heart of a tiger!

D.   That's how I drifted into politics in the Smith-Hoover campaign. Then in 1929 I won a seat in the House of Delegates and became embroiled in my next term in a fight over the public schools. In 1932 some schools were closing in March because the money had run out. Jack Eggleston of Norfolk, a newly elected member of the State Senate, and I proposed to give the localities $5 million to keep the schools open even if it meant borrowing from the highway fund. Almost a visible shock wave ran through the Organization's ranks. We couldn't have touched a more sensitive nerve. The road people hollered and they yelled. They descended on us full force, but Jack and I persisted and we rallied enough support to bring Harry out of the orchards and down to Richmond to caucus on the matter.

He discovered, after he arrived in Richmond, that there was far more support for keeping the schools open than had been thought. He had been firing off statements, but they proved not to be enough. Our support was not bound together, unified, but the public school people flocked to us as did many independents, and, of course, all the Antis. The Antis fell onto anything that seemed to give the Organization trouble.

Harry took us to breakfast one morning at the Westmoreland Club and went over the situation. He realized something had to be done. So he devised the plan for the state to take over the county road systems and unify them in one central highway system, thereby freeing local money for the public schools.

I think it was better than our plan in that it didn't take money temporarily from the highway department which the state figured it would never get back. Our plan would have set the precedent of invading the highway funds, tax funds segregated for road building. Byrd's solution was better in the long run in that it was more enduring, although not as speedy. It lagged in that respect. It didn't give immediate relief. Jack and I were just aiming to keep the schools open.

F.   You were right. They should have found the money somewhere to do that.

D.   Yes, quite. Philosophically we were right; but practically we were not.

F.   Even practically you were right to the extent

that to let the schools close was a calamity. Whether they took the money from the highway fund or somewhere else, they should have found it. You all simply looked around to see where the money was.

D.   We did know where it was, and we had no idea how tender the issue was until we got in the fight. But those were desperate times. Governor John Garland Pollard, a former teacher of government at William and Mary and a splendid chief executive, went to work as required by law to keep the budget in balance, and twice he cut 10 percent off state wages.

F.   Governor, if the Organization had felt for other services the sensibilities it showed toward roads, that would have made a vast difference in the state's progress.

D.   A tremendous difference, but that illustrates what I said sometime back. That the significant development in my lifetime has been the awakening of a social consciousness of the people of the United States.

F.   The awakening was belated in Virginia.

D.   Yes, it was belated in Virginia because we were more dedicated, I think, to Gladstone's theory that he was leaving the money to fructify in the pockets of the British people rather than increasing their taxes. That was a belief fiercely held in this state, to such an extent that Virginians did not realize that the industrialization of the United States had brought new problems. We were no longer the agrarian economy that we had been since colonial days. The First World War ended that with a great industrial push forward. The coming of the automobile and the building of hard roads furthered the impact. In Virginia we lagged not in compassion but in comprehension.

F.   The flaw in that business of leaving the money to fructify is that many had very little in their pockets.

D.   Yes. Well, it's not basically in error. It is in error only when you do not take into account the increasing demands of an industrial society. You have to leave as much as possible to fructify in the pockets of the people. That's very necessary. But the amount that you leave can be much too great or it can be much too small. There is the balance that requires statesmanship. It rests right on that point.

F.   Virginia resisted the idea of social responsibility

far longer than did most other states. Certainly those outside the South fell into it before we did.

D.   Oh, yes. Much before we did. Part of that is, of course, the fact that the race question entered into it in the South. The introduction of slavery, which was the greatest single catastrophe that ever happened in this country, brought in a labor force that was fixed in the minds of people as a part of servitude. Consequently, as the young white people came on in the South, they turned away from work that would have been quite useful and profitable.

F.   The bout over the highway funds raises an interesting point in showing how Byrd and the Organization worked. Critics might contend that two legislators had proposed a worthy remedy and that Byrd had come down and cracked the whip and defeated your proposal. That interpretation would be oversimplified, wouldn't it?

D.   Oh, very much oversimplified. He was devoted to the highway system, but it wasn't a question with him of coming down and cracking the whip. He was devising a plan that would do what was nearest to his heart, and that was hold together the Virginia Organization. He was called to Richmond to help after Jack and I had stirred up so much commotion. There was a bubbling up of people who did not want to see their schools closed several weeks ahead of time because the money had run out, when they thought they could get hold of some money from the highway system. It was the only source where there was any money. It was also the best battleground for the Organization, because it could rally Virginia against us with an argument which had a lot of merit. Once you had started invading highway funds, there would be no end to it, and the tax money that had been collected for licenses would then be funneled off into first one thing and then another, which would not have been desirable. They had no faith at all in our scheme that we would ever repay anything.

F.   The sanctity of the highway fund, its separateness, was nearly as much an article of faith to the Organization as opposition to bonds.

D.   It was fully as much an article of faith because Organization candidates had campaigned on the ground of these being segregated funds and the people were only being taxed by the gas tax to provide highways that they themselves were using. If they didn't use them, they didn't have to pay the tax, don't you see?

F. Also, Virginia, while it has lagged in other services, has prided itself on roads since Byrd's day.

D. And justifiably so. Virginia has not lagged since Harry's time in the development of a good highway system.

F. Yes, sir, but it interests me that the highway system is the one service where we have insisted on meeting high standards.

D. It has. It has been vulnerable only in one respect, and that is that we looked to tolls in Tidewater to cross these great rivers while we did not do it in building the very expensive roads through the mountains to the west. The trick seems to be that if the land rises upward in a small mountain, you are in the clear. If it goes down a little in a basin and is filled with water, you have to finance it in other ways. It's a throwback to colonial days when individuals received a fee for ferrying people across rivers. But for the agitation that Jack and I promoted, along with all of our allies, there wouldn't have been any movement to unify the road system that early. Undoubtedly the state would have come to that because good business demanded it.

F. Let's look at Byrd's technique in meeting your bill's threat to siphon off highway funds for schools. It was not simply a matter of coming down and cracking people's heads to get them in line; he had to find something that would work in the way of legislation.

D. That's right, and something that he felt that he could sell to the people.

F. And he had several priorities. The first was to hold the Organization together. The second was not to let anybody tamper with the road funds, and a third, and indirect beneficiary, was the school system. But he didn't come down primarily to keep the schools open.

D. He came down to head off the raid that was being made on the highway fund. He also did another thing. He was going to find a solution that would make as few enemies as possible. Harry didn't set himself out to make unnecessary enemies, and in the end he devised a scheme that most all of us could join him in. So that what he accomplished was what we wanted done, and at the same time he protected the highway fund from what he thought would have been a very dangerous incursion.

In settling the affair we were able to work out the first road-building subsidy for the cities. This fund has now reached substantial proportions.

F.   The Organization would have been invulnerable to criticism if Byrd had been as bent on maintaining the other services at the same caliber as roads.

D.   I think that's quite true; but, after all, that's asking for something that is rarely, if ever, found, and that is a general overall view of the many needs of the state, instead of addressing himself to one which was very pressing, which was very popular, and which was very manageable. The roads were just that. It was apple pie for political venture.

F.   The issue of good roads was easy for people to grasp and it wasn't complex. It didn't raise all sorts of vexing problems, did it?

D.   No. You do it often in your summary of things. You are talking about a perfect society. Man has never achieved that in his long pilgrimage, and never is going to achieve it. The best we can do is a modest forward step, and the most likely thing is, in the interim, two or three back steps, and then an attempt to regain the ground.

F.   It's just a pity that Byrd had not been as aware of the needs of public education as you were, that he had not recognized that schools are even more important for the future than roads.

D.   I believe he understood the importance of the school system; it was just a matter of priorities. And not only that, you didn't have a people who understood fully the need of a school system. They understood the need for a road system, because they were up to their chins in mud. Virginia's roads were often referred to as the worst in the United States. About the time I got out of the service cartoons used to show an automobile stuck in Virginia. That was regarded as the very top in humiliation.

F.   Who sponsored the bill making roads a state responsibility?

D. Sam Ferguson, a great crony of Harry's from Appomattox. They used to tell around the Assembly the story that lightning had hit the State Office Building and killed half the people in Appomattox County, that Sam had them all up there on the state payroll. But the remarkable thing is, if you will go back and look at the bill, its concluding sentence is: "This Act will be known as the Byrd Road Act," which showed the effort that Harry had made.

They had to call in Harry. Jack and I and the school people had them almost on the ropes, far more than we had understood, even. They formulated the plan because they were shrewder judges of the state than we were. In the first place, they had far more contacts than we had, and the very fact that Sam got in there and said this will be the Byrd Road Act, although Harry was not in the Assembly nor was he governor, indicates the prodigious efforts that he made after they got him to come down out of the orchard to Richmond to help them. The title was a tribute to him and a deserved one because he pulled them out of the pickle.

F. It is almost comic, the frenetic energy he could pour into something when a crisis arose.

D. I don't think so. I think it's quite reasonable. That's the way successful political organizers function. They are all alike in that way. In the first place, they are absolutely dedicated to it. Now in some cases, their living is bound up with it. It wasn't with Harry because he was very prosperous as a businessman.

F. He hurried to Richmond because he was afraid it all might come to pieces before his eyes, wasn't he?

D. He was always afraid of that. You didn't want to let any little rips start because they were apt to spread and tear asunder the whole fabric. Then as he grew older, it became a matter of personal pride. He equated entirely the Virginia Organization with the welfare of the state of Virginia.

F. And with himself.

D. And himself. Well, he was the Virginia Organization. He was head of it.

F. I don't mean "and himself" in a monied sense. I meant he came to look on himself as embodying the Organization.

D. That's right, exactly right. Harry was a very generous sort of person. Willis Robertson and I ate enough off him while we were in Congress to run an ordinary household. Back in the old days we'd go for supper to the dining room on the roof of the Army-Navy Club. Harry would always pick up the check. In any undertaking like that he was outgoing and generous, but he had one single eye, and that was for the Virginia Organization and the running of it.

On the roof of the Army-Navy Club it was perfectly beautiful. Washington was nothing like as big as it is now. The air was clearer and fresher. It was delightful, and we'd sit up there in the cool and plot and plan. Harry would do the plotting, really, because he knew more about it. He had been in it all his life and he loved it with a passion that you can't understand unless you knew him and watched him working.

    F.   Byrd had a masterly sense of timing.

    D.   Yes, he was like a surfer waiting for one of those great waves sweeping ashore in the Hawaiian Islands, hopping on it just before it peaked, and riding in gleefully.

Nothing illustrates it better than his breaking his golden silence in late October 1952, when the Eisenhower tide was coming in, and announcing that he could not support the Stevenson-Sparkman ticket.

    F.   He had a crackling energy, an infectious zest whether climbing a mountain or running a campaign. It was fun to be with him.

    D.   He was dealing with something he loved beyond belief. He just liked to be boss. It occupied every living moment, I guess, of his waking hours after his family responsibilities.

    F.   Once launched on a course, he conveyed a profound sense of conviction.

    D.   And direction. Once having laid a course, he didn't deviate. But he took his time about laying it. Nobody ever got Harry into a snap decision.

Rather, the only one he ever got into, so far as I know, was the Oyster War. While he was governor, he ordered the militia to put down a rebellion by the guineamen around Gloucester. They wouldn't pay any attention to his oyster inspectors.

When the ships brought in the militia, the oystermen met them with oysters and liquor, which was especially embarrassing to Harry because he was dry. The whole crowd got to partying, and

Harry couldn't even find the commanders. He lost complete control of his armed forces. "I couldn't do a thing with 'em," he said. "It's the worst mess I ever got into in my life."

And he got into it just because he got mad and took a snap judgment and jumped up and ordered in the guard—to his eternal regret.

F.   If Byrd had shown the same ingenuity and sensitivity when the Young Turks rebelled in 1954 as he showed in 1932 when you all brought the challenge, it would have changed the course of Virginia politics.

D.   It might have. Certainly that's arguable and certainly there's no doubt that he had become far less flexible in 1954. I think that's understandable. He'd been for years a member of the United States Senate. When he was down pacifying us, he wasn't a member of the Senate, he was chairman of the party. He became chairman of the party when he left the governorship so he could keep his hand in.

F.   Governor, you became associated with Byrd during his campaign against bonding for roads. What motivates Virginians' fear of debt?

D.   Their whole experience with it has been disastrous, going back to our earliest days as a state when many of the leading citizens brought the state into joint undertakings to construct canals. The debt situation became so perilous that the Constitutional Convention of 1851–52 set in motion the pay-as-you-go scheme by providing that the state, when it incurs debt, has to set up a sinking fund for its liquidation. "Pay-as-you-go" as an expression goes even further back to John Randolph of Roanoke who mentioned it in the Constitutional Convention of 1829.

F.   He cried, "I have discovered the philosopher's stone—it is pay-as-you-go!" Did part of our difficulty with debt result from the state's losses in the Civil War?

D.   We came out of it in heavy debt because West Virginia had been torn off and we were then struggling under the financing of the earlier debts that we had incurred in the canal and railroad speculation. The war added to the debt difficulties. It disrupted and paralyzed the trade of a large rich state.

The Underwood Constitution of 1869 broadened and strengthened the prohibitions against using state credit for private endeavors. The 1901–2 constitution put the capstone on it by prohibiting counties and cities from using their credit for such undertakings. In the 1880s and 1890s nearly every locality was bonding itself to get a railroad to come through town. The '02 constitution just said to them: No more!

When I came on the scene and fell in with Harry's army, the battle lines had long since been laid and the immediate issue was whether to bond for roads. I felt that to plunge the state into a multimillion dollar road-building program would be a mistake when we didn't have a highway department to administer it wisely. A good deal of that is hindsight. I'm sure that when I came back here as a young boy from Oxford University that all of that didn't occur to me. It was just a general apprehension.

F.   Where did the state go wrong on pay-as-you-go?

D.   It didn't go wrong. It became rigid. It was not flexible enough. Pay-as-you go is a very sound theory of government. What we should have done earlier was cover by taxation the government's administrative costs and then when we undertook to build a college dormitory or dining hall or any self-liquidating facility, we should have used bonds to be paid by student fees and rents. Furthermore, we should have utilized more extensively the taxing machinery to raise the funds required to meet the social needs of our people.

F.   How would you have the state borrow?

D.   Once authority had been given to pledge the credit of the state, I would avoid long-term bonds and use short-term notes. This would, I believe, save substantial sums in interest.

F.   In other words, after the voters have granted the authority to borrow, say, $125 million as was proposed by the 1977 General Assembly, you would have the state borrow in smaller amounts as the construction of the facilities required.

D.   That's correct. Suppose you issue the full $125 million at once. Chances are they'll be thirty-years bonds. At 5 percent you have well over 100 percent interest. So you are talking about a $125 million loan plus more than $125 million interest. What I would do is to allow the state, now more especially, since our revenue is beginning to rise, to go to the banks and borrow $15 or $20 million at a time on five-year notes and go along with those ventures that have been approved by the Assembly, but not sell $125 million worth of bonds all at once. With a credit as good as Virginia has, it can borrow just as an individual and corporation can borrow for inventory purposes.

F.   How much did we lose by relying exclusively on tolls to build the Chesapeake Bay Bridge-Tunnel?

D.   We could have saved well over $100 million on the Chesapeake Bay venture by using the state's direct credit to undergird the tolls. This also would have freed the bridge much earlier of tolls.

F.   Many Virginians never stop to think what pay-as-you-go means. It has been a litany.

D.   You take an ordinary Virginian and wake him up out of a deep slumber—shake him right quick—and he'll say two words: "Fiscal sanity!" If you woke him and told him that there was starvation, he'd say: "Help 'em, but fiscal sanity!" Fiscal sanity! That became too rigid, you see? The theory was excellent. Perfectly good; it just needed better administration. It becomes much easier to understand if you keep in mind that mankind is struggling for a better system through trial and error.

F.   Had a few more in the Byrd Organization been inclined as you are for trial, there would have been fewer errors. Among the Organization's hierarchy you and a few others were the only ones of stature who would gauge the needs realistically.

D.   It was a natural outgrowth of the agrarianism of the Organization. It goes back to the beginning. Take old Governor Giles in 1827. Read his letters and pronouncements on the future. He was a stalwart citizen and certainly devoted to the welfare of the state and also sure that once the industrialists supplanted the agrarians, disaster was right around the corner.

One of the most interesting stories, and this is kind of personal, but I've laughed about it many times with Connie, concerns her great-great-grandfather, Pierre Samuel du Pont de Nemours, and Jefferson, who were friends and fellow scientists. DuPont wrote an excellent memorandum for Jefferson on public education, which I am sure came out of their conversations on the terrace at Monticello about the dangers of industrialization. They were positive it was the one thing you had to avoid—although Jefferson modified substantially these views when he sought the support of the industrial states in running for president. And Pierre's son, Eleuthère, founded the Du Pont Company, which has plants all over the free world.

F. They may have been wrong about the direction of the development of the country, but they were up there discussing a plan of education.

D. Isn't any doubt about it, and they were basically right in that they were experimentalists in the human journey. They were essentially intellectual explorers wandering around in the long reaches of time. They were together in that.

WORSE THAN WATERGATE

D. When I ran for Congress in 1932, I defeated one of the nicest fellows that was ever in this area—Menalcus Lankford, a Republican from a large Democratic family. He was a friendly, outgoing person, enormously popular. Mac had captured the seat in the Hoover landslide of 1928. He defeated Representative Joseph T. Deal that year and again in 1930.

I won in 1932 because the depression had thrown the Republicans in disarray and also because this district is inclined to vote for the party most likely to be in power. It lives on naval appropriations to a large extent, and the voters figure that a member of the party in power can protect their interests in Washington more effectively. That's the only reason in the world that I beat Mac Lankford. I was swept along on the Democratic tide that by the summer of 1932 reached flood proportions.

The depression was deepening, and Franklin Roosevelt was crisscrossing the country complaining of the Republican party's extravagance. What was needed, he said, was a cutting of federal expenditures and he was the man to do it; and he was for the first one hundred days of his administration. After that he turned into the greatest spender that we had ever had—up until that time. He was just a forerunner to some of these later fellows.

F. Did you beat Lankford soundly, Governor?

D. Not so soundly. The Supreme Court of Virginia had upset the redistricting act of Virginia and directed that the candidates for Congress run at large in the state. I had stated, over the objection of political friends and advisers, that if I didn't carry the district, I was not going to take the nomination to Congress. They could just go on and elect somebody else. I didn't want to go to Congress having been elected by the rest of the state and not supported by my own people.

F. That must have startled your backers.

D. It startled them all right. They came to the conclusion that they had a candidate who really didn't have sense enough to know what he was doing! And I suppose there was some merit to that view. They knew Mac had no chance of winning in Virginia because of the overwhelming Democratic strength. They thought that very likely he'd win in this district because of his personal popularity. They also said it was extravagant to put the state to the expense of a special election, were I to lose. Fortunately, I won in the district as well as in the rest of the state.

It was a first-rate delegation. The others were older than I, but we had a very friendly group. Otis Bland from the First District was chairman of the Merchant Marine Committee. I was in the Second. In the Third was former Governor Andrew Montague, one of the great storytellers of all time. In the Fourth was Pat Drewry of Petersburg who was at work on a life of Randolph of Roanoke. In the Fifth District was Tom Burch, a great friend and political adviser to Harry. The Sixth was Cliff Woodrum, an aviation enthusiast who flew his own plane; the Seventh was Willis Robertson, a great hunter and fisherman and conservationist; the Eighth was Howard Smith, former judge in Alexandria, and the Ninth was John Flannagan, an emerging New Dealer. The Ninth had tremendous unemployment. The mines were shut down. Although John was right of center all his life, he veered to the left of the Organization. The old-line Democrats were stirring up trouble out there trying to oust him. Never could.

Willis and I lived down near the Union Station in the old Capitol Park Hotel. Harry stayed there a little while, and then he figured he had to move to the Shoreham, a much nicer hotel, better suited to a member of the Senate. When my family came up, Connie and I looked for a house. We found a beautiful place in Alexandria.

The Congress then was a legislative body engaged in fairly limited federal issues. Now it is concerned with everybody's private business in the United States, even down to one who's raising chickens. And, of course, the congressman is not only a legislative representative. He's also the business representative of his district resident in the federal capital. He's faced with the necessity of doing everything that can be done to advance every particular business interest in his district. He's their firsthand access to the government, and no living man has that much time.

The Virginia members, Howard Smith particularly, helped me get on the Naval Affairs Committee. Howard was friendly with Fred Vinson, chairman of the Ways and Means Committee that elected new members to the Naval Committee. The Democrats were eager to do whatever they could to hold this district, and they knew the appointment to that committee would give me a better chance of reelection than ordinarily would be the case.

I was part of an enthusiastic Democratic majority. There was an enormous optimism with this fresh tide of people, a belief that they were going to build a new society. Roosevelt's programs seem quite modest when you look at government's operations today, but they were then thought to be revolutionary.

Some of the legislation, you know, was not Roosevelt's. One of the best measures we passed was the guarantee of bank deposits. Had it been passed a year or two earlier it would have saved us from the final plunge into the depression, when people, frightened to death about their savings, were taking them out of the banks. Roosevelt was bitterly opposed to the bill, perhaps because his financial advisers were against it. The Democratic-Republican coalition, and particularly Arthur Vandenberg, just made him take it. Roosevelt would have vetoed it, as a matter of fact, when it finally came down the line, but the public response was so very great that he knew that to veto it would be dangerous. Then, too, Huey Long was looming on the horizon. That scared everybody around Washington to death. Long was promoting the idea that every man was a king. The administration was taking secret polls showing his increasing strength, and after one hundred days it made a complete about-face from Roosevelt's adherence to a theory of economy and thrift in government. That's what Harry used to talk about when he said in his old days that he was one of the few New Dealers left in the Congress. He was, in truth, a New Dealer of the first New Deal. He never was a second New Dealer. He was against the change in face.

F. Byrd had a way of taking one joke, one phrase that appealed to him and hammering at it. He played that theme of being the only New Dealer twenty-five years.

D. He was a valiant New Dealer all right. I blush

when I think about the speeches that we used to run around here and make. Former Governor Trinkle came down and helped me campaign. We'd get up and talk about Hoover's extravagance in having four secretaries. You have to get a telephone book to find out how many secretaries are around the White House now. I mean, it's a small volume. And Hoover had only four. Woodrow Wilson had run the government during the war with one, Joe Tumulty.

I was going around bellowing about that, putting on a great show, in which we believed. Roosevelt was setting the tone. He was the chief economizer. He was the fellow that was going to cut out the waste. Then the switch came.

Roosevelt would come up to the House and make his talks, and a few times he had some of us down to the White House. I remember a special delegation on the bonus bill. Cliff Woodrum herded us down there. We sat around in the Oval Office. The president was giving us the word about holding the line against the bonus bill and saving the country. I remember Governor Scrugham of Nevada, a little bit of a fellow, was far from convinced. I don't believe Roosevelt swung him over, but the rest of us went traipsing along, faithful to the end, and it turned out in some cases to be our end and not his.

F. Was there much socializing by congressmen?

D. They were friendly among themselves in a small way, and we all went down the White House once or twice a year, but in the 1930s there wasn't anything like the partying that goes on around Washington today. The pleasantest parties were Isabella Greenway's in her lovely old house in Georgetown. Isabella was the only member of Congress from Arizona. Her office was just down the hall from mine, and she invited Connie and me to suppers for ten or fifteen people. Alice Longworth was there. She and Isabella were great friends. They'd do charades and all kinds of little games like that after supper, and we'd break up and go home about ten-thirty.

F. What was the makeup of your district?

D. I had a district that swept to the agricultural counties of the west. Farm problems were multiplying. The government planned to assist the major crops—corn, wheat, cotton—with subsidies. Roosevelt was against letting peanuts go in the bill, which was, of course, the major crop in my district, and but for Huey Long

in the Senate we would have been dealt out. We already had been
excluded in the House despite the efforts of influential fellows in the
Democratic majority. All of us piled up together couldn't get peanuts in the bill.

"I'm not going to put peanuts in the bill," the president told one
congressman. "They will laugh it out of Congress, calling it the
peanut bill."

We didn't appreciate that particularly because there were a
number of us whose political fortunes were tied to peanuts. Roosevelt also wanted rice excluded, but when the bill got to the Senate
and Huey grabbed hold of it, that was something else. I don't reckon
Huey knew a peanut, but he knew rice and he said rice was going in
the bill. The minute Long said that, we highballed over there and
asked him to tie peanuts on with the rice. He said he'd be glad to do
it, put 'em all together.

I'll never forget the debate. The Senate was moving on to ad-
journment, and Huey Long had the floor, filibustering, and he said
to them: "You are either going to put rice in this bill or you're not
going to have any bill. You just make up your mind whichever you
want."

Congress adjourned, and he had rice and peanuts in the bill, and
they have been there ever since.

Huey Long used to get up in the Senate to ridicule something
and he'd say: "There's about as much difference in what you are
talking about and what this other fellow's been saying as there was
between the high poppolorum and the low poppohirum that I used
to sell when I was a patent medicine salesman. For years I was a
patent medicine salesman in Louisiana and I had two infallible
remedies that I peddled with great success. There was a lotion for
treating anything you had called high poppolorum, and we made
high poppolorum by skinning the bark off a tree. We'd start up
under the lowest branch and we'd skin the bark down to the ground
and we'd boil that and that was high poppolorum. Now," he said,
"we also made low poppohirum that was just as effective, and the
way we made low poppohirum was we'd cut the bark at the ground
and skin the tree up to the first limb and that was the other lotion
and just as effective as high poppolorum. That was low poppohirum." Now can you beat that?

The most discouraging event I ever saw in my whole life in politics occurred in my first term. That was the trial of federal judges for heartless and merciless stealing. Unbelievable! As a matter of fact, it was more dangerous than the Watergate abuse because when you impair the judiciary you sweep away the last bulwarks of the government. There isn't any question they were thieving. That a federal judge would be engaged in such chicanery had never occurred to me. The judges that I had known here, whose appointments were due in part to political partisanship, were nevertheless honest and decent.

Sam Hobbs represented the House of Representatives in the impeachment proceedings before the Senate. These judges were being tried for their careers. Their wives had moved up to Washington and they were working on the senators to acquit them. It was a disgraceful procedure, really. Even though they were guilty, they were entitled to a full hearing by the Senate, the jury, but few of the senators listened to the trial. I don't think any innocent person suffered. I think the ones convicted were guilty and a number that weren't convicted were guilty, too.

The scheme of the judges had been to rob the bankrupt estates that were moving into their courts for protection under the bankruptcy law. They would levy gigantic fees and then divide them with their old law firms or with the lawyers appearing in the cases. It was just a bunch of rapacious thieves who were hiding behind the federal judiciary. I never will forget Sam Hobbs's examination of one judge.

This judge was maintaining he was innocent, and Sam said to him, "Why was it you had $70,000 in cash in your safety deposit box?"

"Banks were failing on all sides," said the judge, "and I was scared to put it in the bank. I didn't want to lose my money."

That seemed to me to be a sensible answer because although banks had not been failing in Virginia, they had been failing in neighboring states. Then Sam said, "How did it happen you never returned it in your income tax then?"

And that one question convicted him.

Those trials make grim reading. They reached to the threshold of the Supreme Court of the United States. Watergate's impairment of the executive department was vicious and miserable, but to me it never has appeared as dangerous as the corruption that was uncovered in the federal judiciary by Sam Hobbs and others.

When the judiciary becomes corrupt, you're gone. There's nothing that stands between the public and absolute oppression and dictatorship. The fact that the judges and the attorneys that the Watergate gang ran into could not be corrupted explains why the Watergaters ended up face to face with the pokey. But a corrupt federal judiciary would have quashed the whole affair.

ANATOMY OF DEFEAT

D. I was in the House two terms, then I was beaten in 1936 by Norman R. Hamilton. It's not pleasant to be beaten. You always feel that you've been mistreated, when in truth you probably deserve it.

Hamilton owned the newspaper in Portsmouth. The Norfolk paper was with him because Hamilton was friendly with Colonel Sam Slover, its publisher. Their friendship and association in the newspaper business made this quite understandable.

Although I didn't see eye-to-eye with the colonel on my campaign with Hamilton, I've always felt that all of us were indebted to him for his encouraging and preparing his nephew, Frank Batten, to assume direction of the Norfolk newspapers. The community has benefited greatly from Frank's enlightened leadership.

The unemployed, when I went to Congress, stood in long lines outside my office door. They needed help desperately and we were slow getting underway with WPA and like undertakings. I listened to heartbreaking stories, and I wondered how in the world I had ever gotten myself in that situation. The depression hadn't lifted by 1936, and the economic difficulties contributed to the three issues that brought about my defeat.

First, I was one of thirty-three House members who had voted in 1935 against the Social Security Act. Four—Otis Bland, Tom Burch, Willis Robertson, and I—were from Virginia. People looked on us as just a bunch of rascals who didn't want to help anyone. All we said was that Congress ought to provide adequate reserves to safeguard the funds so that when people paid into the Social Security, they got their money back when they retired. Oh, the proponents said, that wasn't necessary. The country would go on forever; and the taxes, half on the payroll and half on the individual, would continue to generate sufficient revenues to keep the fund solvent. Really what happened is the fund started carrying people immediately who had never paid anything into it, and they siphoned off a good part of the money being paid in and that brought on a substantial deficit. Something must be done in the next few years to safeguard the savings of those paying into it.

The problem was further exacerbated by Congress's habit of increasing Social Security benefits every election year and then failing to provide the taxes to support the increase. We simply wanted some plan to make the system secure. You would have thought that we were—well, just antisocial; that's the kindest thing they said about us.

Another issue worked against me, and I've always thought this had much more merit. I voted against the veterans' bonus. Opposition to the bonus had been one of Franklin Roosevelt's planks. He charged into the fray hollering hold the line and soon determined he had to retreat, but he made no mention of the fact to us. Those of us who were stupid enough to stay in the line got cut up badly. The others made their peace and went along as they should have done.

The third factor was the most effective political gimmick I have ever encountered. It was devilish, but it was so clever and really so simple that I've always kind of admired the opposition for thinking it up and using it although it was utterly false.

The employment in the Naval Shipyard at Portsmouth had dropped to a low level. One source of employment was in the manufacture of paint for warships and other naval facilities. The opposition said that my plan was to close the yard's paint shop. I had been working on it, they said, so the navy could give that business to the Du Pont Company. Well, Connie's family controlled the Du Pont Company, and that fabrication fell on tinder and ignited the electorate and aided substantially in throwing me out. The paint issue was totally fraudulent and enormously effective.

I don't think they could have taken the paint issue alone and won with it. But they superimposed that on Social Security and topped it off with my refusal to vote for the bonus—and God knows the veterans needed the bonus. Of course, if I had to go over it again, I'd vote for the bonus with great glee. Had I done that, I might have sneaked by; but when they coupled the bonus and the Social Security issue and then threw the paint in there as flammable material, they had an unbeatable combination.

I never thought that I'd live to see the day that the position that a handful of us took on Social Security would be vindicated, but it is now. The Social Security System is running a deficit of about $3 billion. It is rapidly eating up the reserves. In 1976 the recipient of the first Social Security check died, and the newspaper accounts said she had received a total of $22,000 in benefits over the years; she had paid only $22 into the fund. That is an illustration of why we wanted to bolster the reserves. She should have participated, but Congress should have levied heavier taxes at the start to pick up the slack of thousands of people who had made little or no contribution to the plan. Then Congress should have been careful in not adding to the burden without providing funds to carry it.

In 1935 they just brushed us all off on the ground that we had no idea of looking out for the workingman. Now they are sloshing around—as Carl Vinson used to say—trying to find some scheme to bring this system back into balance.

    F.   Governor, can you learn more from defeat than you can from victory?

    D.   Yes, if you analyze it objectively. Few people are ever inclined to learn from victory. The winners relate the victory too much to themselves, their soaring ability, which has very little to do with it, and in most cases isn't present anyway. An interesting thing I learned from defeat is that attention to the social aspects of officeholding is vital.

I turned down many requests to speak in my district and built up many resentments along the road because I felt that the duties in Washington required that I stay there. After all, a member of Congress ought to look after the business of the nation and his district; but he can't afford to neglect the social activities at home. When I returned to office, I set aside time to go around to meetings, shooting the breeze. It didn't contribute anything to the nation's progress, but it did contribute a good deal toward keeping me in office.

Now, I'm satisfied that Bill Spong fell victim to much the same thing in 1972. He was just as diligent as he could be in attending to the vital issues before the United States Senate; but he was not in getting around his district, which was a big state, and making talks and seeing people.

    F.   Bill realized that belatedly. Some months after

his defeat he said he was too busy looking after a bill for endangered species to go around the state, and come to find out he was one of the endangered species.

D.   That showed a complete grasp of the predicament. His defeat was a substantial loss to Virginia and the country.

F.   Why did you decide to try to return to Congress in 1938?

D.   The demands on a congressman and the time away from home were terribly oppressive, but I was resentful of defeat. What really decided me was sentiment that arose among Norman Hamilton's New Deal followers because of his vote supporting an amendment which President Roosevelt opposed as weakening the Wagner Act. The first repercussions here were not unlike those after my Social Security vote.

Elliott Heath, a prominent Norfolk lawyer and fervent New Dealer who had been one of Hamilton's leaders, came to see me and offered his support.

"I certainly hope you will run against Mr. Hamilton," he said. "You'll never do anything in the world that will suit me, I know, but at least you will never surprise me!"—which I thought interesting. That visit convinced me that the revolt in the Anti ranks was so great that I might win.

F.   What was Byrd's attitude toward your attempted comeback?

D. An interesting lack of enthusiasm. He detached himself from the fray, and that was not usual. I went by to see him after I had decided to run again, and during the course of our friendly talk he asked me not to mention his name in the campaign.

In the first place, I don't think Harry thought I could win, which was a view held by many of our mutual friends in Tidewater, including some of Harry's most substantial supporters. He wanted to be careful not to be drawn into the melee where somebody might take a poke at him. He wished to keep it a local fight.

As I've thought about it over the years, I've concluded that his discretion was quite understandable. The New Deal forces were building in Virginia, and President Roosevelt was bent on undermining Harry any way he could—which was one reason the president intervened in my congressional fight in 1936. Moreover, Governor Jim Price, who had been elected in 1937, was emerging as a New Deal leader. Consequently, Harry's participation in a Second District fight would have put his whole Organization at hazard, and a loss here might have been very damaging.

Harry and Hamilton had been carrying on a long feud going back to the time when Harry ran for governor. I became a part of it when I went to the House of Representatives in 1933. Senator Glass, Harry, and I joined in support of Walke Truxton, former city manager, who wished to become collector of customs, a place desired by Hamilton, who had the backing of Claude Swanson before Swanson left the United States Senate at Harry's not too gentle nudging.

Moreover, Harry's absence from my contest with Hamilton altered its character and permitted a coalition in my behalf between the old Virginia Organization and the many New Deal adherents represented by Elliott Heath and others. Although Harry was on the sidelines, most of the Organization people were helping me.

Another factor in his resolve to stay out of the fight was that his attitude toward Hamilton had softened a little. Prior to my campaign Harry had complimented Hamilton during a speech in Norfolk. This change in relationship probably was due to the influence of Colonel Slover. I've always felt that the colonel had much to do with Hamilton's vote that so offended Elliott Heath.

When I won, Harry was pleased, and he came to a celebration put on in Virginia Beach by Floyd Kellam, a Princess Anne County Democratic leader who always loyally supported me.

Harry's position is a good illustration of his placing the Organization ahead of everything else. Harry believed that his enemies were your enemies, but not necessarily that your enemies were his enemies. He could see virtues in them that you were not readily able to detect.

HOW BYRD CHOSE A CANDIDATE

F. Governor, did you enjoy the day in South Boston yesterday honoring Bill Tuck?

D. It was boiling hot on the fairground, which was in the center of a cinder track out in front of a little grandstand. Down on the track our hosts set tables with lunches for those of us who had come from afar. I bet you the sun was 110 down there.

With all of that, it was a happy day. I saw people I hadn't seen in a long time, and then we went over to the microphone in front of the grandstand, and the speaking and hollering started. It runs in a pattern, but you forget it until it comes again. The eulogies!—you feel that God had never created a person like the one being eulogized.

A week or so before Bill's day I had heard Mills Godwin deliver the tribute at a dinner honoring a prominent person in Norfolk. As half a dozen of us, including Godwin, were flying to Halifax yesterday, I told Godwin, "You know, when you got up to eulogize our friend last night I was confused for a minute about the relative position of him and Jefferson, but after a little while I realized you had moved him substantially and safely ahead of Jefferson, and I relaxed because I knew you had sensed the audience and the occasion."

Godwin laughed. He knew mighty well I had him. He did beautifully for Bill in South Boston.

F. Governor Godwin has a sort of profundity in delivery, almost a sepulchral tone.

D. It is, but it is an oratorical flourish and quite effective—pontifical.

F. It makes whatever he is saying seem momentous.

D. Yes, it does! If he says it is fifteen minutes to twelve o'clock in the way he can say it, you would say to yourself:

Then the world is to be destroyed at noon. Twelve o'clock!

    F.   Or the world is to be saved by Godwin at noon.

    D.   No, it's about to be destroyed. It's kind of inevitable. Crisis has come! Everything is over! Sooner the better!

Bill, I think, was a little overpowered by the tributes because he is a realist and quite modest; but he enjoyed it, and certainly it was heartfelt on the part of all of us. A great many were there, a genuine outpouring.

Between the sun and the oratory that hammered on the crowd, they were groggy by the time they got to me. The oratory was exactly like the sun in its stunning effect, except that it came from a different direction. The oratory flowed with unbelievable vigor straight from the platform over the crowd, crested in the grandstand, then receded to meet another blast that was on the way up from the field. At the end there was utter exhaustion. I spoke very briefly and concluded with this little story.

Shortly after I took office as governor with Bill as lieutenant governor, Bill came in one morning and said: "There's not much to this thing. You look after the office work, and I'll look after the social affairs for the Commonwealth." And with social affairs, I told them, Virginia was never better represented.

What Bill actually said was, "If you'll look after the office work, I'll do the drinking for the Commonwealth!" But I figured that was too much to put on him down there in his home district.

    F.   They'd have understood.

    D.   Yes, they would, completely.

    F.   He brought a conviviality to it.

    D.   He did, but then Bill had a greatness of spirit in whatever he did, and near the close of our administration there was an objective, too. He had made up his mind to be governor and that spurred him to greater heights in his socializing.

    F.   Governor Tuck says that had it not been for you, he never would have been elected governor.

    D.   He had been of incalculable help to me and in a great many more ways than the Commonwealth's social affairs. Tom Burch, his congressman, also was anxious to see Bill become governor. Bill had done a great deal of groundwork, going to conventions, sitting up all hours of the night telling stories.

Bill was one of Harry's great lieutenants and a good friend, but

Harry worried about Bill's conviviality. His apprehension was that Bill was too exuberant, and he figured it would be better to move to somebody else. Tom and I said that we were going to sit along with Bill.

Harry came to Richmond one sunny day in March 1945, and we sat out in the garden on the side of the Governor's Mansion talking about prospects in Virginia. I told him that Bill and I were devoted friends, that he had been lieutenant governor with me, and that aside from my personal attachment I felt that he would make an excellent governor.

Our meeting was not kept secret. Unbeknownst to us, a group in the attorney general's office on the second floor of the State Library building was peeping at us the whole time and subsequently gave out countless rumors.

It's a credit to Harry as a leader that although he had strong personal preferences he was able to weigh the chances. He knew that Bill Tuck knew every constable in Virginia and doggone near every policeman and if a fight split the upper echelons, it might bust the Organization wide open. And he loved the Organization better than anything except his own family. He made up his mind that the best thing to do was to go with Bill, and take a chance on everything working out afterward. As it happened he was highly pleased with Bill as governor.

F.   Would it be accurate then to say that Byrd's choice of candidates for governor was to a degree a case of the survival of the fittest? That at times he let things sort of work out within the Organization and then he said, "This is the man"— that he didn't have always as tight a hand on the selection as it appeared to outsiders?

D.   There's no question about that. He was the overlord and the counselor, but he seldom had the iron hand for which he was given credit or blame. One element of Harry's leadership was the organizing and the sounding out and assessing of the contending forces in the state and lining up with the Organization contender whom he thought had the best chance of winning. The Organization leaders down the line were especially concerned with maintaining the reputation of the Organization's invincibility for their own benefit, and they could best do that by building up Harry. Of course, that's something Harry didn't mind in the least.

F. He didn't stay always within conservative confines. You and John Garland Pollard were acceptable to him, and neither of you were from the stick-in-the-mud segment of the Organization.

D. The determining mark with Harry was what could be put together by way of votes. He often said that the Organization had about a third of the voters in Virginia amongst its friends. Another third would be in opposition, and the effort was to capture the remaining third.

F. He was minimizing the percentage of his backers, because the poll tax and the advance registration cut down the proportion of his opponents. He was running scared.

D. He was erring on the safe side. He was stressing the necessity of everybody's pulling along together.

Harry hit upon Pollard as a candidate in 1929 after Herbert Hoover had carried Virginia in 1928 with the support of Bishop Cannon and the drys. Pollard, a professor at William and Mary, was a dry and and had been a member of the Jones-Glass-Montague faction; but Pollard was no lockstep man. He really was more of an independent than an Anti. The friends of William E. Carson, Harry's former campaign manager, were advancing him and there were others; but Harry figured Pollard was the only man who could pull the state back over to the Democratic column.

F. When the crunch came, and Byrd was overruled, he usually was graceful about it.

D. Yes. That goes back to a thing that he told me years ago. It rose out of a wrangle that Willis Robertson had with a county Democratic committee over some little two-by-four political appointment. Willis got awful mad about it, but finally gave in. Harry said, "One thing you have to remember in politics. It's always important. When you decide to do anything, do it cheerfully. Doesn't make any difference how much it hurts and how much you dislike it, do it cheerfully." And that was absolutely sound. Not to get around and criticize everybody and make everybody mad, but do it gracefully. Now that's what he did. He hated to lose. He was a hard fighter, but he certainly came over in full measure with Bill Tuck.

He did it to a much lesser degree with Jim Price in 1937. Harry was determined that Tom Burch would be governor. Tom—other-

wise known as "Slicky" among those of us who circulated around
with him, because of his maneuverability—was one of the most
faithful allies and devoted friends that Harry ever had. Harry
worked for him mightily and yet in the end the effort fell apart. It
couldn't be done.

     F.   How did Jim Price overcome Byrd's opposition
and win the governorship?

     D.   Through a welling up of countless personal
friends throughout Virginia. Jim Price didn't have any organization. He knew very little about running an organization; but he
had been a member of the House of Delegates, and he had been
elected lieutenant governor on the ticket with George Peery as governor, and he was a leader in the Masonic Order. He knew, it seemed,
almost everybody in Virginia. He was a quiet, gentle, modest individual, striking in appearance. He looked like a governor! He's as
near as I've seen in Virginia to a person being swept into office by
personal friends.

     F.   In Price's case, Byrd didn't seem to follow his
own counsel about losing gracefully.

     D.   The answer to that is quite simple. First, he
resented Price's displacing Tom Burch. Second, he saw Price's election as a movement toward political control in Virginia by a group
that wasn't particularly friendly to him. In that Harry was right
because the forces behind Price became increasingly hostile. Price
came along at a time when relations between Harry and Roosevelt
were cooling. Price was a great Roosevelt man, and that tended
to separate them still further. Harry wasn't dealing with the appointment of a postmaster; he was facing a force bent on supplant-
ing him.

A groundswell was building in Virginia for the New Deal and
Price was part of it although he wasn't as willing to be as aggressive
as the New Deal forces desired. Roosevelt was willing to engage
in straight-out war. Many behind Price were not so much concerned
with him, although they liked him, as they were in building up a
force loyal to Roosevelt. Jim was friendly to many Organization
people. He didn't want to do them injury; he simply wanted to be
governor.

     F.   Is it true the General Assembly made life
miserable for Price?

D. Many of the members were just as hostile as they could be. But remember they were looking beyond Price to the people whom they thought were bent on taking their seats.

F. Did Price eject many Organization officeholders?

D. Not so many, certainly not as many as his followers thought he should. Naturally, he favored his own people in appointments. But the few that Price did oust increased the Organization's animosity. Peter Saunders, Peery's secretary, walked out of Capitol Square and didn't go back until he returned with me. Incidentally, many of the crowd that beat me for Congress in 1936 were red-hot Price men in 1937.

Price's followers tried to exploit his personal popularity and friendship with Roosevelt to the fullest with the aim of building an organization to gain control of the state. Jim Price didn't utilize the governorship to advance his or their interests to the extent that they wished. Many of them were hounding the hell out of him largely for their own advancement.

I saw him from time to time after I had succeeded him. I'd invite him to go to the dedication of school buildings he'd had a hand in. Sometimes he accompanied me to war bond rallies. In our conversations, Jim Price never indicated any personal or political bitterness.

F. But Byrd didn't find it difficult to back Bill Tuck despite his misgivings.

D. With Bill Tuck it wasn't hard because on both sides there were those of us intimately allied with Harry's political operations. All of us had been conniving and talking amongst ourselves.

I think that if the split had occurred, Bill could have won. Bill thinks not. The choice was whether to accept Bill or put in Tom Stanley or John Battle or someone else, but they were the two foremost in Harry's mind. Both were very competent, able persons.

F. In a way, the waiting, the standing back of both Stanley and Battle also demonstrates the process, almost the ordeal, that prospective candidates for governor had to undergo. Stanley was trying to run years before he actually won Byrd's nod.

D. Yes, he worked on it a long time. I remember I went to see Harry one day in his little hideaway almost under the dome of the Capitol. His candidate, Albertis Harrison, had just defeated A. E. S. Stephens for governor in 1961. Irked at Harry's participation in the campaign, "Gi" Stephens had said the Virginia people weren't given to dictatorship. Harry was fuming about the statement.

I was munching on a sandwich, and I said to him, "Harry, you don't think Gi was talking about you, do you?"

He didn't see a damn thing humorous in it. He said, "Who the hell do you think he was talking about?"

F. Why did you support Stephens in that race?

D. We were old friends and political allies from neighboring counties and had served together in the General Assembly. Also I thought his occasional independent attitude was a valuable one within the Virginia Organization.

F. The highlight of his career came during the 1959 special session of the General Assembly. As lieutenant governor he presided over the Senate when the moderates abolished Massive Resistance and adopted the Perrow plan of local option through freedom of choice.

D. That was a highlight in Virginia's history, too.

F. You know the moderates had a one-vote margin, 20–19, and watching those debates and votes, I wondered if the Massives weren't secretly relieved to lose by one vote heroically. Had they won, they would have been stuck with their vows of no-integration.

D. I'm not at all sure they were glad at the time, but the defeat did relieve them of a responsibility that they could not have delivered on to save their lives.

Now, of course, it was the dictatorship element in the thing that gave Harry such infinite personal pleasure. That was one of the things he enjoyed in the Organization. He loved it because he loved the mechanics of power.

Harry was not unlike—though he operated on a far smaller scale— but he resembled Robert Walpole in his love of power and management. Of course, there was one big difference. Walpole had to countenance bribes in the interests of the queen and the British government in those corrupt times.

F. Bribes with money?

D. Bribes with money or, more importantly, influence through appointments. The latter can be a form of bribery, and not infrequently is; but it is an inescapable part of political organization. You cannot divorce political organization from the rewarding of friends if you expect to hold your group together, which in the end gives you the majority needed to govern.

F. Just patronage.

D. Patronage. That's where the puritans run aground. They start off on the assumption that none of these things that cater to the—maybe not the weakness—but the appetites of human existence should be tolerated. And when you get through wiping out all of this, you haven't anything left.

F. The test is whether in dispensing patronage you select within your party able and honest—

D. That's right! That's the sole test! And you get in trouble when you don't.

F. Going back to bribes, I can't remember an instance in which Organization officeholders were involved in scandal.

D. I can't either. I don't believe they existed. I think that as a political outfit we did as well in that respect as any group has done in the country. I think the bill that can be brought against us is that we lacked imagination to a degree. We were not sufficiently abreast of the times; but these times were moving with such rapidity that it was very difficult to be abreast of them if you were going to carry other people along with you.

F. You say we. I would exclude you from that categorization, because you were abreast of the times.

D. I don't exclude myself for the very reason that I was part and parcel of an organization. I'm talking about joint effort through organization. Actually no individual gets but so much done. Government is like a gigantic glacier that moves slowly over the face of the earth. Some individuals draw more attention to themselves by bellowing and claiming credit, but when you cast up all the balances, no individual makes much headway.

F. Not only was the Organization free, more than any other machine that I can think of, from taint of financial wrongdoing, Byrd regarded any such irregularity with positive horror. At the slightest suggestion of misconduct by individuals, Byrd just cut away those involved.

D. He regarded it as a horror on two counts. It was offensive to him personally. He believed in personal honesty.

F. He refused to accept federal soil-conservation payments to which he was entitled simply because he had voted for the bill that authorized them.

D. The next thing, he was smart enough to know that in Virginia that would be death to the Organization. And there was nothing in Harry's whole life except his family that he ever loved as much as he did the Virginia Organization. You might as well have suggested to him that he do something to injure one of his children.

ARMING THE NATION

D. After I was reelected in 1938, I went back to the Naval Affairs Committee. The naval operations in the Norfolk area were huge; and, of course, in relation to the economic life of the community they were paramount. The fleet was being slowly expanded but much of it was on the West Coast. With the transfer of the fleet into the Pacific in the 1930s, we suffered in Norfolk.

I felt that after the Arms Limitation Agreement it was important for us to maintain the strength granted us, but much of the country was not of that opinion. The antiarmament people came down in droves on the Naval Committee. They didn't want to build any additional ships. They didn't want to build to the allowance under the limitation. The Naval Committee and President Roosevelt wanted to do it, but the opponents were so powerful you couldn't even get that done; so finally, to give you an illustration of how strong they were, Roosevelt transferred to the Public Works under Harold Ickes, who wouldn't even have known a rowboat if he saw one, the decision about building some of the smaller ships for the fleet, and Ickes built them under the Public Works Bill. I talked to Ickes about the building requirements for the yard in Portsmouth.

F. Had you all not persisted we would have been in dangerous straits in World War II.

D. Very bad straits. We pushed against great odds during the thirties. A powerful body of opinion in the United States argued that we ought not to antagonize Japan in any way. The theory was that we ought not to strengthen the fleet because Japan would feel that was a threat.

Witness after witness testified to such views before our committee. I remember one fellow, middle-aged, capable, but he was a zealot. He'd lecture the committee about what we needed to do not to give offense to the rest of the world. In his eyes we should set the example for peace-loving people by disarming the United States. You have a certain number of them running around the country now. You can't tell them that having disarmed, that when we are knocked over we won't get to our feet again; we'll be gone. They don't believe that. They believe that the way to show you are peace-loving is to throw away your weapons and leave yourself to the tender mercy of these ravenous powers that are skulking around the world looking for weaknesses to exploit.

F. That was ingenious of Roosevelt, switching some ship construction to Public Works.

D. He could find more ways to bamboozle the general public and do it so pleasantly that everybody was pleased with it. He was enormously skilled in dressing up propositions to enlist public approval.

F. Did he try to bamboozle you?

D. We had some sparring over the appointment of a postmaster in Portsmouth. One of Norman Hamilton's supporters had a temporary appointment to the job, and Hamilton made every effort to keep his man there through his friends in the administration. Finally I went to the White House and talked with Steve Early, Roosevelt's secretary.

"The president is very anxious to make this appointment for you," said Early, "but he can't do it because your candidate is deeply in debt, and it would embarrass the administration to put such a man in office."

"Why," I said, "if you applied that rule to Washington you couldn't open up the federal government tomorrow morning! I'll tell you what I'll do. I'll write you a letter promising that the minute Mr. Roosevelt sends my man's name to the Senate, I'll pay his debt so that he will go into office without owing a nickel, if that's what Mr. Roosevelt wants done."

"Are you serious?" he asked.

"Yes," I said, "I am because I know Mr. Kirby. If he's able he's going to pay me back. Although he's in debt, it's within range that's manageable."

Next Jim Farley called me. He said, "I saw the president this morning, and he's upset about that idea of yours."

"Jim," I said, "what in the world could he be upset about? The only thing I wanted to do was to save the president of the United States embarrassment."

Next day I took to the White House a letter saying that I sympathized with the president deeply and I was prepared to liquidate the sum the day the nomination was sent to the Senate, if he wished.

Jim called me and said, "It's on the way to the Senate, but I'm going to tell you he doesn't like it one bit."

Frank Kirby made an excellent postmaster. I knew mighty well they were never going to call on me to pay any debts. They wouldn't have dared to do so, because they would have been laughed out of town. It wasn't anything in the world but a skin game to refuse the patronage that rightfully belonged to a member of the House. Roosevelt was at war with the Virginia Organization and he thought to tick me off would be all to the good.

Jim Farley and I laughed about it later. I was very fond of Farley. He never flinched on a word he gave you. You could absolutely tie to him.

It's like another story Farley told me. Roosevelt went to dedicate a building in Georgia, and in perfectly outrageous remarks called on the people to turn Senator Walter George out of office and elect Lawrence Camp. It made them so damn mad that Camp never had a chance. After the election, Roosevelt asked Farley to patch things up with George.

"I can't patch it up," said Farley. "I warned you that you couldn't go into a person's home district on a nonpolitical occasion and attack him before his people."

But Roosevelt insisted he try and he did. Talking with Senator George, Jim said, "Of course the president ought not to have attacked you. But you know, Walter, to tell you the truth, in matters like that Roosevelt is his own worst enemy, really."

And George thought for a second and he said, "Jim, not so long as I live."

     F.   What put you in mind to leave Congress and run for governor?

     D.   Just the drift of events. And then dealing with the federal bureaucracy was utterly frustrating. Trying to help the unemployed was frightful. With all of our plans we never cut unemployment to speak of until the United States started to arm for war. The plans were well intended but they were not effective.

F. Your defeat for Congress in 1936 and then your comeback in 1938 had projected you as a possible candidate for governor.

D. Yes, that had some effect, but a greater influence was my being a member of the Naval Affairs Committee when war was coming on. I made a number of talks about national defense, and they inclined people to me. I made friends around the state, and it just turned up that it looked like I could be elected governor.

F. Who were your opponents in 1941?

D. Bill Tuck of Halifax, a state senator; Tom Ozlin of Lunenburg, former Speaker of the House, and Ashton Dovell of Williamsburg, another leader in the House, were interested but finally decided not to declare. Bill joined up with me as a candidate for lieutenant governor.

In the July Democratic primary my opponents were Vivian Page of Norfolk, a political independent and lively and popular member of the General Assembly, and Hunsdon Cary of Richmond, a state senator and a worthy representative of the old order in Virginia. He was an advocate of cottage industries for Virginia.

We had a spirited tussle. The Sunday before the election, as I was driving back from Martinsville, a young sailor flagged me down and got in the car. The boy, an orphan, was on his way to the Naval Operating Base in Norfolk after spending his leave with the doctor who had raised him.

"He wrote me some time ago to come up here and help work for a candidate for supervisor," the boy said.

"It's a pity you can't stay over and see how the election comes out Tuesday," I said.

"Oh," he said, "we've got 'em. Ain't any question about that. We saw every single voter in the district."

Seeing his deep interest in politics, I said to him, "By the way, aren't you all voting on a candidate for governor in Virginia Tuesday?"

He said, "Not as I heard of."

I'd been out shelling the woods, hollering and shouting and carrying on, and here this boy hadn't even heard of it! I had been riding around up there for a week in a little Chevrolet with a few books, staying with friends or in hotels.

F.   What were the books?

D.   I had a number of the Greek tragedies, in little single volumes. I was lugging around maybe two or three other things. It was just a kind of amusement on the side. You get tired driving around the mountains, especially in July when it's hot. I'd just pull off to the side of the road and read a little while. But nothing I read was any more instructive than the conversation I had with that boy. I put him out at the main gate of the Naval Operating Base and wished him well and drove the few blocks on home.

F.   Did you tell him you were running?

D.   No. Didn't tell him I was running. Didn't want to embarrass the boy. I just kept on talking about odds and ends. When that sort of thing happens, you realize that a lot of matters you think are consequential in the world really don't amount to much.

My opponent in the general election in November was Ben Muse, an intelligent and highly literate state senator who had moved over to the Republicans from the Democratic party. I think Ben became a Republican because he thought the Organization wasn't sufficiently sensitive to social problems.

F.   You remember the story about "A hog"?

D.   That occurred during the governor's budget tour of state institutions, which fell between the primary and the general election. As the Democratic candidate for governor, I went along on the tour, which was customary, and Ben, the Republican candidate, joined the tour at Governor Price's invitation, which was an innovation and a very good one.

Tom Stanley, then Speaker of the House of Delegates, was on the tour, and we went by Tom's farm to look at his prize Hereford cattle. Ben raised thoroughbred hogs. That night at supper Ben, who was sitting by me, leaned forward and called to Tom, on the other side, that he'd trade hog for Hereford. Tom, who was as sharp as they come in trading, called, "How many hogs?"

"A hog," shot back Ben.

F.   For the rest of the tour, Muse says, at appropriate moments you'd punch him in the side and say, "A hog!"

D. We had no end of laughing.

F. And then, Muse says, at your inauguration as governor, when you were walking onto the south portico of the Capitol to take the oath of office, coming down to the platform between all the dignitaries in high silk hats, just as you passed Muse, you murmured, "A hog!"

D. Yes, that's true. I A-hogged him at the inauguration. Those things are just irresistible to me.

Ben's departure from the State Senate was a loss to Virginia, but fortunately we have all gained from his penetrating writings on state affairs.

THE SECRET OF CARTER GLASS

D. "If you want to run for governor," Harry was telling me one day in 1940, "you've got to see certain people personally. Don't write them a letter and don't telephone; you got to go call on them. Certainly you've got to go see Mr. Glass first thing."

So I went to Senator Glass's office. He was a little fellow, and his hair stood on end in a topknot which made him look even more pugnacious. He was sitting with his foot on a hassock, his ankle all swollen, as I'd seen him many times before. At those times a visitor would say to him, "Mr. Glass, you're looking better."

He'd always rasp, "I'm here in direct contravention of the orders of my doctor!"

F. He took any optimistic remark as tomfoolery, didn't he?

D. He thought it bordered on the stupid in that it showed no capacity to appraise his physical infirmity. But anybody who felt that you could translate that physical incapacity into intellectual weakness was hopelessly confused.

Senator Glass was a very direct person. When I asked for his support, he told me at once that he had promised to back Bill Tuck but if Bill decided not to run, he would support me.

F. Is it accurate to call him the father of the Federal Reserve System?

D. That's a fair designation. Many people believed there had to be some banking legislation, and as chairman of the House Banking Committee, he was in a position to reflect that thinking.

When I came to know him he was a part of the Organization. Many years earlier, as a member of the House of Representatives, he was leader in the ablest group that ever opposed the Organization. William A. Jones was another leader. In Congress, Jones advocated Philippine independence. The Philippine government constructed a memorial at his grave in the cemetery at Warsaw on the Northern Neck. Then there was St. George Tucker of Lexington, a talented and public-spirited man who organized the Jamestown Exposition of 1907.

The Antis thought they were going to overturn the Organization when Woodrow Wilson went into the White House. They had worked hard for Wilson's nomination, but once in office, Wilson found that he couldn't wiggle without the help of Tom Martin in the Senate and Hal Flood in the House. The Antis had thought that Wilson's election would bring them to the Promised Land. When he came to terms with Martin and Flood, they just lost heart.

Westmoreland Davis, a progressive governor, was another powerful figure in the opposition. Davis appointed Glass to the United States Senate at the death of Tom Martin. But when the Organization supported Glass in his bid for the Democratic presidential nomination in 1920, there was a noticeable change in the political atmosphere. Claude Swanson of the Organization managed his campaign at San Francisco. Later that year the Organization didn't field a candidate against Glass when he came up for election for the remainder of Martin's term. And Glass did not support Davis when he ran against Senator Swanson in 1922.

I've always thought the obligation Senator Glass felt toward Swanson for his substantial effort for his presidential bid caused him to veer away from the Antis and assume an independent position. The Antis never got over it.

F. Was it not then, when the two factions were nearly even, that the loss of Glass proved to be the breaking point of the Antis?

D. Certainly the loss of Glass was a substantial one, but I think the turn came earlier when Wilson found himself unable to reward the Antis for their valiant efforts in his behalf.

Senator Glass's independence gradually merged into friendship with the Organization, although almost entirely on his terms. He was consulted on everything because nobody dared cross him.

F. What was the secret of Senator Glass's success as a politician?

D. He was extremely capable, a very analytical

man. He had a capacity to express himself briefly with great force. He had an awful sharp, harsh tongue. He was a master of invective. The speech he delivered on a nationwide hookup against Herbert Hoover during the 1932 presidential campaign was like a hurricane sweeping over a small boat harbor.

Senator Glass was a great partisan. We used to laugh over in the House of Representatives about his reputation for being uninterested in partisan politics and above party patronage. Well, the reason he didn't concern himself with patronage, he just took everything he wanted and left the balance for the rest of us to divide, and that included Harry. Glass looked over the list and picked whatever he wanted and that was that. Nobody peeped about it.

He wasn't much of a political organizer. He didn't pay any attention to that kind of thing. He didn't go around to groups making speeches. Didn't fool with it. He wasn't an organization man. He didn't think that way. He just went his way. He was utterly fearless. He was a one-man juggernaut. As time went on, he phased out as an Anti leader, and the Organization underwrote him completely.

   F.   It more or less carried him?

   D.   It didn't have to carry him. He marched in the vanguard. Or the vanguard was wherever he marched. He did as he pleased and the rest of us fell in step. Harry was just as cautious as he could be. It was just like walking around a panther.

I remember the Virginia congressional delegation was having a meeting about something one day and some fellow said "Mr. Glass is not going to like that; somebody better go over there and talk to him."

Another said, "Isn't any use going over there and talking to him. The thing to do is simply to find out whether he's agreeable or not agreeable."

I'm sure he talked to Harry a great deal because they were very friendly. You know Harry was his best man at his second marriage. I remember, because the day Harry told me Senator Glass was going to be married again, I was sitting on the little portico on the south side of the House of Representatives. It was the time of the terrible drought in the West. The dust that floated out of the West, borne on those western winds, was plainly visible. It hung like a dark mantle over the city. You could look across the Potomac River and see that heavy haze hanging over Northern Virginia. It had come all the way from the plains.

At any rate, Senator Glass and Harry sat around and did a certain amount of conniving. I don't believe Harry ever made any pivotal move without consulting him.

F. I never considered where Senator Glass's support was rooted. Politics is a cold-blooded operation, and it's interesting that a man could just float there, in sufferance, almost; and yet Byrd was always very respectful in referring to Glass.

D. Oh, he didn't just float in sufferance. He dominated it. And yet as an Anti-Organization person, he had come over. But he was so feared. He didn't float around anywhere. The Organization was just canny enough to know that there were some things that were plausible and possible and other things that weren't. And they all knew that getting in a fight with Senator Glass wasn't going to be profitable to anybody. His strength lay in his personality, his sheer ability, and his acid tongue. I don't reckon any other man in Virginia, except Randolph of Roanoke, ever was in his class when it came to laying the knife on somebody he didn't like.

One day, while Roosevelt was at odds with the Organization, he was holding up an appointment in my district. I went over to see Senator Glass, and he said, "Set up a conference, and I'll go down and talk to the president with you."

Later I was telling some of them in the House what the senator had offered to do, and somebody said: "You've just lost your mind! When Mr. Glass gets through talking to the president, you won't get another appointment as long as you're around here. Mr. Glass is not going to fool with Roosevelt. He's going down there and tell him exactly what he thinks. The best thing you can do is talk to Roosevelt by yourself and not get Mr. Glass in it because he'll just get you in a fight you'll never get out of."

He was a very telling speaker. He could state a case in a way that just took the hide off his adversary. He had the capacity—I suppose it came from his days as editor in Lynchburg—for getting an idea across in as few words as possible. He could organize facts as could few people I've ever encountered. He was utterly merciless in opposition.

I remember his tearing into John R. Saunders, the attorney general of Virginia. Saunders was eking out a puny state salary by selling insurance. During a political meeting in Portsmouth where Glass was on the platform somebody hollered up and asked him about Saunders as attorney general.

"I understand he's fairly good in insurance," Glass replied. "I never heard of him being a lawyer."

My father, who was at the meeting, came home and told me about it.

Another of the old Antis was Governor Andrew Montague. I saw a lot of him after he went to Congress. He lived with his daughter Gay near us in Alexandria. I used to take him to the House Office Building and home frequently. He'd tell stories along the way in a quiet, gentle voice. He had an intimate knowledge of early Virginia and his day and time. He said that when he became governor, Glass got on him about appointing a man to the State Corporation Commission, which had just been created to regulate the utilities and railroads. Governor Montague didn't think the man was very able, but he wrote Glass and said he would certainly give his candidate every consideration. After a long exchange of letters, Glass walked in the governor's office in Richmond one day and said, "I want to know about my candidate for the Corporation Commission."

"Congressman," said Governor Montague, "I've given it thought, but I'm just not sure. That commission has just been set up in the constitution and a lot turns on who goes on it."

"I want to know whether you are going to appoint him or not!" flared Glass.

"If you have to have an answer today, I'll just have to tell you I don't expect to appoint him." said Governor Montague. "He isn't competent."

"Whatever made you think that anybody with any competence would serve in your administration?" snapped Glass.

Can you imagine anything harsher than that? Montague once remarked, "Mr. Glass won't speak to me unless he meets me head on and has to speak. He'll always move away to avoid me."

He was harsh in a telegram denouncing a young University of Virginia professor, Leon R. Whipple, who had made a speech at Sweet Briar questioning America's participation in the First World War. The faculty, the president, and the Board of Visitors joined in Whipple's expulsion in November 1917.

F. That was contrary to Jefferson's wish that the university be tolerant in pursuit of truth.

D. That's the reason the expulsion seems to have been played down in later years; but it shows what can happen in war. It brings to mind something of much greater magnitude, the dominance of Thomas R. Dew at William and Mary. He was a fervent exponent of slavery, and as president of the college did much to steel the 'South against making any compromise as it moved on toward the War Between the States.

F. Why did Westmoreland Davis, who had been a forceful governor, withdraw from politics after he left office?

D. There's a very good reason for that. In retirement Davis kept launching barbs at the Byrd Organization and Harry, but he was realist enough to understand that the balance of power had shifted, that the old independent movement had fragmented to such an extent that he didn't have sufficient base.

F. Virginia is much more fluid now.

D. It is completely fluid now, I should say.

F. People can be defeated and still remain a force or a voice; but not in those days. Those two defeats the Organization handed Francis Pickens Miller—first when he ran for governor against John Battle in 1949 and then when he ran against Senator Byrd in 1952—pretty well quelled him as a major political force.

D. But he gave them quite a tussle, didn't he?

F. He certainly did. And he's not reconciled to defeat even now.

D. I think that keeps him alive. He's just as rambunctious as he can be. He's always been that way. You talk about a real overlord! Had Pickens ever laid his hands on the levers of power in Virginia, Harry Byrd would have looked like a calm afternoon tea. Pickens is—he's an old Presbyterian Covenanter, really. That's what he is. Lord! Lord! Lord! Off with your head! And I've told him so often because we're old friends. Now Harry was adamant at times, but he wasn't a patch on what Pickens would have been had he gained power.

Pickens served an enormously useful purpose in shaking the Organization to its foundations and setting in motion new and powerful currents of thought.

F. What moved Senator Glass and other Antis at

the State Constitutional Convention of 1901–2 to advocate dis-
franchising the blacks?

D. They thought that the black vote was an illiterate mass that was easily manipulated by unscrupulous leaders,
both black and white, who received money for delivering the vote.
In the convention Glass made an impassioned speech in which
he said, "Of course, we discriminate; we were sent here to discriminate, and that's exactly what I expect to do."

F. It seems ironic that the Antis, who were trying
to overturn the Organization, helped to perpetuate it by supporting
measures that restricted the electorate.

D. At that time there was widespread and deep
apprehension of the illiterates in politics. The Antis believed that
with an electorate restricted to those whom they thought had
competence to make a choice in their elected officials, they would
fare better than would the Organization. Also, they felt that their
situation would be improved in that they did not have as much
money to spend in the elections and that they would stand a better
chance in an outright appeal to the intelligence of the electorate
as a whole.

F. It seems to have hurt them because the poll tax
prevented most of the blacks and many whites from voting. And the
black vote continued to be manipulated. The Democratic Organization itself succeeded at times in buying the black vote for its
candidates.

D. The black vote, and the white as well, continued to be manipulated at times, and manipulation, regardless
of race, is always to be guarded against in a democratic system; but
it must be kept in mind that bloc voting which reflects a genuine
unanimity of opinion and objective is sometimes confused with
manipulation.

F. It just interested me that, in time, the Anti-
Organization movement came to depend in part on the segments of
the population which were most vulnerable to the poll tax, and the
Organization endured, in part, because large numbers of blacks and
whites, who didn't take a continuing interest in politics, could not
go to the polls and vote against the Organization if they became
aroused late in a campaign. The poll tax, coupled with requirements to register six months in advance of the election, prevented

any such sudden influx. When the poll tax was removed by Congress, that loosened the electorate. It was a factor that helped break up the Organization. Of course, as governor, you opposed the poll tax.

D. I thought it eliminated many people who were interested in voting: but when I look at what happened in the 1973 campaign for the governorship, I'm not sure my calculation on that was right. There never was a campaign in which as much was spent. A million dollars on each side! And yet 50 percent of the qualified voters stayed at home. I would not advocate a return to the poll tax. I simply say that the lack of interest that I felt was damaging still obtains.

F. I think it took time for the Antis to comprehend the disadvantage to which the poll tax was putting them—that they had to appeal to certain classes of people who couldn't get to the polls.

D. There I think you are right. Many years later they felt that the poll tax crippled them. It had nothing to do with Senator Glass's position in the constitutional convention.

Talking about the plight of the black people in those days, I remember an interesting conversation I had in 1944 with P. B. Young, a black leader who published the *Norfolk Journal and Guide* and one of this community's ablest citizens. We were talking one day about the southern states pooling their resources to support regional institutions offering advanced education for blacks; and he said to me, "Of course, none of that is going to satisfy us. What we are against is segregation, and we are never going to come to terms with anything that maintains it."

And that was so startling that I couldn't get it through my noggin. It didn't occur to me that it would ever be a màtter that I would have to give any consideration in my lifetime. I projected that ahead some centuries. In fifteen or twenty years it was here with us. We weren't quarreling about it. I never had a cross word with him in my life. He was just saying, "As far as we blacks are concerned, that isn't going to satisfy us. We want to get clear of segregation, and that's what we are determined to do." By jingoes! that's what they did, and in doing it they've created a more secure political base for all of us.

There isn't any doubt that you're correct in saying that the poll tax, insofar as keeping an in-group in, whatever it be, this Organization here or any other organization, is a very powerful weapon because its members will have enough patronage to pull a great many people to it and those people can pay the poll taxes of their relatives and keep them as capable foot soldiers.

As I gather it, in dealing with your irony, I don't see that the voting in the constitutional convention was curious by any means. I think it was a general thought that unless something was done to strike the merchandising of votes from the hands of unscrupulous political leaders—both black and white—that the state would be at the mercy of an illiterate mass.

F. I wonder whether the results of an informed electorate, if it's highly restricted in numbers, are any better than would be those of a mass of illiterates.

D. You have a good point there. I think that's what recent years have tended to demonstrate. But the next step on that, and bear this in mind, is whether or not self-government is a viable plan, after all.

F. I think it's more nearly viable if everybody is voting than if a select—

D. Madison thought that, as did Jefferson. They thought that the base of the mass was a protective base. But they also knew that the mass had to be instructed. What they advocated was broadening and instructing the base as much as possible. It wasn't an advocacy of illiteracy.

F. But the state failed to instruct the mass and it compounded the failure by depriving the mass of the vote. To solve the problem simply by saying they couldn't vote was no solution.

D. Yes, well, I think that's valid. But another thing intervenes in there. Neither Madison nor Jefferson, as far as I know, ever contemplated the black force being taken into the body politic. That deluge that came after the War Between the States brought on the acute situation at the end of the century.

F. We have no way of knowing, of course, what Jefferson and Madison would have suggested had they been there after the deluge, but it's not likely that they would have let the problem sit for fifty years without offering some constructive move beyond restricting the electorate.

D. I think that's true, but the training or the

education would have required some years. The threat was on the convention delegates in 1901.

F.   Whatever time was necessary, it would have been better to bear the ills a while longer than to postpone the remedy.

D.   Certainly philosophically you've got much on your side when you say that. Because bearing the ills would have hastened the day when the correction would have come. Don't you think?

F.   I think you've summed it up. The constructive way would have been to bear the ills and move directly to the root of the wrong, which was illiteracy.

D.   But there's another point, and that is whether there shouldn't be qualifications for voting. It's the most important duty that confronts the people. Shouldn't the state say that you have got to reach a certain modest point of qualification if you are to take part in running the state? The other would seem to me about as sensible as saying that we are going to turn you loose to pilot a jet plane with no training.

F.   Governor, that goes directly to your fight to write into the Virginia Constitution the guarantee that every child shall have an education.

D.   That's right. It does.

F.   Now if the state lives up to that mandate, that takes care of the problem. If the state doesn't do its full part in educating its people—as it was not doing at the time of that constitutional convention and did not do for a half a century more—then the state is in a poor position to say you can't vote because you can't read.

D.   I don't believe there is any argument with your principle there.

F.   Many people, anyway, tend to vote their special interests that touch their pocketbook, and the conferring of education on them often doesn't change that reflex.

D.   No, and I don't know that it should. That was Madison's theory of constitutional balance, that you brought these people into conflict and a balancing out of interests resulted. An industrial population's interest is somewhat different from an agrarian population's. It's a conciliation of these differences that self-government requires.

F.   Only when the black people attained the vote with the removal of the poll tax did the majority of the white politicians bid for the black vote openly and take their interests into account. As long as the blacks were disfranchised, the politicians didn't have to consider their special interests.

D.   There's no question on that.

F.   The 1901–2 convention seems to have been the watershed in Virginia politics. When the Antis helped adopt the poll tax, they set the course for Virginia politics in this century.

D.   They did, and, in doing so, they hobbled themselves to a degree. The Antis' very able leadership assumed that as the base was narrowed and purified, their candidates would have a greater appeal than if the mass was just purchased and herded into the fold. But as time went on and the general lethargy settled in, the poll tax operated to exclude a great many good citizens who just didn't want to go to the trouble of going through it. And that diminished the power of the independents.

F.   Well, of course, the poll tax contributed to the lethargy. We are still living with the effects of it. In the 1905 general election after the 1901–2 convention, the turnout was cut nearly in half. Thereafter, for nearly fifty years, it required only about 10 percent of the adult population to elect a governor. Those habitually small turnouts, depressed by the poll tax, resulted in Virginia's being one of the southern states that came under the Federal Voting Rights Act of 1965 because less than 50 percent of their voting population was going to the polls.

D.   But now the poll tax is gone and still many sit around in Virginia and don't vote. I don't think the poll tax is responsible for that.

F.   No, but 50 percent of the electorate going to the polls in Virginia is a millenium when we had been having 10 percent. Compared to what obtained for decades, a 50 percent turnout—

D.   It's very good, but not good enough. Talking about the poll tax and the conditions that prevailed at the time of the 1901–2 convention, I'm not sure that without some drastic action, the situation would not have stagnated. So, taking Glass's statement that they were sent to discriminate, he may well have been on sound ground as an interim movement.

F. The difficulty was the interim extended more than fifty years.

D. Yes, and that was bad. But the problem that they had to deal with when they met in 1901 was almost like trying to combat a fire.

F. The convention's leaders seemed intelligent and high-principled. Yet they couldn't come up with an equitable solution.

D. Had the convention not acted as it did, Virginia might not have pulled itself out. A group of people unconcerned with its welfare might have pillaged and destroyed it. The delegates were faced with putting out the fire and then building something else. We were too slow in taking the second step. Also the Virginia Organization was unwilling to give ground because by virtue of the poll tax, in large part, it controlled the state.

And in that regard there's an interesting sidelight. In 1944 some of Harry's friends were urging him to run for president; and an article in the *Saturday Evening Post*, reviewing his positions on various issues, quoted Harry as saying he favored abolishing the poll tax but that I wasn't agreeable to it!

Of course, I already was on record for its repeal. Harry told me that there had been a misunderstanding concerning this and he regretted it. But it simply was a part of the buildup of his candidacy because even then the poll tax was one of the first issues to pop up in a southerner's quest of the presidency.

An interesting thing to think about is what might have happened had something like a Marshall Plan been applied in the rehabilitation of the South after the War Between the States. Passions were so deep and hatred so bitter that probably it could not have been done, but think of what could have been accomplished had it been done. Solutions to the problems of educating the blacks and of giving a new start to the white people whose base of wealth had been destroyed would have brought what we saw a century later— the industrialization that produced revenues to build hospitals and schools. The rancor and bitterness held us in bondage.

F. Governor, to return to Senator Glass, how do you assess his contributions?

D. You're dealing with an individual who made a profound contribution to one of the greatest pieces of legislation ever passed in the United States and that was the reorganization of the banking system.

If you go back to Andrew Jackson and his fight with the banks and then study the difficulty that the United States had in funding the Union effort in the War Between the States, you'll see the pressing need for reform. Then, after 1865, we entered upon a long period of industrial expansion and the agricultural development of the West without machinery to finance either adequately. The results were recurring panics and great hardships.

The Federal Reserve System provided for a more orderly flow of money throughout the Union. Without the system we would have had great difficulty financing our participation in the First World War.

Senator Glass, more than anybody else, is the individual who through his energy, dedication, and vast knowledge of the banking system placed the Federal Reserve Act on the legislative books. That act alone places him in the vanguard of American statesmen.

A PARDON AT CHRISTMAS

D.   As governor during the Second World War
I worked a great deal on civil defense, especially in Eastern Virginia,
and met at least once a week, in the beginning, with the civil defense
leaders of Hampton Roads. German submarines were sinking ships
right off Virginia Beach at the entrance of Chesapeake Bay. They
had heavy guns that I knew about from my Naval Committee days,
and I feared that they'd surface out there and fire into the populated
areas. I never thought they could land, if they tried, but the shells
would do much to shake morale. We worked hard so that we would
be ready to move quickly to counter any attack. And there were
bond drives and USO campaigns. John Stewart Bryan, publisher
of Richmond newspapers, drove himself mercilessly in those campaigns. In my book he was one of the greatest Virginians. The most
heartwarming aspect of my service during the war was the magnificent response of the people of Virginia. There was no ducking, no
dodging when they were called upon.

F.   You did a good deal of spadework on how to
improve public education, looking to postwar days.

D.   One study that claimed much of my time concerned busing. The Department of Education did a survey on con-
solidating the high schools. We would have had no high school with
less than 2,500 students and that would have assured better offerings and facilities. What convinced me that it was not wise was that
it involved too much busing of children long distances. And yet
at the same time I was sitting there transporting little black children
right by white schools. Not until later was the wastefulness brought
home to me.

F.   Did a study commission prompt you to seek a
million dollars from the General Assembly for audiovisual aids?

D.   That was my own idea. I had concluded that
those teaching aids were needed as I visited schools and talked with

superintendents and teachers. Always it came up that they did not
have enough equipment. The Assembly responded with the largest
appropriation made for visual aids in schools anywhere in the
nation.

     F.   Then you established the Probation and Parole
Board.

     D.   Yes, it was recommended by the Virginia
Advisory Legislative Council and developed under the able
direction of William Shands Meacham. The board has been under
heavy fire recently on the ground that it has been too lenient. The
idea of keeping offenders in jail forever overlooks the need for
attempted rehabilitation, which is vital for both offender and
society. Moreover, it overlooks the fact that you couldn't build
enough buildings in Virginia to house them if there was no probation and parole system.

The Virginia Advisory Legislative Council has been a valuable
arm of the Assembly for developing forward-looking legislation.
It has suffered from the General Assembly's tendency to refer
troublesome issues to a study commission rather than face up to
them. Another advance to come out of the VALC was the beginning
of an adequate personnel system and a retirement program for
state employees, including the teachers.

By all odds the most poignant thing that happened to me while
I was governor concerned a pardon. One afternoon, about mid-
December, my secretary said a lady wished to see me about something important. I went out into the conference room and met a
serious and attractive person about fifty years old. She sat down and
said, "Governor Darden, I've come to ask you if you will let my
brother out of the penitentiary. He's dying. We have been a good
family. Many of our friends and others have not known that he's
been in prison."

His crime had been a violent one, murder, I think. He was in there
for life. She'd been coming regularly to see him and bring him
packages over the years. "If you can possibly let him die at home, it
would mean a great deal to us. I just don't want to think of his dying
in the penitentiary," she said.

She was appealing and dramatic in a way, and yet firm. She
didn't break down, there was no weeping. It was just a calm statement of awfully deep emotion. Reminded me of what Herodotus

wrote about the grief of an Egyptian king who had been overrun by the Persians, as the enemy marched off his people. As his generals went by and his household people and others, the king was very loud in his lamentation. Finally his daughters came by in the train, and he sat immobile and silent as they marched them out. An aide said to him: "Sire, it's strange that you didn't show any emotion when your children went by."

He replied, "There is sorrow too deep for tears."

This lady just sat there and unfolded the story quietly. "Come back here in a few hours," I told her. "I'll see what can be done."

I called Major Rice Youell, who was running the prison system, and asked about her brother.

"He's dying," Rice said. "He's not going to live very much longer. He's been a good prisoner."

"Make out the papers for his pardon," I told my secretary. "I'm going to turn him loose to his sister and let her take him home."

When she came back, I told her, and you never saw such an expression on a human being's face in your life as the one on hers. She took him home. He died in ten days, over Christmas.

She apparently was the only person remaining who cared. I don't think she was married. I don't know where in Virginia she came from. I just remember her sitting and talking with me and the look on her face when she learned he was free.

And you know, there's another interesting thing about it. She had never come in to ask me to pardon him. Only as they moved on toward death and Christmas time, the two together, did she come to my office. She made up her mind that she'd march up there and see if she could get him out. And she did it.

F. Governor, tell me about your dispute over the snake handlers.

D. A group of primitives in the western part of the state insisted that they could handle snakes and drink poison without being affected. They would work themselves up to a frenzy and then reach down into baskets and take out rattlers and moccasins and start handing them around one brother to another, chanting and hollering. A snake bit somebody, and the fellow had a very close call. I told the police to go out there and break up the crowd.

"I don't care about the preachers getting worked on by the snakes, but I'm afraid some children are going to get killed," I said.

The handlers always were near the state line, and as the police would go in and try to catch them, they'd dart into West Virginia or scoot into Kentucky or Tennessee. There was a good deal of commotion about religious freedom. You'd have thought I was attempting to abolish Christianity.

John Flannagan, who'd been a close friend of mine in Congress, was very much offended at my sending the police. He made a number of speeches. Made one when I was on the platform with him in Marion, and he just blistered us, me especially, about the mistreatment of the God-fearing people of Southwest Virginia, denying them the right to pass around the snakes. But I finally made it impossible for them to operate in the state.

        F. That's like not being able to yell fire in a crowded place.

        D. Exactly the same. As Holmes said, "Your freedom stops where my nose begins."

        F. Governor, Harry Truman was president while you were in Richmond.

        D. Yes, I was part of the delegation that helped him at the Chicago convention in 1944 when he came over and asked Harry Byrd to support him for the nomination for vice-president. As governor, I was chairman of the Virginia delegation. I was sitting on the aisle with the microphone. Next to me was Harry Byrd. Truman came over, crouched down, leaned over, and said to him, "I'm not going to ask many people around here to try to help me, but I would appreciate anything you might do." Harry said he'd be glad to see what could be done.

What we were trying to do was stop Henry Wallace. We were all together on that. I never thought there was anything to this hocus-pocus about Wallace being a Communist. I just questioned his economics. For one thing, to forestall massive unemployment after the war, he advocated a vast public employment program. It would have converted, really, the country's economic machinery into a state economy, which would have been far less manageable and less productive than what Wallace had in mind.

I saw Truman not long after President Roosevelt's death. His office called and said the president wanted to see all the governors and ask for help. I suggested that since Richmond was nearby, he fit me into the schedule when somebody else had to drop out. In a week or so a call came from the White House, and the next morning I walked into the Oval Office. There sat Harry Truman behind the great desk piled high with manila files. He was the most woebegone-looking fellow I ever saw, and he said: "Governor, sit down. I want to talk to you. This is a terrible load that has fallen on me, and I just got to have the help of everybody."

"You certainly are going to have the help of all of us, Mr. President," I said. "We realize what a fearful task you are facing."

"I appreciate that," he said. Then he sat there probably half a minute in a pensive sort of way, and he said, "You know, I always thought being governor of a state is about the best political job you could have."

"I don't know enough about the Union to know about all of them, but being governor of Virginia is the best political place you can get," I said. "The people of Virginia respect their public representatives, and their support and confidence really make you do a better job than you are capable of by yourself."

"Yes," he said, "I kind of thought that."

"Another thing," I said, "a state is a small enough unit so that you can do some planning in it and get your plans executed and see something accomplished. That makes it very attractive."

"Yes," he said, "I imagine that is true."

He sat there a while in silence. Finally he looked over at me and he said, "You know, the trouble about this place is, you can't find out what the hell's going on around here!"

Telling Connie about it that night, I said I'd never seen a more dejected fellow in my life. If the good Lord had reached down and said to Truman, "Harry, I know this thing is not to your liking, and I tell you what I'm going to do for you. I'm going to put you back in the United States Senate and nobody will ever know you have been vice-president of the United States. I'll fix it in some way so that tomorrow at noon when the Senate convenes you'll be in your old seat and you can move right on." And I told Connie, the only thing that Truman would have said to Him is, "Could you make it this afternoon?"

My! He was depressed! But then as he got hold of the office he became cocky and sure of himself. I saw him two or three times after that. I remember going to talk to him about appointing a federal judge in Norfolk, and as I walked in the office he said, "The main thing I'm concerned with is not to get some son-of-a-bitch on the bench!"

Truman had been a fine investigator in the Senate. He was a good person. He got mad with us down here in Virginia because he thought we were all in "that Byrd Machine." But at any rate the contacts I had with him were pleasant, and I supported him whole-heartedly.

F. Does that about sum it up, Governor?

D. Yes, I think so. Probably overdoes it.

F. Governor, we focused on your activities in the war effort and three or four advances. There was more, of course. I checked the editorials of newspapers in Richmond, Roanoke, and Norfolk, summarizing your term as it drew to a close in 1946. They say that it was fortunate you were there to gear Virginia into the war, and then they cite a substantial body of legislation to place the state on a progressive course. Let me list some of it.

Your administration managed a striking increase in teacher pay; upgraded vocational education; funded full-time public health offices in every county; coordinated Radford College with VPI and Mary Washington with the University of Virginia; proposed a graduate school in agriculture for VPI and one in education for the University of Virginia; established Norfolk State College—

D. Well, now, hold on! There had been a little two-year school for blacks that began in the old Brambleton YMCA as an extension of Virginia Union University. I helped make it a part of the state system and moved it to larger quarters at the St. Vincent de Paul Hospital building which was being abandoned. Later we made it a division of Virginia State College in Petersburg and moved it along to a former municipal golf course beyond Brambleton Avenue.

It grew rapidly, and Lyman Brooks, the president with whom I worked closely, wanted it to be separate. It wiggled out from under Virginia State, and continued on its way under his able leadership.

But Norfolk State received generous treatment under Virginia State. Virginia State's president, Dr. Robert Daniel, saw to that.

One morning while I was at the University of Virginia, Dr. Daniel came to see me about a problem. He couldn't get laboratory equipment for his Norfolk Division and he wondered if I could help.

"I'll tell you how to get it," I said. "If I had your leverage, there's no end to what I could do for the University of Virginia. The members of the General Assembly shudder when you come into the Capitol, and all they want to know is how much they have to give to get you out.

"You must go see the governor. First thing in the morning, when he's fresh, drive over to Richmond and see him and tell him, not in anger but with just a touch of sadness, that Norfolk State doesn't have money to equip the labs and you see nothing to do but just shut down the labs and send all the students over to the Norfolk Division of William and Mary College. You'll get your money before nightfall."

"Do you reckon it'll work?" he asked.

"I know it will," I told him.

So he went to see the governor and late the next day he called me and said, "It worked!"

I knew he'd get it. When he mentioned sending a mass of black students over to the Norfolk Division of William and Mary he might as well have placed a ticking time bomb on the table.

     F. I'll read more of the list: created a department of corrections; set in motion studies for the hospitalization of the indigent; established a prison farm in Southampton County for first offenders; liquidated the state debt; redistricted the state to give urban areas better representation; extended workmen's compensation; recommended the creation of a pollution control board so that the localities and the industries could be brought into line on waste treatment plants.

     D. That's a lot of stuff I don't remember. You reckon that's right?

     F. I pulled it out of the editorials.

     D. That may be, but I've seen editorials that are wrong.

     F. If so, all of these were wrong in concert.

     D. Go ahead. I pushed along on those things with the help of many other Virginians. Remember, nobody acts alone in this world. The older I get the more I'm inclined to believe an observation I heard many years ago: There's no end of what can be accomplished if you don't concern yourself as to who gets credit for it.

F. The list continues. You succeeded in getting a reduction on interest rates on small loans—

D. That was the bitterest fight I encountered in Virginia. That was a fearful fight! The loan companies were permitted by law to charge 42 percent interest. I thought that excessive. We cut it to 18 percent.

F. Did the lenders work on the General Assembly through lobbyists?

D. Did they work on them? I say they did! They worked on them all around the state; but there was a great groundswell for reform, helped along by the newspapers.

F. Didn't you call the General Assembly into special session to liquidate the state debt?

D. Oh, yes. The liquidation of the state debt was very simple. Under the provisions of the bond issue, I simply bought federal bonds of comparable maturity and put them aside. In other words, if the state had $5 million mature in ten years down the line, I bought federal bonds ten years down the line.

I said in my message to the members of the General Assembly that there was no use doing this unless we were willing to make it a permanent commitment. They agreed, but they disestablished it in a few years. The Organization scrapped it to find funds to counter the telling thrust of Pickens Miller's educational proposals in his gubernatorial campaign against John Battle. Since it went for schools, that never troubled me.

F. The editorials note that you put the idle funds of the state to work.

D. Well, I put the idle funds of the state to work in that instead of just carrying these big cash balances with no interest, we put some of them into savings accounts and that brought in considerable revenues.

F. Tell me about the dispute over contributing the Capitol Square fence to the scrap metal drive.

D. That was when Mrs. John Garland Pollard came to the rescue in a magnificent way. There was quite a sentiment around and about to take down the Capitol fence and melt it into scrap for the war effort. Simply to say no, we are not going to give up the fence because of aesthetic or historic reasons would have been quite difficult. Mrs. Pollard wrote me a lovely note and said, "Tell them that you'll put the fence in the furnace when the White House fence goes in."

And when they came back to me I said, "Your idea is first rate. It is a great emergency. Let the White House fence and the Capitol Square fence go in the furnace together." That's the last word I ever heard on the fence. But that was her idea, not mine.

F. Then you told the board of William and Mary that you thought fraternities and sororities at state institutions ought not to have houses off the campuses.

D. That's right. I remembered that Oxford had more clubs than you could shake a stick at; but they were not separate residence clubs. I proposed that sororities and fraternities not live apart from the student body.

F. I hadn't realized that you tried twice during the war to return to active duty in the Marine Corps.

D. No, only tried once. When we went to war, I communicated with them and explained that I was on the retired list and available for duty. The commandant of the corps thanked me and said that under the circumstances I would not be called up.

F. You were forty-five then; but you felt you ought to go into active service?

D. Well, I felt they had a call on me. There would have been quite a commotion because I already had been elected, you see. But I never tried twice. The twice thing came up because I talked to Jim Forrestal and some others about returning to the service when my term concluded if they wanted me. I didn't know the war was going to be over by 1945. It looked then that we had two or three more years ahead of us.

F. You held frequent press conferences while you were governor.

D. I had a constant press conference going on because the reporters hung out at my office, just sat around a long table and argued and talked. Nobody in the world ever had more press conferences than I had because we were engaged constantly in press conferences, aided by my able press secretary, Virginia Davis.

F. One report notes that you had two press conferences a day, morning and afternoon.

   D. That's a modest statement, I think. It was a continuing thing, and I bowed out for lunch at the Mansion and they'd go downstairs to the little sandwich counter and get their lunch. We'd come back and sit down and go to talking again about one thing and another.

   F. Then it was what is called today an open administration, wasn't it?

   D. 'Twas a very open adminstration and thoroughly delightful.

WORKING ON THE
CAPSTONE

F. Governor, as your term was ending, the newspapers reported that you were the overwhelming choice to succeed
ailing Senator Carter Glass when he retired. The difficulty was that
you didn't seem to want a seat in the United States Senate.

An editorial in the Richmond *Times-Dispatch* observed on November 16, 1945, that if you intended to retire from public life at the conclusion of your term in January, "there should be an uprising on the
part of the people, and a firm demand from them that he change
his mind."

Two days later the *Times-Dispatch* reported that "the cold fact is
Colgate Darden doesn't like Washington" and that "the whole
matter seems to add up to that rarity in politics—a case where the
office actually seeks the man."

Finally on June 20, 1946, the Associated Press carried your statement rejecting a draft. Why were you so determined not to accept
either an appointment or a convention's nomination to the Senate?

D. While I was in the House of Representatives,
then when I was in Richmond, I found myself away from home
much of the time going to meetings—first one place and then
another. I concluded that if I was going to see anything of my family,
I should change this. The other reason was that I decided I wasn't
going to bring our children up in Washington. Not that it was a bad
town, but it is to a degree a rootless town. It is mankind in motion.
It is blocs and individuals on the move toward something. Whether
you think highly of it or not, you find there is a propelling force
moving them in first one direction and then another. And private
life was infinitely more attractive to me than public life.

So when I left the governorship I left Richmond with an idea of
settling back. I had in my own mind closed the door on Washington.
A good many of my friends didn't take that seriously. They thought
that I was angling to get to Washington, and it wasn't until the

nominating convention of 1946 that I got to a point of making it stick.

Sometime before Senator Carter Glass died, I was advised through intermediaries that he was prepared to resign from the Senate if I'd take his place. I didn't have any idea of resigning the governorship of Virginia to take a place in the Senate. I wouldn't resign the governorship of Virginia for both seats in the Senate rolled into one.

F.   Years later Senator Byrd told me that you were the only man he had ever known to reject a seat in the United States Senate. He couldn't comprehend why anybody would do that. And in 1946 he didn't believe you would do it until you insisted on becoming chairman of the nominating convention so that you could, if the delegates put your name up, block it.

D.   I pleaded with my friends not to put my name in nomination, but they did and it led the first ballot. Then the convention recessed for lunch, and when it reconvened I told the delegates that I had consulted the best lawyers who assured me that if nominated I would be under no compulsion to accept or run, and that was final.

F.   Meanwhile, you have been working in one cause after another. I have never seen anybody outside public office as active incessantly in public life as you are.

D.   Yes, but that is different. Now what you have witnessed is my engagement in undertakings at my own option and on such terms as suited me and the people with whom I worked.

F.   The work you did during twelve years at the University of Virginia was demanding because you were trying to change its course. Weren't you working as hard as you would have in the Senate?

D.   There's no doubt I was working hard, but I solved the question of being with my family. Then there was another point. I felt that altering the course of the University of Virginia, if it were possible for me to do so, would be an infinitely better piece of public work than being a member of the United States Senate.

F.   So often during these past two decades you have tried to educate or persuade the community or an individual to remedy a situation. Couldn't you have exerted guidance more directly as a senator?

D. I don't think so. The size and momentum of the Senate is such that the individual member is considerably restricted. This was not the case at the University of Virginia. The president there had many opportunities, particularly with a fine board such as I had, to improvise and experiment.

F. How do you rate your experience at the university?

D. Oh, I'd rate that as the top undertaking. Working with these young people from day to day is exhilarating. They are an intellectual elite, really. There are disappointments among them, but when you look at them as a class, they are the hope of the Commonwealth. A tremendous amount happens to young people between seventeen when they enter the university and twenty-one when they come out. They grow up in that time. They are different people. You realize that what you are watching is the development of enormous power. That is Virginia; that's America, and that's the future right there multiplied many times over. Of course, the student body of the University of Virginia wasn't a large one, but it represented a segment of the United States at its best.

F. I believe many persons wished you were in the Senate because they recognized that you embodied the best of Virginia's traditions and also were attuned to the needs of modern society.

D. That's an overassessment arising out of the partiality of old friends. The question to be resolved is whether the individual can in his own opinion make a more substantial contribution in one place or another. And, of course, the ultimate consideration is what you want to do in the limited number of years you have in your life. Having served in the House, I was well aware that insofar as the family relationship, which I think is paramount in our society, I couldn't carry on. And I resolved it as I should have, in favor of getting back into a position where we were together. The state ordinarily has no call on anybody superior to the family's.

F. For a little more than a year you were chancellor of the College of William and Mary.

D. The chancellorship carried no administrative duties, and though I enjoyed the association it made no consequential demands on my time. After it became certain that I was not going to the Senate, a few people who were interested in the University of Virginia talked to me about going there on John Lloyd Newcomb's retirement. The demand that I go to Charlottesville wasn't overwhelming, but I felt the need was overwhelming to get along a step further with Jefferson's idea of making the university an integral part of the public school system of Virginia. Many people with whom I'd been associated in politics didn't think the idea amounted to a damn. They figured that I'd gone off my rocker when I could go to a place like the United States Senate and strut around with the various perquisites but chose instead to join the academic world.

        F.   Of course, Jefferson didn't look on it that way.

        D.   Oh, no, Jefferson didn't look on it that way and a number of other people didn't either, but it is fair to say that the political thinking was paralleled to a degree by some of the faculty members' thinking, that I was moving in on them totally unequipped and unprepared to assume the headship.

I knew the undertaking in Charlottesville required time, patience, and unremitting effort because you don't change the direction of a great institution quickly. When I left the university twelve years later, many things remained to be done, but we were well on our way. We had set the direction. You know, this idea that individuals accomplish great things is a lot of moonshine, really. What you do is work along with others on a general line, and mankind moves along, but slowly.

It reminds me of a story my administrative secretary at the university, Mrs. Anne Davis, told me years ago. She came into the office laughing one day, and said: "I just had a funny experience. I was coming from downtown, and behind me on the bus were two students, an older student pointing out to a newcomer the things of importance. We passed through the underpass and he said that was the C&O railroad and then he pointed to the medical center on the left and the beginning of the university grounds, the gateway and the walk up the hill to the Lawn, and then the bus came along to the Rotunda and stopped at the traffic light at Rugby Road. The older boy explained about the Rotunda, and then the new boy looked up at Carr's Hill, and he asked the older boy, 'What's that house sitting up there?'

"And the boy said, 'That's the president's house. There he sits up there in that great big house drawing a great big salary, and he don't do a damn thing!' "

The point that I tried to make was that Jefferson had built the university as the capstone for public education. An effective system of public schools required at its top a university. That had not obtained in Virginia. Jefferson passed from the scene, and the university drifted into the hands of individuals who nourished it and protected it, but who, by and large, were the graduates of private schools because the South had been so slow in developing public education.

Even after the Underwood Constitution in 1870, the development of public education in Virginia was painfully slow notwithstanding the heroic efforts of William H. Ruffner, our first superintendent of public instruction. During that time the university furnished a steady flow of graduates to the southern colleges as teachers; and a steady flow of southerners came there as students, many from private southern schools. But for these the university would have suffered terribly.

There were few high schools in Virginia when I was young. Great growth in public education came during my early days when President Edwin A. Alderman, Governor Andrew Montague, and others in the state organized a crusade, the May Campaign of 1904, and set about strengthening public education. After the First World War there was another great impetus to public education, and it moved along; but in its moving along, it never had really come to look on the University of Virginia as its head. I'm not sure that it does now, as a matter of fact. There is a warmer feeling between the university and the public school system than there was when I was a boy; but it isn't comparable to the feeling that you find in North Carolina between Chapel Hill and the public schools. To a North Carolinian, going to Chapel Hill is almost like going to Mecca.

F. I'm trying to get your term as president of the university in perspective. Really, you lifted that school. In so many ways—academic standing, professorships, capital outlay—it had been undernourished.

D. I'm not sure that it was a question of lifting so much. It certainly had been undernourished. I was able to get more funds. In the first place, more money was available; and then I was close to the political hierarchy and it was very generous in trying to help me out. But basically what took place at the university was somewhat a change in the emphasis.

My predecessor, John Lloyd Newcomb, had served the university admirably. He was an engineering professor, and he was a good, hardheaded person who labored under the greatest difficulties of not having money enough to carry on during the war years. He stayed on in an advisory capacity and was invaluable in helping me. He had a small house down beyond the gymnasium and I used to go down there frequently Sunday mornings and talk with him.

As a student I used to see President Alderman from a distance. He was one of the grandest looking people I ever saw. He had a fine head and fine face and was very kind to all of us, but we kept our distance. Not a one of us ever would have thought of opening our peepers about anything that he did or said.

He had a magnificent cloak he flung over his shoulder. You felt that this at least was a Roman senator moving along the colonnade by the Lawn! He was an absolutely superb speaker. He had a beautifully modulated voice, and occasionally when he'd get us together in Cabell Hall to give us the word about something, he charmed the whole student body. He was like some magician who stood and waved a wand over us. He performed the same magic when he made the memorial address about Woodrow Wilson, an old friend, before Congress.

He would go over to his office sometime between eleven and twelve—I lived on the Lawn for a year, and I would see him—and then move on home for lunch, and so far as I was ever able to learn, that completed his day's work. I'm sure that what he did was work in his library at the president's house. Also, he did a good deal of traveling in promoting the university and raising funds.

A great many faculty members were never entirely reconciled to the creation of a president of the university. Alderman, as first president, allayed much of their fear by maintaining the excellent scholastic standards of the university. Newcomb was the second president, and I was the third. Then came Edgar Shannon and Frank Hereford.

Edgar Shannon was a first-rate scholar, he knew university life, and he was close to the faculty. He picked up the duties very rapidly and discharged them with rare ability. The difficulties that arose out of student unrest in the 1970s were unfortunate, but they probably were unavoidable and had they not been handled as he decided, they might have been much worse. He presided with ability over the profound changes as desegregation flowed from the court decisions, and his innovative academic programs were most helpful.

The choice of Frank Hereford also was a very good one. As a matter of fact, I made him a full professor ahead of schedule on the recommendation of the physics faculty; but for that, we would have lost him. He'd had considerable experience because he was Shannon's provost. He came into the presidency with excellent training. He's a fine scholar and an indefatigable worker.

The faculty ran the university for its first seventy-five or eighty years. Many never had believed they needed a president, and even in my day some of them resented a young upstart like myself. They thought that was just rank heresy. And then somebody drawn out of the political hierarchy in the state was even worse! Of course, Jefferson, Madison, Monroe, and Joseph Cable were not altogether political novices.

Even President Alderman, with all his prestige, had his trials. They were always sharpshooting at him. That was not apparent to us as a student body. We didn't understand that. If we saw it, we didn't know what we were looking at; but in some of the minutes that I read after I became president, it was apparent that they were bent on making life quite trying for him.

        F.   What were your relations with the faculty?

        D.   In the academic work, I relied heavily on the deans. While we did not always agree, I never undertook to make an appointment without securing the approval of the appropriate faculty committees. I didn't follow all their recommendations, but I felt that in that field they were better equipped than was I. Too, I knew that the person appointed would have to work with them to be successful. When we disagreed, I simply asked the committee to give me another name to submit to the board.

When I went to the university, the enrollment was not quite 4,000. Under the stimulus of the GI Bill, it rose rapidly to 5,300, and then when I left there it was in the range of 3,500. The tide of veterans had swept through. Then the enrollment rose again fairly rapidly until now it stands at about 15,000.

The veterans and I arrived together in 1947. They were admirable. Their experience was such that they realized the necessity of getting their work done. Many were married. Their wives were working for the university and they rode herd on their husbands' studying, and they weren't having parading and drumming around on the weekends. The veterans stayed home and worked, and as a result they were better students than the rank and file.

The fellow that I am deeply indebted to in getting along with the veterans is Dick Poff, who is now on the Supreme Court of Virginia and who used to be in Congress. The university had a veterans' village called Copeley Hill, and Poff, as a law student, headed its government. We called him the mayor. I call him that now.

We had no end of trouble at Copeley Hill over the children and the dogs. The parents wanted their children to play out in the yard and the street, and they did not want the dogs running loose across their front yards and knocking their children over. The dog-people wanted the parents to build fences around their property to keep the dogs out. It was just that simple between the two camps.

A little town council governed Copeley Hill. One night in a discussion of the dogs-children issue, a councilman jumped right over on another councilman and pulled his shirt off. They had quite a set-to. I made up my mind that something had to be done, so I sent for Poff.

"Poff," I said, "there is a lot of trouble at Copeley Hill. Take it over, and I'll back you up, but I want some peace and quiet. I'm tired of listening to mothers hollering at me about the children and the dogs." I never had another peep out of Copeley Hill. Poff organized it perfectly.

My relations with the faculty were pleasant. Some, while not unpleasant at all, were aloof simply because they thought that the faculty committee ought to run the university. I had no argument with that, because I was inclined at times to agree with them.

Those who opposed the president were convinced that the state employed him to make life unpleasant for the faculty members, young and old. Consequently they were in a constant state of new combinations to the common end of putting your eye out.

There wasn't a day but what at least a dozen presidents weren't walking around the grounds. That was an average day. Some days it went up higher. A few days it dropped below that, not many. Now of that dozen there would be seven, say, from the student body, and five from the faculty. I knew that as long as that existed things were reasonably all right. It's when a student body gets to be quiet that there is trouble ahead.

But the students reacted quite reasonably to the tremendous liberty. They would leave home, where they were under the careful tutelage and chaperonage of their parents, and come to the university, and overnight they were to be treated as grown men. You can see how with the exhilaration of the new freedom they could come to the conclusion that everybody there was an old fogey and didn't know what he was about and that the university would be far better off if turned over to them.

The only limitation that the itinerant presidents placed on their activities was that I should continue to raise the money for the university. That was a simple arrangement. I was to get together the money to finance it, but in all other and more important matters they would take charge. But with all of that I developed— and interestingly enough, it still survives—a good system of student government. I gave the student council authority to deal, subject to my review, with student offenses against the university. At first it didn't work smoothly, and I concluded that it wasn't well to have the council that brought the charges act as a court. So I had the student council bring the case and created a judiciary committee to hear it.

I've always felt under great debt to the student body. Students are prolific beyond belief in ideas about what ought to be done with the university. Now, in that, it's like searching for gold, I imagine, back in the old days in the West. Occasionally you run across a nugget of great worth. Most of their suggestions are not particularly good, but they have so many of them that if you listen to them, you learn. They used to come by the office and sit down and talk with me. They were very open, coming in and telling me what was wrong with the university. I found that occasionally we'd hit on an idea that was priceless, and I would adopt it.

F. Did they just drop by or did they make an appointment?

D. In those days it was nothing like so hurried,

and they'd look in the window and if the office was clear, they'd come in and talk.

F.   How old was your own family when you went to the university?

D.   Our oldest child, Colgate, was at Deerfield Academy. He came back to the university. Pierre was at Lane High School and Irene, a little bit of a thing, was at St. Anne's, down the road. I made a lot of miscalculations in my life, but not going to the United States Senate, getting out of politics and getting back home, that was absolutely sound, that decision.

F.   Did your boys live at home?

D.   Colgate was there at home and then he married. Pierre moved over into the dormitories for a time so he could get a touch of college life. In his last year he moved to the Lawn. He had my old room: 21 West Lawn. He wiggled around and got 21 out of the university in some way. Colgate joined the fraternity I'd been a member of. Pierre never joined one. He'd seen enough going on around there so that he didn't want to be a member of anything. He stayed an independent.

One of the many fine things about the university was the reception my children had from the student body. Certainly nobody was more unpopular with many of the students than I was at times. The dislike of me was deep over my support for a student union building. Many fraternity members felt it was an intrusion of their preserves. But I never encountered and I don't believe my children ever encountered a single thing that indicated that the students wished to take out on them their displeasure with me.

OPENING UP THE
UNIVERSITY

F. Governor, when did you first feel the need for increasing admissions of public school students to the university?

D. From my student days. That feeling was reenforced in talking about the university to people when I was in the General Assembly and later when I was governor. We didn't do much then because the state was terribly restricted by the war effort. I did arrange a substantial appropriation for dormitories to encourage high school students to come to the university.

The underlying difference—and this wasn't anything that unified great groups of people on either side—arose because my idea about tying the University of Virginia to the public schools differed from what many of the powerful people that were associated with the university thought ought to be done. But the difference never brought on any unpleasantness. I knew that they felt one way about it and I felt another way, and I had to keep working along on my plan and see if it had any merit.

Many people with whom I talked were sympathetic. They simply didn't believe that the public school students could do the work at the university. The view was very widely held, and it was a damaging one. In those places where public schools were weak, the answer lay in improving them, not in weakening the university. In fact, I found that well-prepared public school boys gave just as good or better account of themselves as did the private school boys.

Neither the faculty nor I were willing to lower standards. There is no use watering down good education simply to admit people to build up enrollment. That's self-defeating. The point was to develop a good system for those with ambition and sharp minds.

The domination of the private school influence remained great during the time that I was at the university, and the public school system was slow in understanding what I was trying to do and frequently it didn't encourage students to come to the University of Virginia. Now the university's relationship to the whole scheme of education in Virginia is much broader.

    F.   Much of that stemmed from what you did.

    D.   In part, perhaps; but much is due to the efforts of Presidents Shannon and Hereford. And, of course, much is due to the improvement in the public school system itself.

    A focal point of difference between myself and the fraternity members was the student union building. Influential student groups, the student council and that crowd, were bitterly opposed to building it. They saw no need for an entertainment facility because the fraternity houses monopolized social activities, a dance or anything like that, any weekend.

    The fraternities recognized in the student union a threat to their supremacy, and they fought it fiercely. Not effectively, because they ran up against Governor Tuck, who was ready to dehydrate them at the drop of a hat. He didn't have any patience with their opposition anyway. Just before I let the contract, the student council sent Bill resolutions roundly condemning the venture. Bill called me on the phone and said, "Don't ever take your eye off them. I've got this resolution here, and I don't think a thing of it."

    Now, I'm told, if you'd put to a vote of the students what building they'd do away with, the student union would be one of the last ones they'd let go.

    F.   Somebody told me that you opposed fraternities because they had refused to take you in as a student.

    D.   That piece of gossip originated in Richmond. I joined a fraternity after I got to the university in 1914. What influenced my thinking more and more as the years went on was that my father had been in straitened circumstances because the outbreak of war in Europe had wrecked the cotton market.

    When I looked back on the fact that it cost him $100, a tremendous amount of money then, for me to join a fraternity, I realized what an unnecessary burden had been imposed on him. He did it because the social stratification was such that otherwise I'd have been at a decided disadvantage. As I turned it over as the years went on, I realized that a nonfraternity boy at the university wasn't given sufficient chance. There were no recreation places other than the living rooms of the fraternities. During Easter Week dances, when girls would come up, the only place for parties was at the fraternity houses.

Now it was my idea that the opportunity of enjoying the university to the fullest should be open to all the students. The answer didn't lie in striking down the fraternities, but in striking from their hands the absolute advantage that they enjoyed over the others.

F.   It's revealing that your critics couldn't conceive any other explanation as to why you would be against fraternities.

D.   It's very interesting because that was given great currency. It was immediately seized upon as gospel. It was such an easy explanation. In defending the status quo, they used to say to me that the university was "a way of life." An old friend came in to see me one day and said, "There isn't any use talking about the University of Virginia's educational offerings. Really what you learn here is a way of life."

"It may be," I said, "but it's going to be something more than that while I am around here." So they were very angry with me, and that was the basis of much of the stubborn opposition that I had as president of the university.

The institution had a vested interest because the fraternity houses quartered a great many students. By using them as rooming houses the university authorities were assisting indirectly a group that tended to fragment the university.

F.   During the period how did the students express their opposition?

D.   Various ways. Many came by and talked with me. At one stage some of them got mad about something—I forget what it was—and they came up on Carr's Hill several times at night and burned a kerosene-soaked cross propped against a tree. My reaction, published in the *Cavalier Daily,* was that I didn't have the slightest objection to individuals burning crosses so long as they didn't lean them against the oaks that had been growing there two hundred years. They never burned another one.

Since the construction of the student union building, Newcomb Hall, the university's social life has changed because that's open to everybody. All you have to be is an enrolled student. I think the fraternities have forgotten their animosity toward me. There's one letter buried in the university archives that is going to cause somebody to laugh when he comes across it. When I came back from representing the United States at the United Nations, a fraternity president invited me to talk to his chapter. They kept me answering questions until after midnight, and I said to them finally, "Boys, I've had a nice time, but I have to work tomorrow, and I must go home and get some sleep."

A few days later a letter came from the president. He was very generous in his praise, and at the close he wrote: "Mr. Darden, to tell you the truth, we did enjoy it, and speaking for myself, I never did think you were as bad as a lot of the fellows around here think you are."

Those kinds of things that popped out made life at the university interesting. Pierre was a great fellow for telling me stories he had heard. He heard more of them because although most of the students knew Colgate was my son, a great many didn't know Pierre.

We had dug a deep hole near the Rotunda for some telephone equipment, and Pierre came along as a boy was standing and looking down in that yawning hole, and the boy said, "That's about the right size for Colgate."

"What have you got against Colgate?" Pierre asked.

"Oh," he said, "I haven't got anything against him. He's just the president of this damn university!"

It shows the complete abandon of students' thinking.

    F.   Did it trouble Pierre?

    D.   No, he was amused by it. Students, you know, run like a great current through a university. In a few years they're gone and others have taken their places. The resentment toward me gradually faded around the grounds. The anger lingered among some of the old boys who had graduated.

One day at lunch Pierre and I were discussing a funeral that the students had given a dog, Seal, a dearly loved mascot. They had turned out in force for Seal. I said to Pierre, "You know, I don't believe the university would give me as big a funeral as Seal was given."

And Pierre said, "Daddy, I think probably you're right. I don't know that you'd draw that big a crowd from among the students; but if they could keep you out two or three days and send word to the old boys and give them a chance to come back, you'd have the biggest funeral ever seen in Virginia!"

In the disagreement over the university's relation to public schoo.s, I didn't have any unpleasant experiences with the faculty members; but there was a vast gulf between the university some of them believed in and the university I believed in. They thought that my chief concern was going to be to build up enrollment any way possible. Until they got that out of their heads, as they did as the years went on, they constantly were on guard, and rightly so, to see that the academic standards of the university were not impaired. They believed it was not possible to increase materially the admission of public school students without dropping the standards. It didn't follow because we guarded that very carefully. We could easily have run up the enrollment had we been willing to make concessions on admissions; but that we were never willing to do.

F.   The admission standards have risen.

D.   Yes, no question about that. But you can see how when I began talking about increasing admissions from the public school system, the skeptics had grounds for fearing that I was attempting to make it another Great State U. That was their favorite expression: Build another Great State U. that was to be filled by lowering admission standards.

F.   Even had that happened, it would have been better than to have a private club.

D.   Yes, as a choice between those two, it would have been much better, but that choice did not have to be made. Time demonstrated that there was an unending supply of good students in the public schools.

F.   The difficulty now is that an overabundance of well-qualified applicants has made admissions a headache. Part of the pressure arises because, with the admission of girls, who soon will account for half of the enrollment, the university has to turn away the sons of alumni.

D.   And well-qualified sons, amply able to do the university work. It's important, though, not to underestimate the value of educating the girls. For one thing, you are, in effect, putting a teacher in every home.

F.   Some parents of sons contend that the university ought to be for boys because they have to earn a living. Of course, that's decreasingly a good argument because the girls in these days earn a living, too.

D.   Quite. It was overpowering when I was a boy, because only a handful of women were in the work force. Now they are a big part of it. That isn't a sound reason. The real reason for educating both boys and girls is to give them the opportunity of developing their talents.

F.   Yes, I understand that; but given this continuing tussle over admissions, the point of the mother serving as a tutor counters the argument that girls go there just to get husbands.

D.   What's wrong about that? Wouldn't you likely by that kind of arrangement upgrade a civilization? Of course, you must be careful that the girls toe the mark intellectually. You can't make it a hunting ground for husbands at state expense by allowing these girls to sit up there and do no work. They do work, and they give a fine account of themselves; and, after all, it's the state's responsibility to equip them to support the large number of husbands they later fall heir to.

F.   Girls are just smarter than boys.

D.   Quicker. Of course, Congress may correct that. It is undertaking everything else. Like the British Parliament. Wasn't it Walter Bagehot who said that the only limitation on the British Parliament was that it could not make a man a woman or a woman a man?

F.   I don't think Parliament and Congress together could solve the admission problems with which colleges have to cope.

D.   The most recent difficulty arose with the law school at Charlottesville in connection with the admission of out-of-state students. Several years ago the pressure reached alarming proportions, and at the urging of the governor, the law school reluctantly took in an additional number.

F.   The law school faculty feels that to maintain the quality of classes it must admit superior out-of-state applicants.

D.   To deny the out-of-state admissions would be to impair the intellectual quality of the school itself. You can't build a great university along parochial lines. Jefferson always had in mind that the essential test should be the quality of education offered, and it should be open to all qualified to profit from it.

Just now the law school at William and Mary is growing very rapidly. It's a fine school, but it lacks the facilities that would help take the pressure off the state for the restriction of out-of-state admissions at the University of Virginia. That's one reason I was interested in helping Governor Holton in the project of building larger facilities for the law school at William and Mary adjacent to the National Center for State Courts. Between that and law schools at Charlottesville, Washington and Lee, and the University of Richmond, we shall have ample provision for the education of lawyers in Virginia.

If we take away from Virginia students the opportunity to associate with good minds drawn from other areas, we fail to provide the highest quality of education.

THE COLLEGE ON THE HILL

F. While you were president of the university, you established Clinch Valley College in Southwest Virginia. How did you manage that breakthrough on barren ground?

D. One day three leaders from Wise County—Kenneth Asbury, Fred Greear, and Bill Thompson, Sr.—came to see George Zehmer, the university's director of extension services, about enlarging the extension work in Wise. George had no money in his budget, but they said as long as they had come all the way, they'd like to talk with me. So they trooped into my office. George, by the way, was a very capable, energetic, dedicated person, an old marine from the First World War. We named the first building at Clinch Valley for him.

That day they told me that they had some room at the county farm that was being abandoned, and we began discussing the possibility of setting up a little school out there on the poor farm. The Commonwealth didn't have any colleges in the far west. It is an area that has never shared, really, in the development of Virginia to the extent that it deserves.

That was the reflection of the dominance of the slaveholding east through the centuries. It showed up strongly in the Constitutional Convention of 1828–29 and later in the Convention of 1850–51. There was a steadily widening gap between the plantation society of the east and the nonslaveholding western part of the state. The growing division between the two areas eventuated in the tearing off of West Virginia during the War Between the States.

F. Southwest Virginia still feels slighted. It's an orphan complex.

D. Yes, it is, but it tends to be exaggerated now, because a great deal of attention has been paid to that area. In talking with them you always gather the impression that they feel they are being dealt out and unless they are very vigilant, the east will run off with everything.

F. They have fared well in appointments and in political office, but they have been shortchanged in other ways. I recall three Organization governors from the Southwest since the turn of the century, and yet, save for roads, officeholders from Southwest Virginia did not seem to try to obtain for their own people the advantages the east enjoyed. Why was that?

D. It's fairly simple. You could make a pretty good case that in those early days the existing institutions in the east were sufficient to care for the needs of the population. Many in Southwest Virginia came east to college. Many went north to school. And, of course, the tragic thing was many went nowhere to school.

F. The vast area between Blacksburg and Cumberland Gap had no state college.

D. The population was very sparse, too, you must remember; but then it's not a question of resolving it on the basis of sparseness, anyway. The state's responsibility is to take care of its citizens wherever they are. An oversimplified example of it would be building highways through populated areas and then halting construction when you get to a sparsely inhabited county.

I was anxious to set in motion something that would give a forward thrust to the whole system of education out there. Moreover, I knew that if it were done under the direction of the University of Virginia, it would be well done. They were trying to get the university to come in there with extension courses; but in talking, we hit upon a scheme that we'd make a larger than ordinary extension center, and that was the genesis of the little college.

"I can do it in a minute," I told them, "if I can lay my hands on some money."

"We can get the money," they said. "We'll go on down to Richmond where the legislature is in session."

"Go down there then," I said, "and put the money in the appropriation bill and we'll go to work."

I knew they couldn't ask for $100,000. It would scare the General Assembly to death, so I suggested they get $5,000 or $10,000 in the budget bill and get established and we'd start from there. Once we had the extension division in place, I believed that we could obtain legal authorization for the branch college. We got the funds and we were out there and at work in no time and opened in September 1954.

F.   But think of opening a college on $10,000 in a poorhouse!

D.   That's right; but after all, you don't know the drive that was bound up in those fellows, and they hit exactly the thing that I'd been thinking all along, although I had never gone so far as to develop a plan of how to do it. When they walked in, it was just like swinging the door open. And also I knew another thing even better than they knew it. I knew that with their political muscle nobody could slam the door.

F.   Joe Smiddy, the chancellor at Clinch Valley, remembers that the County Board of Supervisors deeded the farm-land and appropriated $16,000 to renovate the poorhouse, and businessmen donated furnishings. Many individuals wanted to build down by the road, but you were determined to set the college on the hill.

D.   Yes, that's when we had the set-to. My God! we had a time. The pressure was in the town of Wise because everything there was built on the road. I walked over the property and I said, "Don't let's do this. Let's go put this school on a hill. It will overlook the country." They went along with it finally, but I think in truth they did it to humor me.

All of us agreed that the school was a necessity. So there was no difference of opinion on the main point. Nobody was lying behind the corner sharpshooting at you, as frequently happens in an endeavor in public life.

F.   You all had to have a graveyard removed from the top of the hill; and Smiddy said that when you asked Sam Crockett how many graves were up there, Sam was such an optimist—that's the way Smiddy put it—he said there were about forty.

D.   There were about 123, as I remember it. Anyway, I paid for moving them. I knew I couldn't get the college up on the hill unless I agreed to pay for it. And I could not have moved the graveyard but for the fact that it was county property where the poorhouse people had been buried.

F.   Why didn't the county know how many were up there?

D.   Came about very easily. We took up the bodies

of which the county had a record, but many of the poor people in the community had buried their dead there without notifying the county.

Word would come to me by way of a letter or by way of a visitor from up there, or it'd be slipped over on me gently when I'd go out there to look around and see how we were getting along. Things were moving along but difficulties had been encountered. More bodies had been found, and they were consulting with me about how we could deal with that problem. Of course, there wasn't but one way to deal with it, and that was for me to go on and pay for moving them.

After that, Connie and I bought a hundred or so acres that had been mined and gave the tract to the school. I figured it would be better for the college to have it than to have somebody building up too close to the campus. Then we bought some other property, including two lakes, between there and the town. And then I bought a house so that they could build a road going into the campus.

I enjoyed it very much because the need was so great. We did whatever we could with pleasure. The only difference we've ever had out there, I wanted the front of the hill left in an open terrace, but later the library was put there. And yet, as time has gone on, I've concluded it's probably a good location. Maybe what they've done is better than what I had in mind.

F. It's a handsome building. With those slashes for windows in the walls, it looks like a Tibetan monastery sitting up there.

D. In 1967 it became a four-year institution and two years after that held the graduation of the first full four-year class.

F. An academic procession marched down those steep terraces, and the teachers and students, black gowns flapping at their heels, seemed like devotees of a solemn religious order, except for a gale of laughter at the end of the line where you and Smiddy were walking, and he was urging bystanders to join the "parade."

D. Smiddy was telling me stories as we went along, always one of the pleasantest parts of my visits. I'd told him my remarks at the graduation were going to be brief, and that reminded Smiddy of the visiting preacher in a church back in the hills, who droned along until an old fellow on the front row took out a pistol and placed it in his lap. The preacher brought his sermon short, and, later, when the congregation was filing out, he asked the pistolpacker: "You wouldn't shoot me, would you?"

"No," said the old man, "but the fellow who invited you here is in deep trouble!"

The college's steady advance was interrupted only once, during the second year, by a sharp drop in attendance. We investigated and discovered that the mountain public school system had begun hiring students for teachers as soon as they finished their freshman year.

That was the year, too, we had trouble putting in the sewer line. It hit rock, and we couldn't get through. We were using prisoners to do the work. The officials at Wise would take people out of the jails and use them over there, and because we didn't have enough skilled workers they scuffled around in some of the neighboring areas for help. It was not true, as was charged, that they caught people and put them in jail in order to get them out there to build the sewer line. They did not do that!

      F. Who in the world brought that charge?

      D. Just some wag. You know, there's no end of storytelling in Southwest Virginia, and we were over there heart and soul, all of us struggling mightily to build the sewer line. We were using prisoners, which was not unusual. They used prisoners in various community endeavors out there, so we were no different from those building roads or something else. But some fellow cooked up the idea that we were catching people and putting them on the sewer line to get it built. Wasn't a word of truth in it, not one word!

      F. How did the young people respond to the college?

      D. In Charlottesville there were always some discipline problems, nothing of consequence, but just enough to worry you. Numbers of students at the university felt they were doing the state a favor by going there. Strange theory, but it was entertained by some of them. During a visit to Clinch Valley, I asked a college official: "What are your disciplinary problems?"

"These children are so thankful to be in school—they realize it's their only chance—that we don't have any trouble," he said.

That's what led me to say many times that Virginia has in value received gotten more for every penny spent in Clinch Valley than in any other place in the state.

F.   But it is still inexplicable that although Southwest Virginia, the Fighting Ninth, for so many years was the Byrd Organization's finishing punch and E. R. Combs from the heart of the Southwest was Byrd's main strategist, all of that clout was never translated into a program of uplift for Southwest Virginia.

D.   It was never fully translated. And yet the spirit was there. Nobody in the world ever got greater support than I did in that effort.

F.   Doesn't that intrigue you, that they should have delivered the votes so many times—

D.   And they did deliver them! There isn't doubt about that.

F.   And yet the leaders let the people, who should have benefited, sit there in poverty and ignorance?

D.   Bear in mind, though, that there was not any building in the eastern section during that period. The eastern effort had been made long before. These people were in a period, at least when I knew them in politics from the time of the depression, during which construction was almost at a standstill statewide. So that the leaders cannot be charged with neglecting the area from which they came.

F.   It seems a long, long period of waiting. After all those years of loyalty at the polls, they had to wait until you got to the University of Virginia to establish Clinch Valley College before they sat down at the table.

D.   Nobody labored harder and to greater effect in the building of Clinch Valley College than Sam Crockett, and he was followed by Joe Smiddy, who never lost sight of the fact that what the university wanted there was a first-rate educational center. What made Smiddy a good teacher also made him a good adjuster of difficulties in the community. An outstanding example was his treatment of the controversy over strip mining.

F.   He made the school a forum for airing the issue, even though the mining interests tried to keep the college from discussing it. Smiddy told me he didn't blame people for being upset with the college at times; but, he said, people will kill themselves for a living, and it was the college's function to present both sides and to try to find the truth.

D. That's education at its best.

I NEVER FELT I HAD
DONE ENOUGH

F. Governor, a great deal of building occurred at the university during your presidency.

D. Oh, yes, but actually that's incidental. The main thing is the interaction between a first-rate faculty and a top-flight student body which has marked the university from Jefferson's day. The building, much of which continued through the Shannon and Hereford regimes, probably is leveling off.

F. You call it incidental, but without it the university would not have been able to grow.

D. You're quite right on that, but even with it the university could not be a great one without the others. I had a very sympathetic General Assembly. I used to tend to my business with the governors on the telephone. You can't do that now. There are all kinds of forms to fill out and a flood of paper floating back and forth between Charlottesville and Richmond. In my day I used to phone Bill Tuck or John Battle or Tom Stanley.

F. Governor Tuck once told me he would give you anything you wanted for the university.

D. He used to put out that stuff. He was just as good as he could be. He was just telling me to feel free to call him, assuming, of course, I wouldn't impose on him; but he kept his hand on the state budget; and, of course, we all had to operate within the limits imposed by the General Assembly.

F. Walter Newman said that when he was trying to win appropriations for VPI your influence was such that all you had to do was call the governor, whereas he had to go the long way round and bring pressure on the General Assembly through the farm lobbies.

D. He was awfully effective the long way round. He opened up shop down there in Richmond and rallied the VPI people, and he was a powerful advocate. In addition, he is a fine person and laid the foundation for VPI as we know it today. Never will forget, Governor Battle called me one day and he said, "You've got to come on down here. Newman is organizing VPI, and if you want this stuff for the University of Virginia, you better do some work on it." It really wasn't necessary because Battle lived in Charlottesville, and he was very popular with the legislators. All he had to do was tell them what he wanted.

F.   Governor, what was the origin of the School of Business Administration?

D.   In 1948 I was asked to Lexington to a joint meeting arranged by the Department of Highways and the Virginia Manufacturers Association. Henry McWane of Lynchburg headed the manufacturers, and Jim Anderson was highway commissioner. The war was over and we were getting squared away for a long pull and what we thought was going to be a far happier and more successful pull for the nation than it has turned out to be.

In reviewing the needs for the group in Lexington, I suggested that we set up a graduate school in business administration because we needed one and furthermore we were losing many of our people who went outside the state for a business education.

From there we moved to plans of getting together a million dollars to start the school. That took several years. We had help all over the state in gathering the money, and I persuaded the board at the university to let us have Monroe Hall so that we could use the income from the million dollars as a supplement to run the school.

Although we were in an era in which there was greater support for higher education than there had been ever in Virginia, convincing the General Assembly that it should put its shoulder to a new graduate school wasn't easy; but we did it in part because we had the million dollars in the kitty. After that we searched for the faculty. We were fortunate in obtaining Professor Charles Abbott from Harvard to head the school. He spent a year organizing it and acquiring a faculty and opened it in 1955.

The school is over twenty years old and has moved into its new quarters on the North Grounds. We're landscaping it. You see the necessity of it when you look at those giant buildings. In twenty years you'll go into a magnificently green area and through the trees will see these massive buildings that will be not offensive at all. The grass and the shrubs will help soften the masonry, but the main thing was to get the trees in place.

The success of the planting venture turns on whether we keep the young trees watered. I've done no end of planting in my life for other places and sometimes the trees died simply because they weren't watered. People don't seem to understand that for a year or two, until the trees get their roots out, you've got to keep them watered just as you do a flower.

I have always loved to look at tree catalogs, sketch out things in my mind about how I want them. It is the pleasantest part of an administrative job. I did a lot of it at the university. It is the one thing about which there is little controversy. Most everybody will fall in with you and say, "Well, that's worth doing." They may not think much of it. They may not think it is as important, certainly, as I think it is; but they are not yowling at you about something all the time, complaining.

When I walked around the Grounds at Charlottesville, I saw a lot of old impaired trees that had to be taken out; and I knew also that the first time I took out one of them, I'd be in a row with the old faculty and everybody else up there. The Lawn was the tenderest part; touch anything there and they were ready to lynch you. So I got a tree committee, made up of four or five top people in the university. I set them to work and they laid out the trees that had to be removed. If you go there now, you'll see the young ones are really beginning to take their places on the Lawn and elsewhere in the university. That, you see, was twenty-five years ago. It's the only way you can do anything like that and not get into a commotion. They still have the tree committee, although I think they have a fancier name for it. Dean Ivey Lewis headed it first and then Dean Runk took it over.

      F.   Governor, what prompted your interest in the offering of ethics in the business school?

      D.   Even before Watergate, I felt that instruction should be given in the ordinary morality of business and life. The men who engineered Watergate came out of the top law schools in the United States and joined in a scheme that struck at the very heart of American government.

For years the law school in Charlottesville has had a course of ethics, but it has never been given the emphasis it deserves. I was so pleased a few years ago when the university set up a Center of Applied Ethics in the Business School and encouraged the law school to join in. It holds real promise. It is general in its instruction and yet definite enough to get in the minds of these boys the responsibility they assume when they enter business.

Interestingly enough, in appealing for funds to support the undertaking, I found a great many people who were indifferent because they felt the instruction was coming too late, so my fund-raising efforts were ineffective. They believed that if a student had not received a good moral foundation in his home, church, and early education, nothing could be done about it in graduate school. I think the subject deserves attention from grammar school through graduate school.

     F. In August 1959 the *Times-Dispatch* noted that the students had voted you the Raven Award and that the faculty attitudes had undergone an even greater transformation in your favor. From being suspect as a politician on your arrival you had won near unanimity of support. The faculty gave you the Thomas Jefferson Award and later adopted a resolution of thanks for raising salaries, constructing buildings, and adding well-qualified teachers. It also said:

   "More than once you have stood at the gates, and to outside pressures have said: 'Thus far and no farther.' . . . You have given wise leadership and administrative guidance worthy of the tradition of its great founder."

What does the reference to standing at the gates mean?

     D. It came out of a continuing insistence on my part, from the McCarthy days on, that the university must remain free.

     F. How did you know when you had done enough at the university?

     D. I never felt I had done enough. I simply wanted to come home. You run out of ideas, and what's needed is somebody to come along with other plans, many of which may prove wrong; but if you do a few things right, the cause moves forward a little bit and that's all you can expect of life.

Shortly after I requested the board to look for a replacement, a friend was at the Farmington Country Club and ran into one of the main props of the bar downstairs, a good mutual friend of ours, who had been having his usual afternoon drinks. And the fellow at the bar said, "What's Colgate going to do?"

My friend said, "I don't know. He tells me he's not going to do anything but go back to Norfolk and sit around and gossip and complain."

"My God! I'm glad to hear that," said the fellow. "There'll be no break in the continuity!"

L.R.P.

G.   Mrs. Darden knows as much about nature as you do about politics.

D.   Her specialty is birds, their flights, habits, calls, and she learned photography to portray them. She has for years charted the arrival, nesting, and departure of the yellow-crowned night herons that roost in the tall pines around our house on Crab Creek. There seem to be two or three herons, and she doesn't want to be tied in with the wrong ones.

G.   Where did she acquire her deep knowledge of nature?

D.   Through her own interest, reading about it and observing. Her father, Irénée du Pont, was avidly interested in rocks and the like. He had a wing in his house for a rock collection he had made over the years. He also was interested in astronomy and getting the magazines and watching the little star charts showing what constellations were appearing.

G.   She knows about ferns and flowers as well as birds.

D.   Yes, she does, but it has been a leisure activity. Her first love is music. She went to Friends School in Philadelphia and Baldwin in Germantown. Then she studied art and music with teachers in Philadelphia and played the violin and moved over to the viola d'amore, which isn't played very much. She organized the Society of Ancient Instruments and still runs it and journeys to Philadelphia for concerts. Here in Norfolk she is a member of a string quartette that gets together to play every week.

G.   Mrs. Darden told me an adorable story of how you came into her life. Her aunt was riding on the train with a friend for a vacation in Palm Beach. The two ladies were having difficulty reading the railroad timetable, and you in your uniform stepped forward and helped them. She said she had quite an assortment of nieces and invited you to meet them.

D. I was returning to the air base outside Miami from some kind of leave. Later, I went to visit her aunt in Wilmington and that's where Connie and I met. Her aunt's home was always full of young people, and Connie and her sisters lived just across the lawn. While I was at Oxford, Connie accompanied her family to England and they came by to see me. We were married in 1927.

G. How many sisters has she?

D. She is the third child in a family of eight girls and a boy. One sister, Doris, died, so there are seven now: Sophie, Margaretta, Constance, Eleanor, Marianna, Octavia, and Lucille.

The boy is Irénée, who takes after his mother. She was one of the finest individuals I ever knew. She put her whole life in those children. Looking after her family came ahead of everything else for her. They have a deep attachment to one another, and I've always attributed that in considerable part to her unfailing attention to them. She taught them that ideas were far more important than things.

G. Does that account for Mrs. Darden's naturalness?

D. Yes, in this way. They were fortunate in being people of a great deal of means, and the children could have had anything they wanted. Their mother taught them that things were inconsequential compared to what they did and how they got along with people. It was an emphasis on ideas and relationships with others rather than on possessions.

Connie's father was a compassionate, tolerant person. I don't recall ever having heard him say an unkind word about anybody, and surely with his vast business experience, he must have had some very decided views. He was the Du Pont Company's specialist on safety. He did more work than anybody else in improving the safety of their plants to the point where its record was at the top in industry.

He retired from the presidency when he was forty-eight. Connie says that during the years he was working at its head it was an event when his family could be with him any length of time. He would come home and eat supper with them and then go into an office in his home and work and they wouldn't see him any more that night. He would have breakfast very early and go to his office before they got up. That's one reason, I think, he gave up the presidency. He wanted to see something of his family. He enjoyed his children.

Of course, that was one reason I quit public office. My being in politics threw the burden on Connie. So often she was by herself taking the children to museums, plays, and picnics and reading and talking to them about everything in the universe.

     F.   In a way Mrs. Darden was trained for that role.

     D.   She certainly saw her mother go through it. That was the tradition in her family. They put the operation of the Du Pont Company first. Her father was running that company and everything else gave way in front of that. Her mother stepped in and did her part with the family, and did it superbly, as did Connie with ours.

So far as my being away at politics at times, Connie just felt it was dedication to what I was supposed to be doing and she had to make the necessary adjustment to it. She did it in a very effective way and a noncomplaining way. There wasn't any whimpering around about it.

     G.   Where do her sisters live?

     D.   Most of them live within hollering distance of where they grew up, and a remarkable thing about them is that they all have the husbands they started out with. The sisters are just as close and clannish as any people that God ever made, and while they deny this vigorously, they would put their husbands out tomorrow morning before they would allow the slightest division amongst themselves. They would pitch us all right out the front door.

They are all great family people, traveling around amongst themselves, finding out what each other is doing. Connie especially is that way, keeping in touch with them. The first thing she does every morning is get on the phone and check on each one.

When we first moved down here, you'd have thought we had moved off to the South Pole. They had no idea of coming to Norfolk. It took overnight, you see. You'd go to Washington or Baltimore and get a boat to come here. In the old days, going to Wilmington, we'd leave here early in the morning and take the ferry to Cape

Charles and then drive up there and reach Wilmington late in the afternoon. It was an earthshaking accomplishment, very much like now circling Mars and coming back down.

It's interesting. I never saw just such closeness and attachment of children in my life. In my own family we are very close but very different. My brother is seven or eight years younger than I am. My sister is about two years younger than I am. Our interests in my family were quite different. It doesn't affect our devotion to each other but it's just a different pattern.

      G.   You are all interested in the community, though.

      D.   We are interested in the community, yes; but I think anybody who has his wits about him realizes that unless you are interested in the community it doesn't work.

      G.   A lot of people aren't, though.

      D.   I know they aren't. They are to a degree, not altogether, a dead weight on the community, because many of them are very good families that are self-contained, not interested. They leave the burden of public service to be carried by their friends and others.

      G.   Mrs. Darden treats every human being with dignity.

      D.   Yes, and among her activities for others she runs a taxi service at all hours for the church.

      G.   In all the years that she's been with you in all your campaigns and offices, I bet there's never been anyone who disliked her.

      D.   You're right about that, but then I'm somewhat partial in the analysis.

      G.   She speaks to everybody as if that person is royalty. She has a gift for putting people at ease.

      D.   Connie's a great conversationalist with cab drivers or anybody else who'll talk to her. She always engages them in conversation. One time she and Irene were returning to Charlottesville from a trip and they caught a cab at the depot downtown. They got in and got settled. The driver wasn't sure as to the whereabouts of the president's house, and she told him how to get there, and then she asked: "Didn't the president of the university used to be governor of Virginia?"

"Yes," he said, "and he won't much of a governor!"

Then Connie wanted to know why he felt that way, but he clammed up and that, along with a timely poke in the ribs from Irene, settled the matter.

Connie is the most self-effacing individual I've ever known, but, with her, self-effacement doesn't mean retreat from responsibility. The other side of the coin is her dedication to serving others.

    G. She does it gladly, and she never complains privately, does she?

    D. Not a bit! She thinks they're doing her a favor to let her work for them. She goes about it as her duty as a Christian. But I think—I tell you where I saw her interest in nature and her religious belief help. When our son Pierre was lost at sea in 1959, they simply saved her life. They just sustained her and bore her along through it.

    G. The only thing that I know that will give you any feeling of security outside, as you say, of your religion is to have something concrete to do.

    D. Yes, and also it's much more interesting in the long run than lighter diversions.

    G. Did Pierre look like Colgate?

    D. Very much like him, yes. They were about the same size and they were both deeply interested in making things go. They were always buying secondhand cars and repairing them. On Carr's Hill they converted a garage, an enormous structure which had been an old stable, into a repair shop. I had to leave my car outside because they kept dismantled motors all over the floor and around on various pieces of wood and boxes.

You needed a compass to find your way through Colgate's room. It was strung with wires and packed full of electrical equipment and gadgets. He filled the attic with electrical apparatus and worked on one project after another, a continual line of them. Colgate learned to fly and then began putting together old planes as he had done with old automobiles. For the past ten years he has been teaching nuclear physics and astronomy at the University of South Carolina. Now he is on a sabbatical that allows him to work with a research firm in West Germany in nuclear power and energy.

While the boys were mechanics, Irene was largely a horseback rider, to my consternation; but she became a fine rider. She is an independent operator. I don't think Irene ever wanted to be a little girl. I think she wanted to be a man running a country somewhere. Her husband, John Field, is in the British foreign service, and they enjoy that tremendously. It allows them to travel throughout the world, and at each place Irene finds a job among the people. In London she had some work with a company publishing a dictionary equating English and American terms. In Japan she worked on a book about an English trader who formed a big trading company after Japan was opened up to the West. In Russia she taught American literature at the University of Moscow. She's industrious and has a good tough mind. There's nothing fluffy about it. It's hard, concise. With their two children they have a close-knit little family devoted to one another.

G.   Pierre was interested in exploring nature, too?

D.   Yes, and he and the Coke and Irene were naturally inquisitive. Pierre had picked up somewhere a little trick saying he popped back at you. He would ask a question, and I'd say, "What do you want to know that for?" and he would say, "I ask only to learn."

Pierre became a great reader. He was reading C. S. Lewis while he was in college and joined the group that was sending him CARE packages during the Second World War. In Lewis's autobiography, which I read years later, he mentioned that one thing he appreciated so much was receiving from the United States CARE packages which he shared with friends and students.

One of the last things Pierre did, he took my set of *The Decline and Fall of the Roman Empire* with him when he was living in New Jersey, working in the Bell Laboratories. When Pierre went to work for the telephone company, they asked him to write an essay as to why the telephone company was not a monopoly. Well, he came out with the fact that it bore all the resemblance to a monopoly so far as he could make out, which probably didn't please them.

G.   That's exactly what you would have done.

D.   Well, I don't know about that. But then, before he set out on this voyage that cost him his life, he had left the telephone company. I think he was planning to go to work for the Du Pont Company. He said that the telephone experience convinced him that he was not willing to spend his life simply in higher mathematics; he thought that in the end it was too restricted an existence.

While he was still in college he was rejected for military service in the Korean War. That altered his whole life. At the university he was in the ROTC, but he was let out because of poor vision, and then his draft number came up. He hurried to Richmond and reported for the draft, but was rejected because of his eyes. And I think—I don't think, I know—that that had a tremendous effect on him. He took up motorcycle riding and he was incredibly reckless in riding around over the Grounds. At Carr's Hill he'd go over the terraced part of the lawn with a motorcycle, and I was certain he was going to break his neck. I believe it was a reaction to that rejection that led him from one adventure to another entailing far more than the ordinary risk. I can't help but believe that was true in his final adventure, because he'd sailed for years and knew what boats could do.

He'd arranged to go off on a cruise to the Caribbean. Of course, it never occurred to me that he'd try to take a little open sailboat from Hampton Roads out in the North Atlantic in the late fall. He kept the boat at a yard in the upper reaches of the Chesapeake when he was working with the telephone company. He'd go there and sail. He knew mighty well the general rules of buoyancy. I think he figured that he could just stretch the point and get away with it. Of course, he got out here in the Atlantic in a season given to storms. He and a friend, who was also quite a mathematician and engineer, had brought the boat down here. I think they had her overloaded and either she went down in a sudden squall or she was run down at night by some ship that never saw them.

F. Governor, tell Gin what Pierre did at graduation from the University of Virginia.

D. It was the doggondest thing that ever happened to anybody. He had earned degrees in mechanical and electrical engineering and they both were awarded at the same commencement. The deans were calling out the names, and I was standing there handing out the diplomas and shaking hands with the students and wishing them well, and along came Pierre for his second degree. I handed him his diploma and grabbed him by the hand and he turned loose in the palm of my hand an electrical device that spun around and gave me a shock that lifted me straight up in the air about a half a foot. I never was more provoked in my life. I came within an ace of just giving him one awful kick in the rump. He gives me that gadget and holds my hand so I can't get it loose, you see? And finally detaches himself and shoots off the platform!

F.   Did it make a buzzing?

D.   Yes, it made a buzzing, but what it did was you felt you were being electrocuted along with it. It was an absolute surprise. It never occurred to me anything like that was coming down the road, and—bam!—it was just like being hit by lightning! I reckon the spectators thought I'd lost my mind. I suppose they thought that the long hot afternoon had finally gotten to me, that I had just lost control and was jumping up and down on the platform. In a second it was all over and he was gone on his way.

G.   Nobody but your son could ever have done that, and think of where he did it!

D.   Right in public. No shielding, no place to retreat. Here I was passing out these diplomas, wishing these children well, and he arrested and stopped the whole thing in mid-flight! It was a calculated trick. He got it in my hand and wouldn't turn it loose. So he had me. It was what our children used to call L.R.P.

F.   What is L.R.P., Governor?

D.   L.R.P. started in Charlottesville when Anthony Steel, principal of the University College of South Wales in Cardiff, came to visit us with his wife Aileen. In great commotion or difficulty, Aileen Steel would dispose of it by saying, "It's simply life's rich pageantry!"

Pierre picked it up and shortened it, and that's what happened at graduation—L.R.P.

SERVING IN THE UNITED NATIONS AND ELSEWHERE

F. How did you happen to go to the United Nations, Governor?

D. John Foster Dulles telephoned me one day in 1955 from California and said that he'd like for me to go as one of this country's representatives to the Tenth General Assembly. The university's Board of Visitors was agreeable. I had a grand board. The members were just as generous and considerate as they could be.

I was there from mid-September until mid-December on a kind of disjointed leave of absence from the university. I'd stay in touch by telephone and get back down to Charlottesville every now and then. The fall term had started, and the faculty had been employed. There wasn't much to do, except miss the football games. Nothing suited me better than that. I got so tired of football that I haven't been through the gates of a stadium since I left there.

They put the delegates up in great style in suites in the old Vanderbilt. We had our seats laid out in the Hall of the Assembly. The delegation was run by the State Department from Washington. Nobody ever wiggled without going out and calling up the State Department and asking what to do next.

F. Did you draw any hope from watching the UN?

D. I didn't draw much hope. I'd been a fervent League of Nations supporter. Had we been willing to adhere to the League of Nations and put into it a small part of the money and effort that we have put into the United Nations, the Second World War could have been prevented.

I was a less fervent United Nations man, and my service there dimmed my hopes further. It was the most frustrating and exasperating task I had ever undertaken because it seemed we were constantly engaged in picayune, inconsequential matters.

There was a good deal of pettiness. One time when a member of our delegation asked the head of another delegation why he voted against France on an important matter, the head said the French ambassador had walked past him the day before and didn't speak to him. So he wouldn't vote for him simply because the ambassador, worried to death as he was walking along, didn't see this clown.

The talking was incessant and in most cases utterly trivial. Until I went to the UN, I thought Americans were the most vocal, but stacked up against the Indians they were practically tongue-tied. I once read that useless talking is better than war, but I can't see why we have to have either of those afflictions. We spent hours and hours arguing about little two-by-four things. And then there was too much entertaining and too many parties. We spent the afternoons going to parties at one embassy after another, floating, it seemed to me, on a wave of affluence generated by the United States. Also, I sensed that there was a general movement around of countries making alliances against each other. The dominant impression I received of the United Nations was that rather than being engaged in keeping world peace, it was engaged in forming the coalitions for the next war, and I haven't changed my mind. It is not workable as it is now.

There is an imbalance in membership brought about by the proliferation of small states as the colonial empires broke up. The time may come when the major powers will demand a readjustment of the financial burden among those participating and that may force a restudying of the whole concept.

F.   Would Americans agree to this country's surrendering sovereignty without checks and balances in the UN?

D.   Oh, we'd have to have checks and balances. The charter would never have been acceptable in the United States or in the other countries if there hadn't been the power of veto by a single permanent member of the Security Council. Now they have gotten around that to a degree by interpreting proposals that can be handled by the General Assembly without requiring the Security Council's approval. I don't think Russia would have ever agreed without that veto provision, and I'm certain the United States would have balked.

There is no way you can get a real grip on world peace without a genuine commitment to concerted action by the world powers; and that concerted action must have due regard for the small nations.

F.   It seems imperative we do something in the way of a world organization; and yet, as you say, the United Nations has been so barren.

D.   And then it's so self-serving. All of this marching and countermarching, for instance, about aggression in one place and another in the world, and yet there's no ability to come to grips with the crises.

F.   They say very little about the major powers' suppression of minorities, for that matter.

D.   Well, to keep that subject out, the charter provided that the United Nations should not take cognizance of any domestic quarrel, unless—and this is where the interpretation has been made in recent years—that domestic quarrel threatens world peace.

The United States, for instance, was very careful to join others in supporting this provision because it didn't want the UN calling up a state in the Union on its racial policies in the late 1940s. So it was an agreement that was widely supported by the great powers for their own reasons.

F.   Did anyone there catch your admiration?

D.   No, but there were a great many able people. I thought Cabot Lodge was very able. Dulles was a very strong individual. He ran the State Department absolutely, and he ran our delegation. He'd come up there occasionally and sit around and represent the United States. The hardest fellow I saw was Molotov, who occasionally was guilty of a faint smile that involved only his lips. The upper part of his face remained immobile and his eyes cold as arctic ice. You didn't feel that he was hostile, especially, but you felt that he was impenetrable, that nobody knew what went on behind that mask. Dulles said that he was the ablest foreign secretary that he ever encountered.

F.   Wasn't there a high degree of futility in Dulles's efforts at forming coalitions that so often proved ineffective?

D.   Certainly a good many turned out to be ineffective, but some of our foreign commitments have been enormously helpful. Dulles's work on the Atlantic Community has been of great value. The Marshall Plan in Europe was a stunning success. It gave the Europeans the opportunity and materials to reconstitute their industrial machine, and they did it in a magnificent way of making it more modern than ours was.

F.   Did the Marshall Plan stem from an altruistic desire to rebuild their machinery or a desire to check Communism?

D.   They were closely related. Europe was prostrate and hungry and would have fallen victim to some form of authoritarianism. Communism was the most dangerous because the Russian divisions were on their borders and would not have hesitated to have moved to the Channel but for the strengthening and rehabilitation of Europe.

Winston Churchill called the Marshall Plan the most unsordid act in history, and it's well to remember that we offered to include Russia—but Stalin refused.

F.   Can you remember any other instance after a war when a country has gone to such lengths as we did to put the victims, including the vanquished, on their feet?

D.   No, there's no other example in history, and it may well be regarded as a milestone in the slow advance of civilization. One of the most interesting developments, if you look back over those years, is that the Marshall Plan was so successful, but foreign aid, as we tried to apply it around the world in first one place and then another, hasn't always worked as we had hoped. The reason it hasn't worked is that we have assumed that if we gave them economic aid they had the skill to use it and the background to reproduce our form of government or something resembling it. Now Europe had the labor force, the skill, and the cultural background, so that when we gave those countries the material help, they moved rapidly into a fairly safe position. The undeveloped countries couldn't do that.

F.   A revisionism of Truman in the popular mind depicts him as a person of plainspokenness and a man of decision; but the wisdom of some of those decisions is debatable. Yet his policies worked in Europe.

D.   Certainly the Marshall Plan worked brilliantly. That cannot be said of some of Truman's other plans. A case in point is his political decision, over the objections of many of his advisers, to recognize Israel at the termination of the British Mandate. The recognition of Israel made inevitable the drawing together of Russia and the Arab world which caused such apprehension both here and in Europe. It was the forerunner of the Arab oil embargo that struck with such devastating effect several years ago.

There's reason to believe the problems can be worked out if calm minds and sane counsel can prevail; but it is a very dangerous situation as evidenced by the recent Israeli elections when the hard-line group under Begin turned out the moderate government.

    F.   What should have been done?

    D.   Of course, that is not easy to say even with the advantage of hindsight. I have thought that what should have been done was to continue the policies that were being pursued with some success prior to the Truman recognition. That was to assure the Jewish people protection and opportunity to participate in government in the areas where they lived. That seems to have been the view of Justice Brandeis, who worked so hard for the Jewish cause in the early part of this century, and it appears to have been the basis of the Balfour Declaration.

My uneasiness arises from observing the activities of the Israeli delegation to the United Nations at the time I served there as a member of the United States delegation. The Israelis were unlike the Jewish citizens whom I had known in the United States and who had contributed so much to the development of our country. In the United Nations they were abrasive, overbearing, and exceedingly aggressive and seemed bent on forwarding their own interests without regard to the effect of their activities upon the position of the United States or anybody else. And, interestingly enough, through skillful political organization they were able to dominate United States foreign policy in matters concerning Israel.

These tactics would not have been effective but for the fact that they were joined by many political leaders in the United States determined to make personal political capital out of what was a great emotional issue. However, we are now beginning to understand the extreme danger of such a state of affairs.

Given the present situation I see no way whereby it can be resolved short of an agreement by the Arab world of Israel's right to exist and the creation of a Palestine homeland wherein the occupants of the refugee camps can be settled. To this must be added a guarantee by the great powers of the Israeli borders finally agreed upon. This suggestion is not unlike the partition plan put forward in the closing days of the British mandate—a plan which met with such disfavor in the Arab world. However, it is the only solution that I can see and without which I believe war is inevitable.

F. Is it fair to trace our involvement in Vietnam to Truman's theory of containment?

D. I think it's fair to trace it to the theory of containment, but that responsibility doesn't rest entirely on President Truman. It grew out of a mistaken belief, not entirely dissipated until the tragedy in Vietnam, that the United States single-handedly could settle the affairs of the world to the betterment of mankind.

At the risk of oversimplification, we lost the Vietnamese War the morning that the marines waded ashore, because what happened in the minds of the Asiatic world was the reassertion of white supremacy. Basically, the Asians wanted the white man back in the West. They had had enough, and they wanted to get clear of us. When those troops marched ashore they represented a perpetuation of white rule. True, they were Americans, not French. It's also true that they were not sent ashore to build a colonial empire. We thought we could help in a situation concerning which, as it turned out, we had made a terrible miscalculation. Unwittingly we provided the one weapon necessary to arm the Asians against us and from then on it was an uphill fight and, in fact, a losing fight.

North Vietnam, as some military people argue, could have been destroyed and brought to terms. However, the destruction would have left an autocratic, repressive regime in South Vietnam that ultimately would have provoked other revolutions on the part of the people wanting to shake it off their backs. The regime that we did espouse in South Vietnam became more and more autocratic, which appeared to support the suspicions our intervention aroused.

F. Americans have a tendency to assume heavy burdens of guilt when a policy goes wrong.

D. We have guilt, but we also have a great deal of claiming to be related to God in all our operations. We didn't hesitate, for instance, when Roosevelt was telling Churchill that England had better free India and that he had better give up Hong Kong as well. I think it was inevitable that the Indian subcontinent break free, but we have an extraordinary capacity to equate our own theory of things with righteousness, and we are heavily freighted with piety.

F.   I was thinking more about the mass of the people than the leaders when I said we have a tendency to suffer these terrible guilt pangs at setbacks. That the concept that worked in Europe didn't work in Asia, has shaken us.

D.   It has shaken us very deeply, but it also has educated us. The drive of the American people has been for stability, but evolving regimes are not necessarily stable. Movements toward independence or self-government contain forces that of themselves create instability. We could count on the stability of Europe because cultural patterns were set and fixed. The support of governments in South America, Africa, and Asia moved us into much more turbulent waters.

F.   Isn't it strange that we who were founded in a revolution should have expected that we would be able to confer instant democracy?

D.   I don't think so because I think we have been overly self-confident. We've had a lot of luck going with us. We've been protected from the rest of the world by these great oceans, and had come to believe that the American way was the only way, and therefore it's so simple to say to others that what they need is the American system.

But look at the way it's working here. Look at the stuff we've taken control of, the railroads bankrupted, the airlines pushed to the brink, the mail service deteriorating. There isn't any doubt that the space program has been a spectacular success. That has shown technical capacity of rare promise. When I look at that I am encouraged to think that if we will simply address ourselves to it, that we can overcome the fuel crisis in a reasonable time.

It's my belief that the future, not only with us but with the rest of the world, turns on the development of new forms of energy. Somewhere ahead of us is the controlled fusion of hydrogen. If you can arrive at that, you've bypassed coal, oil, and wood and hooked the industrial machine of the world directly to the sun. You will have all the power—and clean power—that anybody can possibly use, lasting until long after the time when the human race has departed from the earth, as the sun millions of years from now grows dim and the planet moves on to being a lifeless mass floating in space, cold and silent.

F. And when you find that limitless source of
energy, available to everybody, have you removed the cause of war?

D. Certainly you will have removed the greatest
basis of contention that so often has driven nations to war.

F. The work at the United Nations was one of
several assignments you undertook on the national scene. Tell me
about the committee on foreign aid that Eisenhower got together.

D. We set out to study foreign aid programs
around the world. It was disheartening in a way. Many of the
countries wanted heavy armaments, but weapons were the last
thing they needed. Money to build hospitals would have been
infinitely better.

Benjamin Fairless headed the committee, and one of his old
adversaries, John L. Lewis, was a member. They were both Welshmen, and they'd both risen to the heads of their groups, Lewis of
the United Mine Workers and Fairless of U.S. Steel. In the wars
between labor and steel, they had been antagonists, but that was
all in the past, and they had become friends.

"One point about John, he had a clear idea of the necessity of
mechanizing the mines," said Fairless. "He never raised any objections to that. The only thing is, John wanted his share; and his
share was every single penny saved by mechanization. But other
than that, he was very easy to get along with."

On the same trip when we reached Paris, Lewis darted out to the
embassy commissary to buy presents for his daughter. He was devoted to the child and talked about her frequently and was always
on the lookout for things she'd like. In Paris he bought her a bottle
of expensive perfume.

Back at the hotel we were sitting around talking and I said to
Lewis, "This is the kind of information I'd like to have if we got
into a political battle. I'd go out in Southwest Virginia and tell
the miners about your struggling around Paris buying French
perfume with their money. That's all I'd have to tell them," I said.
And he said, "Hell, they'd never believe you!"

And that, of course, was a fact. Had anybody gone out there and
told them John Lewis was hopping around Paris buying French

perfume, they'd have said, "Well, everybody knows he's a liar, and this proves it. John Lewis doesn't know what French perfume is!"

When we concluded our report at a meeting in the old War and State Department building across the street from the White House, one of the members said, "All right, come on, let's walk over and give the president our report."

"Oh, no!" Lewis said. "Oh, no. We won't walk over there. We've got to go up in style. You phone and get a White House car."

And I said, "For God's sake, you don't get a car just—"

"Oh, yes," he said. "We have to have a car. We're going in the main entrance."

An aide phoned for a White House car and we went down and got in a Cadillac and moved slowly all around the block and rode to the main entrance of the White House. President Eisenhower greeted us pleasantly and asked us to lunch. But that was Lewis's showmanship. The idea of anybody walking across the street and taking a side entrance to the White House, just as an ordinary pedestrian, was nonsense. You were going up to see the president of the United States and you had to go up in style.

Lewis was an extraordinary fellow in appearance and behavior. My child used to tell me that his were the most gorgeous eyebrows she'd ever seen on anybody. And they were. Gigantic things! We got to be chummy on the foreign aid committee and we met again when the University of West Virginia invited us to receive honorary degrees. In the case of Lewis, the degree granting had stirred up a row because some people opposed his having one and others believed that he should have had it long ago.

While Lewis and I were standing in our academic gowns and gossiping, photographers were circling us, and Lewis said to me: "Turn around, they want to get a picture of us—and I'll say to you it won't do either one of us a damn bit of good!"

He didn't dress anything up. It was all just cold steel with him.

I worked on Eisenhower's Commission on National Goals for the 1960s under the leadership of Henry W. Wriston, a knowledgeable fellow, vigorous in debate, who used to be president of Brown University. Our two most significant recommendations concerned education. One called for a doubling of expenditures for education by 1970. We've done more than that, but part of it, of course, is printed money. The second, and by all odds the most important, urged that racial discrimination in higher education be overcome by 1970 and every state make progress in good faith toward desegregating public schools. Actually, we should strike down discrimination wherever it exists.

For a while I was on a commission of civilians that Congress insisted on setting up to review the CIA. I went to several countries along the West Coast of Africa. The CIA had many representatives, and I was talking to them, trying to find out what they were doing and how they were getting along. I went frequently to meetings in Washington where we talked to Allen Dulles, head of the CIA, and reviewed the difficulties in the world. Dulles was careful to point out that it was vital that the CIA not attempt in any way to operate within the United States since it was forbidden by an act of Congress.

The CIA committee was brought into existence to monitor the very large expenditures. The government feared that a public disclosure would endanger the lives of agents abroad. After serving there, I was on an advisory group to the National Security Council set up by Gordon Gray, former secretary of the army. Gordon would sound us out on various ideas.

In that group Kenneth Royall told an interesting story about George Marshall. One day when Royall was assistant secretary of war his phone rang, and a voice said: "This is George Marshall. The secretary is away, isn't he?"

Royall said that the secretary was out of town, and Marshall said, "I'm sorry about that because I have put my affairs in order and I'm retiring this afternoon. I wanted to tell him goodbye."

"Have you told the president?" Royall asked.

"No," he said. "I'm going to call him shortly."

"General," said Royall, "we want to have a ceremony, but I can't organize one on such short notice."

"Oh, don't bother about any ceremony," said Marshall.

Marshall hung up the phone and Royall called Truman and asked, "Did you know George Marshall was going to retire? He just phoned and said his time is out, and he's leaving this afternoon."

"No!" said Truman. "What are you going to do about it?"

"Mr. President," he said, "there's nothing I can do. We haven't any troops here. We can't arrange anything in an hour."

"You better damn well think of something!" said Truman. "I'll be over there in a few minutes."

So Kenneth called Marshall and asked him please not to go home early and then he had the telephone operators ring every office in the Pentagon and tell the people to drop everything and turn out in the big central open area. Didn't make any difference what they were doing. Hang up the phones and get out there. The president came over, and Kenneth said you never saw so many people in your life. Out there by the thousands.

The president and Royall made speeches commending Marshall and then General Marshall made a little speech and put on his hat and went to Leesburg.

F. Isn't it interesting that Ike picked you for all these commissions?

D. I had worked with a lot of these fellows. Gordon and I had been friends for many years. I tell you the truth, I think it's an evidence of how much they had to scuffle around to get people to help them out.

F. Tell me of your role in erasing sectionalism in education.

D. In late 1959, at the request of the Southern Regional Education Board, West Virginia Governor Cecil Underwood and Tennessee Governor Buford Ellington appointed a commission to examine southern education and asked me to be the chairman. I was happy at the opportunity to say something that had been on my mind.

The night we gathered in Atlanta some of us were sitting around talking about what we ought to do. "I'm willing to sign any report you all want to make about improving southern education," I told them, "if you'll just say that the South will be judged on the basis of the nation. Let's get away from salary differentials for the North and the South. Let's set up standards on the grounds that we will be judged against the United States. This idea of cringing in front of other parts of the country is utterly repulsive.

"No economy is more impoverishing than that which is achieved by paring the cost of education, because by so doing we diminish substantially the opportunities of those generations who will come after us."

To raise the necessary funds would not be easy, I told them, but unless we were willing to pay the price we would continue as a second-rate mediocre region. That became the theme around which the report—*Within Our Reach*—was organized. Ralph McGill, the Atlanta newspaperman, responded enthusiastically.

F.   Governor, you left out one important group— the commission that met once a year to hear a report on the upkeep of the Washington Monument.

D.   In truth, I did! The commission was chaired by Earl Warren, chief justice, in the absence of the president. I'd known Chief Justice Warren very pleasantly when he was governor of California and I was governor of Virginia.

The meetings never varied. First we heard a report from the Interior Department that the monument had moved two hundred thousandths of an inch, which meant it wouldn't go off balance for the next million years. Then came the report on the annual count of visitors, which always disclosed that a good many more tourists went up in the monument than came down, at which Earl Warren would become terribly worked up and demand to know if anybody had been left up there. Interior's man would explain, patiently, that the count didn't include those who walked down the monument's steps instead of using the elevator. Between annual meetings Warren would forget the explanation and when, alarmed all over again the next year, he raised the question, it was worth the trip to Washington to see the look of consternation that swept over the members' faces at the thought of all those people hung up there somewhere. Only inertia and God working together keep this country going.

A REVOLUTION WITHOUT BLOODSHED

G.   Senator Robertson loved the outdoors, didn't he?

D.   Yes, he was a great sportsman. As a matter of fact, I think Willis would have been happier at that than he was in the Congress. He was commission chairman of the State Fish and Game Department, a thing he got up when he was in the State Senate. He loved it. He enjoyed politics, but only to a limited degree, I think.

F.   When he entered the State Senate in 1916 he saw that without some protective laws there soon wouldn't be any fish or game to hunt. He became a one-man conservation movement.

As a freshman in the House of Representatives in 1932, he co-sponsored legislation applying fees to sporting goods for conservation. He also drafted the Duck Stamp Bill for game refuges.

But when it came to campaigning, he wasn't as complete a politician as Byrd. He lacked his zest for the minutiae of politics.

D.   They were totally different in that Byrd understood intimately and well the detailed planning required for political leadership, but Willis never did. Willis didn't have the flair for organizing. Matter of fact, that was the reason he was beaten by Bill Spong in 1966, plus the fact that his friends didn't take Spong's candidacy seriously. There were enough votes in Lexington to have elected Willis, voters who sat around the house and never even took the trouble to go to the polls. Willis never had the faintest idea about how to organize. His whole life had been spent with the Virginia Organization. It had carried him, and when the end came, and he was out on his own, he just didn't have sufficient knowledge of operating a state campaign.

F.   His friends used to say that he had hunted and

fished with enough people in Virginia to assure his election. He was
fond of history, too.

D. He certainly was, and he knew how to express
it. I had a conversation with Harry after a speech Willis made in
Luray at the dedication of the carillons. I asked Harry how the day
went.

"Fine," said Harry. "I learned a lot about carillons."

"I'm sure you learned all about them," I said.

"No," said Harry, "Willis, in his history of carillons, had only
reached the time of the birth of Christ when night fell, and we had
to shut down."

F. That happens to us all. One time Robertson
and Lindsay Almond were seated on a platform outdoors while
Tom Stanley plowed along in a campaign speech. Darkness came
and Stanley, standing by a naked light bulb on a pole, had to
pause frequently to fight off a swarm of gnats.

Robertson, his hands locked around his right knee, was rocking
back and forth, and Almond asked, "What's the matter, Willis?
What are you doing?"

"Praying for more gnats," said Robertson.

D. Tom Stanley never received the credit he
deserved for his administrative work. Nobody paid any more attention to detail than he, and he had an intimate knowledge of the
business of Virginia. One day I went to see him about a proposed
physics building at the university. It was a costly project, and Tom
had the plans spread out on his desk in the governor's office.

He said to me, "Why do you need this spigot here in this room
on the second floor?"

"Tom," I said, "I don't know, but if it displeases you, cut it out."

F. While Lewis Webb was president of Old
Dominion University, Governor Stanley came to inspect proposed
capital-outlay projects. He was so familiar with the details that
he asked to see a particular closet to make sure an inordinate
amount of paint hadn't been requested to spruce it up.

D. You know, one person who knew both Willis
and Harry well was M. J. "Peachy" Menefee. After Peachy came
close to defeating Willis for Congress in the Seventh District, Willis
took him to Washington as his secretary. Then after many years
with Willis, Peachy worked a long time for Harry.

One day in the early era of surging good feeling between Congress and the Roosevelt administration, we all trooped down to Union Station to welcome Roosevelt on his return from Warm Springs, and then we paraded back to the Capitol, Willis and Harry and I, in the ranks with the rest; and as we marched up the hill like a bunch of penguins, Peachy, standing on the curb, said to us in a whisper that was audible but not loud, "You'll be sorry!" We walked manfully on, unaware of the accuracy of his prediction.

One of the most arresting things I ever saw happened on a visit to Peachy's house in Luray years ago. We went up in the attic looking for some papers, and there, thrown very carelessly over in a box, were the three highest awards of the French government for valor. He had the Médaille Militaire, the highest award, given only for combat, nothing else; and the Croix de Guerre, and on top of that the Legion of Honor.

I had never heard Peachy refer to them. I asked him about them and he said, "Yes, they were given me after I was wounded." That boy had been shot in the head. I never saw him wear the rosette of the Legion of Honor that you see worn by many people of some importance, at least in their own minds, strutting around with them. Peachy never mentioned them again.

F.   There was something jaunty about him, blithe, as if he had faced the worst and saw other troubles in that perspective and had reached a sort of truce with life.

G.   Can you remember when you first became interested in politics?

D.   I grew up in it. My father was a Martin man, a stout no-compromise Organization man, and he hated the Republican party in Virginia with a passion. But it is understandable when you realize the age out of which he had come—the invasion of the carpetbaggers, the followers of the Union Army in the southern states, and the bitter poverty.

F.   Governor, your sister told me you made your first campaign speech as a boy in high school.

D.   That occurred when Henry Stuart was campaigning for governor and came to a rally in Courtland. I made a little speech as a representative of the school children in the community.

F.   How was it received?

D. Very modestly. Father made only one comment. He said, "If you expect to take up speaking you better prepare yourself."

G. Is your sister interested in politics?

D. Loves it. More than any of the rest of us. She understands the mechanism. She's a fierce one in her loyalties. Got out with Mills Godwin, who had always been very generous and kind to her. She'd been a violent supporter of Mills. But when Mills went over to the Republican party, it almost killed Katherine. You would have thought that some close member of her family had run away or robbed a bank or something like that. Been sent to the penitentiary. She just never could come to terms with it. Her partisanship more nearly resembled my father's feeling about the Martin outfit in Virginia than anything I've ever seen.

Martin must have been a superb organizer, although I don't think any better than Byrd. Harry in organizing was as good as any I've ever seen. It reminded me of a thing I've read a number of times about Bonaparte setting his artillery in place. His skillful use of artillery contributed more than any other single factor to his mastery of Europe. They said of him that after he had arranged his artillery and had given the word to commence the battle that he could stand in the place chosen for himself to oversee and listen to the guns and tell his aides what gun and what battery was firing. Now Harry in his capacity for detail was that good. Moreover, he was indefatigable in following up.

He'd arrange his battle and he would give you a task that he wanted you to do, say in the morning, and that afternoon he'd call you up and want to know if you had done it. You hadn't had time really to get out and do it. That night he'd call you and want to know if you had done it, and the next morning he'd be on the phone again. He did that running all through his whole Organization, and it was awfully effective.

It was that which threw him into panic when he lost Sax Holt and Billy Wright. Billy Wright was managing Sax's campaign for lieutenant governor in 1937 and they had gone down to some places in the Valley. Harry knew where they had gone. He had followed their movements by phone to a fish fry or something. But then they disappeared hook, line, and sinker. Both vanished from view. Pandemonium broke loose in Harry's office. I thought he would go crazy. For about forty-eight hours he could not find them. He couldn't get them on the telephone and he couldn't get in touch with anybody who had seen them—other than a few who had seen them depart in high spirits from the fish fry, from which Harry imagined the worst. That's the last that they had seen of them. Well, sir, it just tore Harry all to pieces until they reappeared.

F.   Wasn't he upset when he couldn't lay hold to John Battle in the gubernatorial campaign of 1949?

D.   I don't think Battle ever gave him the jolt that Sax and Wright gave him, and he repaired the difficulty with Battle very quickly because Bill, John's son, was brought in to drive his father. John was deliberate and Harry thought a candidate should be more active in getting around. John just took the thing more or less in his stride, which, in truth, was part of his strength. They arranged for Bill to deliver his father in places and keep him on schedules, and it worked out beautifully.

Harry was a great detail man. But he also paid a great price for it because that attention to detail in Virginia diverted him from important national issues.

G.   Did you think his fiscal conservatism in the Senate was good most of the time?

D.   I think the conservatism in the nation was very good. I don't know that he foresaw the complete recklessness that obtains today, which is so very dangerous. Nor did he see in Virginia fully the needs of a great urban industrial society. And understandably so. Harry was basically an agrarian. His whole life around Berryville was wrapped up in his orchards. The Organization's rural roots resulted in our failing to move forward as rapidly as we should have moved to meet the changing industrial climate in the state.

Jay Wilkinson spells out accurately in his book that the Virginia Organization was founded around courthouse rings. Those groups or associations, whatever you want to call them, were almost all farming people. For that reason the Organization was less aware of the needs of a rapidly industrializing Virginia. The best illustration was the crushing of the Young Turks in 1954. They were not Young Turks. They were young progressives. There was nothing revolutionary about their proposals. Their plans were as modest as any plans could be that undertook to meet the needs of an industrial society. Their defeat was a very unfortunate thing for the Organization. For the state it was a tragedy. Had they won, the orientation of power would have changed, but the fact that the Organization was in charge would not have changed because they were part of it. But they were beaten down because the Old Guard was simply afraid of them. The Old Guard was saved temporarily by Massive Resistance. The movement of the state was toward an accommodation to an industrial society, and that would have happened much earlier but for the fact that the desegregation issue was thrown into it.

F.   Mills Godwin was a major advocate of Massive Resistance. Yet later he rode the progressive thrust that the Young Turks had espoused.

D.   Yes, but I think it's to his credit that in those intervening years he grasped the state's needs. There isn't any question that in the State Senate he was adamant in his opposition to the young Turks. He was part of the Virginia Old Guard that beat them down, and yet he accepted their program and more later on, which indicated that he had learned more of what was needed.

And he was a great friend of young Harry Byrd. They were sitting by each other in the State Senate and I believe they shared a firm belief in thinking that integration was an onrolling disaster. Mills came to understand, though, given the federal system, that it was an inevitable thing and that the solution was to make the best of it.

F.   It just always struck me as ironical that he should have inherited the Young Turks' place.

D.   There's nothing unusual about that if you go back over English history. That is what preserved the ruling class so many years, both Whigs and Tories. The strength of the English political system has been its genius for compromise.

F.   Yes, I can see that. It was a long gap, although not in the eyes of history, between the Young Turk rebellion in 1954 and the progressive General Assembly of 1966.

D.   That's a very short time, really. And then, also, you have to realize that Harry played a decisive role in that because he was as apprehensive about the Young Turks as anybody else. And he still was the dominant figure running the Organization.

F.   We can be philosophical about a long view, but

what went on in that twelve years was very turbulent, particularly Massive Resistance. I'm talking about not only the failures to meet the needs of public education, but also the risks in following Massive Resistance and closing the schools in Norfolk, Warren County, Charlottesville, and Prince Edward. The state survived, but it was a terrible chance to take.

 D. It was a mistaken policy, but I don't think the risk was so great, given the political temper of the people of Virginia.

 F. Yes, sir. What saved us was the fact that they are good-natured, calm, and reasonable; but to play on that and to close the public schools was the cardinal mark against Byrd and the Organization.

 D. It may well have been, but I don't believe the period was anything like as dangerous as the years surrounding the British Reform Act of 1832. As a matter of fact, when you consider the revolution through which we have lived since the Supreme Court's desegregation decision in 1954—taking the country as a whole now, with all of the violence that is constantly in the headlines and on television and radio—the remarkable thing is that there was so little of it when this vast transition took place. The comparative lack of violence gives the indication of a far more stable political and social system than many appear to think.

 F. It does, and it's remarkable in two ways. One is, the whites were calm, but even more than that, is that the blacks were calm.

 D. Isn't any question about that!

 F. So often when observers remarked on the good temper of the Virginia people, they seemed to be thinking only of the whites.

 D. What I said to you is inclusive of the blacks, because without that stabilizing force, which had enormous strength and great wisdom, we would have slipped into unspeakable violence.

 F. Exactly. I didn't mean you. In the height of Massive Resistance when so many persons were issuing denunciations, the black people apparently seldom registered in their minds.

 D. That's probably true.

 F. But it was the black people who as much as,

and maybe more than, the whites accounted for the calm that permitted the Massive Resisters to make those rancorous statements.

G. That was the saddest part about it—that the blacks were sitting there really not being thought about as human beings, almost.

D. Quite. It's a great tribute to them really; but it is a great tribute to both of the races that we managed to muddle through. All in all, with all of its trials and tribulations, the change is not a discouraging one. It gives indication of a political stability that might yet rescue us from this terrible dilemma, the malaise, in which we are now. The vital thing is that the country passed through a revolution with a minimum of bloodshed.

FROM MODERATE TO
MASSIVE

F. Governor, what was your reaction to the Supreme Court's school desegregation decision of May 1954?

D. I was surprised. I had regarded the decision in *Plessy* v. *Ferguson* in 1896 as settled law. In fact, when I testified in an early challenge to Prince Edward County's segregated schools, I had taken the position that "separate but equal" was the law. That was all swept away by the May decision of *Brown* v. *Board of Education*.

F. Did Governor Stanley seek your advice after the Supreme Court's May decree?

D. Yes, not long after the decision John Battle called me at the university and said Tom wanted to talk with us, and so John and I drove down to Richmond. Tom said he wanted to devise some way to meet the court's decree. His mood was thoughtful and temperate, just as his first public statement had been temperate. In our conference with Tom, John and I encouraged him in his thinking.

F. In late August 1954 he appointed the Gray Commission of thirty-two members of the General Assembly to look for a solution. In mid-November 1955 it recommended a plan that permitted some local option integration and called for state tuition grants to assure that no child would be compelled to attend an integrated public school. The commission's plan could be construed as a temperate response in contrast to what came later.

D. That was a good commission and a remarkably good report. Don't you think so?

F. Considering the makeup of the commission, yes.

D. It was remarkable when you look at the composition of the commission and also the climate out of which it came. It is one of the best examples of effective commission work that I've seen in Virginia. That report, embracing opinions of many people who differed in many respects, was an extraordinarily able achievement. The turning away from it later was a mistake.

F. The Gray Commission's membership was weighted heavily to the Southside, but there were able spokesmen from other areas, and each side had to give.

D. And did give, and each side received a full hearing over many weeks of deliberation.

F. Senator Charles Fenwick of Arlington, a workhorse for moderate causes, was able to give by accepting the idea of tuition grants for children whose parents did not wish to send them to integrated schools; but the Southside members from constituencies with tremendous black populations, such as Senator Albertis Harrison of Lawrenceville, also gave by contenancing a little integration.

D. Not so little, either. There was a remarkable degree of integration there, provided the localities wished it.

F. In a four-day special session ending December 3, the General Assembly provided for a referendum on January 9, 1956, on whether the Virginia Constitution should be amended to allow tuition grants. Near the close of the campaign leading up to the referendum, some of the Gray plan's supporters noted that it would permit integration, and that caused quite a stir.

D. I made a great many speeches around the state for the Gray Commission's recommendations. Delegate Tayloe Murphy, a commission member, had come to New York where I was serving in the United Nations, and asked if I'd be willing to come home three or four days early and begin campaigning around the state for the plan. Part of my reason for agreeing to help was that John and I had encouraged Tom in his moderate course.

Time after time when I was asking support for the plan, a listener would bring up the point about the plan's admitting some integration. I would reply that it would, but that the integration was based on the decision of the locality in which the school was located.

F. That would mean no integration in some localities.

D. But it also would mean there would be integration in some localities, and the force of that example, in the minds of many of us, would accomplish more than anything else we could do.

F.   Though there were no blacks on the commission and though it was stacked with Southsiders, it did offer a meeting ground for two extreme constituencies.

D.   It did, and also it was an example, really, of the genius of the people of this state in dealing with a difficult subject. The Gray Commission report was the Virginia legislative machinery at its best.

F.   During the campaign on the referendum, you issued a statement that shook the electorate and those campaigning both for and against the plan. Your statement erupted in somewhat unusual circumstances.

D.   While we were struggling in that December campaign looking to the referendum on January 9, Willis Robertson became alarmed about quite another matter: the abuses, as he saw it, in subsidized athletics, particularly football in Virginia's colleges.

F.   So he summoned you and the other college presidents into session at Natural Bridge to confer on the troubles of big-time football.

D.   And settle it all at one fell swoop. I took off from campaigning for the Gray plan and joined the other college presidents to ponder the problems that alarmed Willis.

F.   Senator Robertson came prepared with his definition of amateur athletics. Do you recall what that was?

D.   No, but I know he was loaded and prepared for the whole thing, because he had gotten highly exercised. I don't know what moved him so, except probably a deep puritan instinct. And also a desire to take charge at a critical moment when he knew the rest of us were in a position where we couldn't do anything or wouldn't do anything.

F.   It was his own background of being an athlete himself, you know.

D.   Oh, sure. That gave him the entrée.

F.   My recollection is he earned letters in all major sports at the University of Richmond.

D.   Willis was one of the great athletes of his day.

F.   And played every minute of every game on offense and defense.

D.   Yes, they had no relief back in the days when he played. They just put them in there and let them die!

F.   This was his definition of an amateur athlete: "One who receives nothing in excess of necessary expenses."

D.   Which, of course, would have embodied everything.

F.   Another thing you all did at that meeting was to recommend that the various colleges within the state play one another. You all agreed to that, but said, on the other hand, if any college wanted to go outside the state it could.

D.   Thereby giving latitude to our cogitations.

F.   Both those decisions were what you call open-ended.

D.   That's right, and stamped with the majesty of the Congress. Here Willis was a member of the United States Senate down there settling this matter for us. Willis came rightly by the fervent spirit that drove him on because his father was a great evangelical preacher.

F.   After two and a half hours in private session, the presidents began lunch in the motel dining room. I was sitting at the end of the long table with two or three dozen sports writers from throughout Virginia, and suddenly, in the middle of the discussion of old-time athletes and so forth, I heard you booming forth at the head of the table: "There must be categorical assurances that no public school will be closed in Virginia!" We had jumped from the issue of subsidized athletics to the question of desegregation of public schools. What moved you to make that statement then? Had it been on your mind?

D.   There never was any question in my mind about the unwisdom of abandoning schools anywhere. Closing schools is simply self-impoverishment. The topic just happened to come up in conversation at Natural Bridge because we had, I think, grown tired of wrestling with the athletic difficulties and Willis's scheme to save us all. He'd brought us together and at lunch we'd gotten off on to something that seemed simple. We fell to discussing the Gray Commission plan.

F.   So you told them, number one, that there should be categorical assurances from the state leadership that the public schools would be kept open. Number two, you said that the state should not flinch from its responsibility as set out in Section

129 of the Virginia Constitution to maintain a free, efficient system of public schools.

D. In campaigning around the state for the Gray plan, I had encountered no end of groups who said this is nothing in the world but a skin game leading up to the closing of the schools. That was firmly implanted in their minds. Why, I didn't know, but it was there. It never was in my mind because I wouldn't have been out campaigning on any scheme that looked to the closing of the public schools under any circumstances.

F. After the newspapers published your declaration at Natural Bridge, I went into the Gray Commission's campaign headquarters. Some of the staff seemed to be reflecting the leaders' feelings of hostility over the story.

D. They were not enthusiastic because they got on Tayloe and asked him if he knew what I meant by my statement. Tayloe told them he thought it was easily understood and there was no use in his inquiring of me as to what it meant. It was spelled out in English. That reaction led me to believe that there were grounds for the suspicions which I had encountered.

F. What had happened was that Senator Byrd had received a copy of the Gray Commission plan when he was on a congressional trip overseas, he told me years later, and he read the report and said, "This won't do." And when he got back from Europe he began planning to change the thrust of the report.

D. After I came back from New York I went to Richmond and talked to Tom. He told me it was very important that the plan be ratified and he would like for me to stump around the state. I never will forget it because I made an early talk before Christmas over radio in the District of Columbia beamed to Northern Virginia. And that night, having fired off my piece, I began the drive back to Charlottesville. About an hour out of Washington I ran into a snowstorm, not a heavy one, but one that was enough to make you look sharply at the road. I had the radio on, and I heard this fellow on the 11 o'clock news in Richmond saying Governor Stanley and his family just boarded the Coast Line going down to their home in Hobe Sound for the Christmas season. I said to myself, "You saphead, you are getting exactly what you deserve! Here you are pulling around on these lonely roads in Virginia by yourself and Tom's highballing it down to Florida taking his ease over the holidays."

F. Even as all of you were out promoting the Gray Commission plan, Senator Byrd had determined to abandon it.

D. That I did not know, because I had only one talk with Harry about the court decision. He and I were having supper at the Army-Navy Club in Washington, and in a discussion of the political situation he got on the matter of segregation and the necessity of maintaining segregated schools and the danger of the Supreme Court desegregation decision. I remember he said, "Nobody ever need plan to run for public office in Virginia that's not on the segregated side of this issue." And I said, "Harry, that's academic as far as I'm concerned because I'm never going to run for public office anyway." Some months later, Tayloe Murphy told me that Harry said precisely the same to him.

F. The Organization's shift from the Gray plan of local option to Massive Resistance was a delicate operation. In a statement in December, Byrd endorsed tuition grants but refrained from comment on other features of the Gray plan.

The Massives had to secure the passage of the amendment for tuition grants because a defeat there would have been a disastrous setback; and yet, feeling they had to throw out the other half of the plan, they had to be careful how they lined themselves up. Also, had you and others known their intentions, you could have withdrawn from the campaign.

D. Certainly Harry was enough of a planner to know that would give trouble. There would have been nothing for us to campaign for. I would not have been coming home in a snowstorm while Tom and his family were heading for the sunshine of Florida.

F. On January 9, 1956, the voters approved by nearly three to one the holding of a constitutional convention to clear the way for tuition grants, and a six-day convention early in March amended the constitution. In late July, Governor Stanley presented to the Gray Commission a new plan that would cut off state aid to any public school allowing any integration. It also stripped local pupil placement boards of powers and centralized authority in a state board. Nineteen of the thirty-two member commission, including Chairman Garland Gray, repudiated the original plan.

Byrd endorsed the new plan at his annual orchard picnic on August 25. He urged the state to fight the Supreme Court's desegregation order "with every ounce of energy and capacity" and said, "If Virginia surrenders, if Virginia's line is broken, the rest of the South will go down, too." The destroyers of public schools, he said, would be those "who try to force mixed schools upon us—something a large part of Virginia will never take."

The General Assembly's special session convened August 27. On September 1, in the first expression of opposition from a major figure within the Organization, you called the new plan an illusion that "will simply close many schools in Virginia" and offered nothing to help localities hard-pressed by integration problems. To deny them their money was unfair and of questionable legality, you said, and added: "Just when help and support are needed most, the state retreats to the sidelines."

D. Tayloe Murphy and others then asked some of us to appear on September 5 before the General Assembly's joint committees and try to persuade the legislators not to go over into Massive Resistance. I told them that the fund-cut plan meant the abandonment of public education and pleaded with them to accept the original Gray Commission plan that left the localities free to work out the problems their own way.

I told them I didn't think any plan short of closing schools would prevent integration. The fund-cut plan, with its accompanying disturbances in public schools, would do irreparable harm to the supply of teachers. It was bound to get us in trouble, I said. You simply can't treat people that way.

The people of Norfolk wouldn't be willing to surrender their school system because some integration occurred. I added that we shouldn't close schools in black counties but should operate them alone for Negroes, if necessary, because we could not afford illiteracy.

Southside Virginia was in a desperate situation, but it would cause other sections to lose patience if it insisted on adoption of a single plan by the entire state, I warned, and anyway, I said, integration wouldn't come in our lifetime in Southside Virginia.

That prediction just shows what can happen when a chump

takes off from the launching pad and begins freewheeling. It was
brought home to me a few months ago when I attended in Southampton County a celebration for the winning football team. The
gymnasium was packed with blacks and whites, and they showed
no difference in their enthusiasm for the team. And that celebration
took place on the very ground where Nat Turner's insurrection, the
largest slave revolt in the United States, had occurred.

      F.   You asked, "What would happen in any case
where we have a society of laws . . . and we say we can refuse to be
bound by the decision of the highest court?"

That didn't mean that Virginia agreed with the decision, you
said, and noted that you yourself had testified in favor of segregation in the first Prince Edward County trial; but the way to end the
trend toward centralization, of which the decision was evidence,
was to convince the people that the trend was wrong.

If the state wanted to resist, all that was needed was a resolution
by the Assembly telling the governor to stand firm. "That," you
said, "will bring the state face to face with the federal government."

      D.   An assault on public schools, democracy's one
instrumentality for improving itself, was bound to be terribly
damaging, I warned. If you turn away from that you draw down a
curtain of darkness.

Among others who spoke were Dabney Lancaster, chairman of
the State Council of Higher Education; Tom Boushall, a member
of the State Board of Education; Charles Martin, president of
Radford College, and H. I. Willett, superintendent of Richmond
schools. We were courteously but frostily received.

Resistance had hardened rapidly. Spurred by Jack Kilpatrick's
editorials in the *News Leader,* the Organization had thrown its weight
behind interposition—which had little legal foundation but considerable popular appeal.

After my appearance before the General Assembly, I went by
to see John Dana Wise, general manager of Richmond Newpapers,,
about a university matter. I found him quite stout in opposition
to integration. He told me about being given a standing ovation
a few days before for a speech he had made in his neighborhood
about holding the line.

      F.   The fallacy in polls and the like during that era
was that people would say overwhelmingly that they favored Mas-

sive Resistance—until the time that it was about to close their schools. In the General Assembly as the legislators shifted from the Gray plan to Massive Resistance, some would vote for the fund-cut legislation and then admit privately that it wouldn't help.

Until Byrd intervened, Virginia seemed headed on what many whites felt to be a somewhat reasonable course.

      D.   An accommodation.

      F.   Yes, they were trying to accommodate.

      D.   I don't share your view about Harry's strength in executing the change. I think he reflected a rising tide of resentment in the state and without that I doubt that he would have been able to bring about a change in the Gray plan. The favorable sentiment of the early days of the Gray Commission probably would have disappeared.

      F.   North Carolina, which had citizens fully as embittered as ours, adopted the Pearsall plan copied from the Gray plan and went through the period under moderate leadership without school closing.

In Virginia, Byrd genuinely believed that in the long run integration wouldn't work. And yet, I never saw a trace of prejudice in him. He simply was sure that integration would not work, and he was an example of how powerful one man was in one state, reversing a legislative commission and turning around Governor Stanley from moderation to Massive. Then Governor Almond went to the brink before he drew back.

      D.   That was Lindsay's finest hour and a fine hour for Virginia because to have continued to resist might have provoked violence.

I'm not certain that Harry, even if he had felt differently, could have dammed the rising tide against integration. During the campaign for the January 9 referendum I didn't feel that the lines had hardened. Now they hardened very rapidly after that, and unquestionably because he helped harden them; but I believe the hardening process would have taken place with or without his leadership.

      F.   My feeling is that he generated the harsh climate to a large degree and that he could have moderated it and led the state into reasonableness.

      D.   Certainly the Gray plan was the preferable

course. It was a rendezvous with moderation that didn't work out. Don't you think so?

F. Yes, and had Byrd felt and acted differently, he would have gone into history as a great leader.

D. I can't argue with you on that score at all because the moderate course was the better one. What I've never been able to settle to my own satisfaction was whether or not he could have won on the issue. Now the reason that there is no conflict between us, I think, is that a loss on the issue would have added to his stature. It was not an issue you had to win to prove you were right.

F. Governor, now the former Massive Resisters contend that they were buying time, channeling public debate, and thereby helping avert violence and giving people a chance to adjust to the inevitable. What is your feeling about their assertion?

D. I think it's an illusion.

PASSING THE WORD

       F. Governor, you mentioned once that Senator Byrd offered you the leadership of the Democratic Organization. When was that?

       D. In 1944 or '45, we were walking from Capitol Square to the Jefferson Hotel to a meeting, chatting along, and Harry said to me, quietly: "I'm getting mighty tired of this thing. I wonder if you wouldn't like to take over the Organization and run it?"

"Harry," I said, "nothing would suit me less than that. There are several reasons. One is, it's your Organization. You've built it up with great care. Two, while you may think you are tired, nobody would be more unhappy than you would be if you gave it up. You wouldn't be up in the orchards a week before you would be bitterly sorry that you had ever given any indication that you didn't want to run the Organization. All your old cronies in Virginia would be phoning you and telling you what a mess everything was in, and imploring you to come back and straighten it out. Don't give a damn how well it was run, it wouldn't suit them and it wouldn't suit you.

"Over and above that," I said, "I have not the slightest idea of spending my life wrestling around with people over appointments and this thing and that. I've enjoyed being governor, but even if everybody in the Organization agreed to my running it, I still wouldn't do it, because it's just not the kind of thing I want to do. Plenty of people around Virginia have the ability to do it, and if you are looking for somebody to slip the mantle over on, you'll just have to look further. But the truth is, you are not going to slip it over on anybody, because you wouldn't be happy."

       F. Was he perhaps sizing up your ambitions? You said once he was good at guarding his flank.

       D. Any man that runs a political organization is

bound to be. It's just like a field commander in the army. You can't run an organization on a half-time or third-time basis. It's a full-time hard job, and a disagreeable job unless it's what you like to do. And Harry loved politics. He loved the wear and tear of it. The thing that bore heavily on other people, he took in his stride, because he was physically in good condition. He was a strong person and took regular exercise.

F.   He made a definite move toward retirement in 1958. Where were you when that news broke?

D.   I was in New York, walking through Times Square, and saw flashing around the Times building the bulletin that Senator Byrd planned to retire. I didn't know the details because while Harry and I were friendly, we were never particularly close after Massive Resistance. I was not one of the faithful in Massive Resistance. But the bulletin didn't bother me because I figured that there wasn't much to it and when the chips were down, he'd be going back to the Senate. I got home and in a few days quite a storm blew up because Delegate Baldwin Locher of Lexington was organizing for John Battle to succeed Harry. And Bill Tuck had told Tayloe Murphy that he was going to run. There were all of the makings for just one helluva wrangle that would have ended in the Organization's being terribly hurt because we would have torn it apart in that fight to such an extent that nobody could have put it back together again in a reasonable time.

Anyway, shortly after I returned from New York, Harry called. Already there'd been requests that he reconsider, and he said to me, "You reckon you can get the old governors to come together in a statement?" He said, "Don't tell anybody I'm talking to you." (Harry would always say don't tell anybody about something.) "You reckon you can get them together in a petition for me to stay?"

And I said, "You couldn't have gotten a more willing person than I to work on it because after a fight over your successor the state would be torn asunder and I wouldn't be able to get a satisfactory budget for the university through the General Assembly to save my life."

Battle was right there in Charlottesville and dearly loved and very popular and a good friend of all of us and then Bill had been my lieutenant governor and was a close friend, and when we got through scuffling there would have been just nothing. So I drafted

a ringing declaration as to our need for him. They all went along.
John said he didn't see any special reason why we had to get up a
statement, but joined in with us. I didn't have any trouble with any
of them. I think there was some thought on their part it was strange
that I was interceding when I wasn't one of the faithful of the Massives.

F.   It must have baffled them.

D.   It did, completely. It would work because I held
absolutely to what Harry asked me to do. I never breathed the secret
to anybody. I went right on it on my own, which I was glad enough
to do. No deception in that. As I said, he couldn't have hit on a more
willing collaborator than I was because I was sitting right up there
next to the fire. And I fell into the task with vigor. I drafted up a
pretty good statement, if I may say so myself. It pointed out the
dilemma that we would be in and the difficulties Virginia would
face with the loss of his powerful committee assignments. I fired it
up to Harry's office with all our names on it. And he fired it into the
newspapers.

F.   I've never seen such a comic interlude in politics. Shortly after Byrd indicated he would retire, Ben Lacy, clerk
of the Senate, called me very confidentially into his office—he was
like an elephant tiptoeing through daisies—and gave me Tuck's
statement announcing his candidacy. "The minute Battle an-
nounces that he's running," Ben said, "you release Bill's statement."
And the Battle people gave me his statement with the same instruc-
tions. Had Byrd not changed his mind, it would have made a fine
story.

They talk about passing the word. Byrd's asking you to ask the
governors to ask him not to retire is a prime example of Byrd's
passing the word to himself.

But don't you see the comic aspect? Calling you, of all the
governors, the one that was least in his camp, and asking you to
do it but not to tell anybody?

D.   Yes, but that, of course, was also part of his
maneuvering. Now, of course, the telegram went to him. Only the
governors knew that I had framed it. And they didn't know for certain that Harry hadn't framed it and phoned down to me, although
I never suggested to them that Harry phoned me about it. He said
don't tell anybody about that. So I kept it absolutely.

F.   Governor, what sort of Organization was Byrd offering you on that walk to the Jefferson?

D.   The Organization that Harry loved and ran was a fairly simple operation. I'm not certain he could have managed the complex political organization that would have accompanied the development of an industrial state. Certainly the type of organization that he used would not have worked under those conditions because he would not have been able to base the power on the local courthouse officials through the state. That was the basis of the Virginia Organization. It would have had to have been a much broader base.

F.   Of course, he tied it in closely with the wealthy businessmen. It was a combination of agrarianism with big business.

D.   Yes, but the large business interests were also fearful of the expense that might be entailed with the enlargement of social services. For instance, in the whole time I was in the General Assembly, I do not remember that a single proposal for improvement of working conditions and other things in the state had the support of the Virginia Manufacturers Association that was represented by a substantial lobby. It was a very good lobby—nothing wrong with it, so far as I know—excepting that it did not see the breadth of the problem, the whole of what had to be done.

In fairness it should be noted that under the leadership of W. T. Reed's commission, business played a determining part in the reorganization of state government—which was one of the best things Harry did as governor.

What we are witnessing now is that the counties no longer are dominant in the General Assembly. The cities have reached a point that the industrial areas are as restrictive and as punitive as the old county system used to be. It means that the pendulum is swinging too far the other way.

F.   The retribution won't be any worse than the crime. It's as bad under one as it is under the other.

D.   It won't be any harsher than what was done to the cities under the old crowd, but it's something that ought not to happen. Excesses are never good.

F.   Except you are not going to get the major cities in control because the suburban counties have united on many issues with the rural counties.

D. I would exercise great caution in making an assessment on that.

F. The rural and suburban counties and the new cities have given little consideration to some of the older cities' deep concerns, such as integration of public schools. Virginia Beach is an outgrowth of Sidney Kellam's masterminding the merger of the resort city and Princess Anne County to avoid annexation by Norfolk. The thrust of much of what Virginia Beach has wanted has been not far different from what Princess Anne County sought.

D. That's quite true. It's more or less the same, isn't it? But time will change that.

F. Yes, it's beginning to change with the incredible growth in Virginia Beach. Only when the big suburban areas become so populous that they themselves feel urban problems acutely, as is happening in Northern Virginia, will there be a marked swing to urban domination.

D. Oh, I don't mean what's happening is a complete reversal of the old days. But certainly we are seeing a vast shift in political power.

F. There's no doubt about that. I only meant that the General Assembly is not so much more attuned to the cities' needs—

D. Than in the olden days?

F. —as you would think if you classify legislators as rural and urban.

D. Well, maybe not, maybe not; but I think that's cutting it too thin. Really there's far greater awareness of the needs of the cities than when I was a member forty years ago.

F. You have the awareness, but the General Assembly doesn't always back it up with the money. You come back to the schools. The suburban counties and new cities are not overly concerned if the older cities have a mass of ghetto pupils to educate. When you go into a suburban school you immediately feel a world of difference between that school and one in the city.

D. And yet I don't see any other engine but the public school system powerful enough to make this system of ours work. That's our only hope.

There is an awareness, much beyond anything in the early days, of the need of equalizing school facilities among localities. Now when I went to the General Assembly, we had an equalization fund of about $5 million given to help. It's $436 million today. That's a tremendous advance to wipe out inequities.

F.   It's certainly an advance, but that equalization fund applies statewide, naturally, and it was a part not only of increasing concern but also increasing inflation. But beyond that general effort the inner cities have a very special need because they are trying to lift a race two or three grade levels. The schools have borne the brunt of the revolution amazingly well, and they deserve help and understanding. I don't think that the General Assembly has addressed the problem to the extent that it should in the core cities or, for that matter, in the rural Southside counties.

D.   I have no quarrel with that; but certainly it is well underway toward being addressed. The general sentiment in the Assembly today is vastly different from what it was twenty years ago.

F.   It's loosening, certainly, but the older cities have had to wait while the problems of integration intensify.

D.   That's right. That's true.

F.   Richmond, Norfolk, Roanoke, have not been able to call the tune—

D.   That's true.

F.   —as might have been expected, say in the 1952 reapportionment, when we began to urbanize rapidly.

D.   Yet careful thought on it would have led you to conclude that the satellite counties to the core cities, say, would tend to throw their weight on the other side because they were created out of fear of the core cities. For instance, the tremendous growth in the last twenty years in Henrico, Chesterfield, and Hanover counties has come about in part because of apprehension over the problems within Richmond. Now consequently it's not reasonable to suppose that their delegations in the Assembly would line up with the core city people completely in addressing their problems.

What you are witnessing is the slow working of representative government. When you look at representative government, you don't see a temperate, well-thought-out scheme to address problems as they occur. What you are looking at is water rising behind a dam until it reaches a point and then—swish—it's over.

F.   My feeling is that if someone who had been in

the Assembly in the 1950s came back in the 1970s, he would find that things had not changed nearly as much as the purely demographic trends might have led him to expect.

D.   But on the other hand, I think he would feel that they have changed far more than you think they have changed in your witnessing it over the years.

F.   There has been a great deal of change. Your own work in upgrading education—

D.   Let's put it another way. There has been change but not as much as you would hope for.

F.   One always hopes; but simply as an observer I'm interested that there has not been more change.

D.   There's another very good reason, and I'm sure that you realize this. Those were the impoverishing years of Massive Resistance that you are talking about. The Massive Resistance movement slowed the forward thrust, not only in education but in other areas as well.

F.   Yes, it certainly did, because it consumed the attention of the General Assembly.

D.   Not only that, it consumed the attention of the people in the state.

F.   In a sense they were feeding each other there.

D.   Yes, exactly.

F.   That French proverb—the more things change the more they stay the same—applies with particular aptness to Virginia.

D.   Well, it applies to the human race.

F.   But Virginians are among the more conservative segments of the human race.

D.   I don't know enough about the race to pass on it; but I should say they are conservative enough. Wouldn't you think so? I would say that Jefferson and others might at times in my lifetime have had difficulty making their way around the state. They might have been locked up because they were dangerous revolutionaries.

A LITTLE THING
FOR ALBERTIS

F. In August 1963 you agreed to try to reopen the public schools of Prince Edward County which had been closed four years to avoid court-ordered integration. How did you become involved in that effort?

D. Brooks Hayes called me one day and asked me to meet him in Richmond. Brooks was a part-time Baptist preacher, as well as being an assistant to President Kennedy and a former congressman from Arkansas. He was on one of his preaching missions. Brooks said, "The president feels he has to have the schools open in Prince Edward. They want to know if you would be willing to undertake it. They plan to use defense funds on the theory that the failure to educate is a failure to prepare the United States for war."

I said, "That Virginia has a county without public schools is indefensible. It's impoverishing both white and black. But it's the state's responsibility, and the state should meet it. Moreover, only the state can do it with any chance of success because the effort must have public support. If the state wanted to do it, I'd feel compelled to help. I called on so many people when I was governor of Virginia that if the governor asked me to do something, I'd do it, almost regardless."

Some weeks later I was in Richmond at a board meeting, and the secretary called me to the phone. It was the governor, Albertis Harrison. "I have a little project," he said, "a thing I want you to do for me. I can tell you on the phone in a minute or two."

"Albertis," I said, "we're about to end our meeting here, and I'll come by your place in a few minutes."

"Come on up here then," he said, "and I'll tell you. Won't take but a minute."

It never occurred to me what he had in mind. I thought it was some trivial thing, that he wanted me to make a speech for him. So

I went to his office. Albertis is a very deliberate sort of fellow. He said to me without even batting an eye: "I want you to go down to Farmville and get the schools open."

I said, "You do?"

"Yes," he said. "I'll tell you, this situation is bad. I don't go anywhere to make a speech but what somebody jumps up and wants to know when are we going to open the schools. I don't mind that so much, but I'm afraid that something like the trouble in Cambridge, Maryland, could happen in Prince Edward. I'm just afraid there is going to be violence. Something has to be done about it."

I said, "Albertis, I feel that this is something that you want done as governor of Virginia, and it's up to me to try to do it, but I have to find what the people on both sides are willing to do. I want to know whether the blacks are going to stop parading up and down the streets. I'm not talking about the right of protest. I'm willing to join with anybody in guaranteeing that right; but you just can't educate children who are marching continually and getting all excited. Another question is whether the county officials will let us use the public school facilities. I'll begin there by talking to J. Segar Gravatt."

I began walking out, and at the door I turned and said, "Albertis, is there any other little thing around the Commonwealth you want done?"

He didn't even crack a smile. He said, "No, that will be enough for the present."

Next day I went to Blackstone to meet Segar, who was counsel for the County Board of Supervisors and who had been a very able member of the university's Board of Visitors while I was in Charlottesville.. We conferred with local officials at a restaurant near Farmville.

It was not my purpose, I said, to interfere in any way with court proceedings. The committee's sole function would be to run the schools while the case was under consideration so the children would be in school rather than straying around by themselves; to do that, I had to have support, friendship, and help.

So, really the quarrel over segregation versus integration was not brought into play. It wasn't a compulsory school system that was planned. We were working as a private independent committee, the Prince Edward Free School Association. We needed to use the county's buses and buildings, but we were not acting under the authority of the state and consequently could not compel attendance. I told them we would raise the money. A Justice Department official had assured Albertis that money could be raised privately. The county officials said we could have the four buildings and buses. They pledged their support—and gave it fully.

Next day I went to confer with the black leaders in the Capitol. In the Old Senate Chamber I talked with the Reverend William Griffin, the blacks' leader in Farmville; W. Lester Banks, head of the Virginia National Association for the Advancement of Colored People, and William J. vanden Heuvel from Attorney General Robert Kennedy's office.

"I'm willing to undertake this," I told them, "but I can't do so unless you all can stop the marching. I haven't any objection to protests on anybody's part, but I don't believe you can teach children under those circumstances. I know that the education can't resume unless you underwrite it. Now if you can stop that for the time I'm down there running the school, I'll do my best."

"No," they said, "we can't do that. This is too deep an issue with us. The children have a right to march around town, and we are not going to tell them they can't do it."

"You are on sound ground as to their rights," I said, "but I'm not going to open a school down there under conditions which I deem impossible."

I went upstairs to Albertis, who was with Segar Gravatt and Collins Denny, another lawyer for the county.

"Albertis," I said, "I just can't do it because I can't get the commitment to quiet. I'm going back to Norfolk."

"Oh, you can't do that!" Albertis said. "We've got to get the schools open!"

We had a break for a few minutes, and I was getting ready to leave. I walked to the elevator and vanden Heuvel overtook me.

"I have talked to the leaders," he said. "They are right. They're not willing to go to their people and tell them they can't march. They just can't do that and have the people trust them; but I can say this to you: if you'll go work on the schools, there won't be a parade while you are there."

So I started work. We never had any demonstration of any kind. Their word was just as good as a bond. The federal government put the bite on people around the United States for donations to a committee headed by Harold Geneen of IT&T. We also received many contributions from people throughout Virginia. We recruited teachers from all around. With maybe one or two exceptions, we received splendid cooperation.

F.   Vanden Heuvel said you were the one person indispensable to the venture.

D.   That's very generous, overly so. The rest of the committee was invaluable, as was vanden Heuvel. Working with me were Fred Cole, then president of Washington and Lee University; Thomas Henderson, president of Virginia Union; Robert P. Daniel, president of Virginia State College; Earl H. McClenny, president of St. Paul's College, and Dean F. D. G. Ribble of the University of Virginia Law School.

The superintendent, Neil Sullivan from Long Island, said, "I don't see how in the world we can keep these children in school. That's what's worrying me."

There was no way in our setup to compel children to come to school. Even under the best of circumstances, where there are compulsory school attendance laws, children play hooky; and the children of Prince Edward County had not been in any school for four years.

Remembering the little crowd that got together for cold lunch in my day in school and the pleasant friendships growing out of those modest meals, I thought that such an operation, greatly expanded, would accomplish what we wanted to bring about. We could think of the students in Prince Edward as an enlargement of the little group that assembled in Southampton County many years ago. The question was where to get the food.

Then I remembered reading in the paper that the Agriculture Department had a tremendous number of surplus chickens.

"I can tell you how to do it," I said to Sullivan. "Get in touch with the Department of Agriculture through vanden Heuvel. Rent a warehouse in Lynchburg and lay in a supply of frozen chicken. Give these children a half of chicken for lunch every day. Don't worry about their getting tired of chicken. They've had an awful hard time. If you'll do that, you won't have a falling off of one of them during the whole winter."

We stocked the warehouse in Lynchburg with chicken, and we

rolled them into Farmville. We had a cafeteria running, and we had the help and the teachers and all, and you never saw such lunches as we shoveled out to them since you've been born. It hit at the right time, because I knew the government had the surplus, and I knew, of course, with the temper of the country and the race issue being what it was, and with the Kennedys so anxious this be done, that all we had to do was ask the Department of Agriculture to let us have the chickens and we'd get them.

Then, of course, in late fall tragedy befell us. The president was killed in Dallas. His interest in Prince Edward made his loss especially painful. Some time later Robert and Ethel Kennedy paid us a visit. It was a carefully planned event. We went out and met the Kennedy party at the airfield. They came down in an army helicopter and rode in a motorcade through Farmville, stopping at Longwood College where the students rushed out. From Longwood we went to the high school auditorium for a display of oratory.

Then Robert Kennedy talked to the boys at Hampden-Sydney College, and they raised directly the question of the justice of integration. He met it head on and said segregation was wrong and that the court decisions had to be obeyed. Many in the student body disagreed with his position, but he was well and courteously received; and he gained their admiration for his forthrightness.

F. To keep those schools functioning smoothly was a long pull, wasn't it?

D. I'd get the early morning train and go up there and then come home at night. Damn near killed me because I wasn't very well at the time, but I got a lot of help. I did not encounter any unpleasantness, and yet it was something that the community could not have had any deep sympathy for. Barrye Wall was running his newspaper, the Farmville *Herald*, and what was that phrase with which he used to close his editorials? "Stand Firm!" And yet Barrye never at any time advocated anything other than adherence to what he regarded was a constitutional right. He wasn't a violent man at all.

I have been taking Barrye's paper ever since. We subscribed to it for the members of the board to keep them abreast of what was going on. I kept it up because Barrye writes the best travel editorials of any I've read. He detaches himself in the fall and goes up in the mountains of Virginia, first one place and then another, and describes the turning of the leaves.

F. You had to go between the two camps and win an agreement from each.

D. Yet the pressures to come to an agreement were very great. Neither side wanted violence. Neither side wanted the situation to degenerate into something that would be uncontrollable. And I'm satisfied that both sides wanted the opportunity given the children.

In December 1963 my old friend, Virginia Chief Justice Jack Eggleston, gave a sure sign of things to come in a solitary and penetrating dissent to the majority's opinion sustaining the school closing in Prince Edward.

Warning in his conclusion that the majority opinion was a clear invitation to the federal courts to step in and enforce the people's rights, Jack wrote, "I am sure that that invitation will be promptly accepted. We shall see."

Thereafter when I saw Jack I'd sing out to him, "We shall see!"

THE BATON IN THE
LUNCH PAIL

F.   Governor, what has been your objective in working so many years for the public schools?

D.   My great interest was equalizing the opportunities for education. The charge, so often leveled, that the program would prove too costly for the state is an inaccurate one. That loses sight of the fact that nothing is more costly than a poor education.

My idea was that a child should obtain a good education wherever he lived just as a county gets good roads no matter where it is or how poor it is.

F.   Shortly after you left the presidency of the University of Virginia, Governor Almond appointed you to the State Board of Education in 1960.

D.   Lindsay called me and said, "I'm in just terrible straits up here about the schools. If you could help me on the State Board of Education, I certainly would appreciate it."

I said I'd try because when I was governor and asked people to help me, they always responded.

Lindsay was in a terrible row after he altered his position from Massive Resistance to compliance with court orders for desegregation of schools, and he needed all the friends he could get to help him. He was at odds with many of his old supporters and they were not available for appointments. Also, I thought that his change in position was right.

F.   You became cochairman of the board with Lewis Powell?

D.   That was Lewis's generosity. He was the senior member and chairman because he had been sworn in a day before me. I was delayed by a snowstorm, but he insisted on appointing me as cochairman.

F.   You all functioned in tandem in improving the schools.

D.   We just kind of worked together, but Lewis really was chairman.

F.   How would you evaluate your old friend's performance now on the United States Supreme Court?

D.   He's doing exceptionally well. Lewis's very strong point is his capacity to compromise, to resolve differences in an amiable way that doesn't lose sight of the great objective and yet gets away from the little irritable things that can break up conferences of great consequence. He has a rare ability to synthesize differences of opinion.

F.   Isn't it interesting the way the governors call on each other? I don't recall any other state where that's done.

D.   You don't know any other state that has the kind of close friendly relationship that the leaders of the old Organization had. The Organization always—practically always—won and the governors were old buddies and anxious to help each other.

F.   Perry Morgan, publisher of Norfolk Newspapers, says that Virginia is the only state he ever saw where a former governor can go around telling the incumbent governor what to do. Of course, he said, part of it is that they had you to consult.

D.   Well, they knew that I didn't have anything to do after I left the University of Virginia, and they figured that they could ask me to do thus and so, and it didn't make much difference. And in that they were right.

F.   It's a remarkable turn that Governor Almond, who very nearly capsized public education, hollering about integration and metaphorically throwing down his arm to prevent it, should in the end have made so constructive a move in reaching out and picking you two who were progressive—

D.   And middle-grounders. Lewis was on the school board in Richmond, you know.

F.   —in thinking and wanted to reshape public education, after all the furor had died.

D.   Those of us on the board got a fair amount done, I reckon. It's such a prodigious task. When you take a public school system, a million or so children in it, schools everywhere—

some very good and others mediocre, and poor counties and rich—
it's just a task that staggers the imagination when you sit down and
try to dope it out; and you've got to convince, and properly so,
people to go along with you, and then you have to be careful not to
encroach on local school boards.

F. I'm looking at these steps in education: your
efforts to upgrade education as a member of the House of Delegates,
and as governor, president of the University of Virginia, member of
the State Board of Education, the leader in reopening Prince Edward's schools. Then there was your work on the Commission to
Revise the Virginia Constitution, which really tied down what you
and Lewis Powell had been trying to do with the Board of Education.

D. That was finally winning acceptance for a plan
I'd worked on for years. Mine was a very simple, single proposition.
I've always felt that if you are going to get anything done you better
make it as simple as possible so people can understand it and you
can explain and you can keep on working on it. It's like Antonio
Mendoza. Charles V said that Mendoza was Spain's greatest colonial governor, and historians are inclined to agree.

The emperor called upon Mendoza to go to Mexico City and
break up the terrible coalition between the Spanish army and some
members of the church who were heartlessly oppressing the Aztec
Indians. One side or the other had succeeded in undermining the
governors who had served before Mendoza.

Mendoza was a member of one of the most powerful families in
Spain and Charles paid him $50,000 a year, which wasn't hay back
a little after 1500, and Mendoza went out there and succeeded. He
came back and the emperor said to him, "I want you to go down
to Peru and straighten that out."

So Mendoza went to Peru, though very reluctantly. One day
someone asked him: "How was it you achieved so much?"

"I did little, and I did that very slowly," Mendoza replied.

I don't think anybody ever spent more time thinking and projecting about education than I have, and I doubt that anybody has
accomplished less. But the objective was that every child in Virginia
should have an opportunity for a good basic education. Many
poorer counties offered courses every third or fourth year or stag-
gered them so that the children came out without a basic education.

That, to my mind, was wrong. I wanted to see in the constitution a commitment that when a child goes to a school that has Virginia Public School written across its front door, that child is going to get an education, and that whatever it costs, we are going to pay for it.

It is like buying a brand of goods. If you buy it in Wise County, if you buy it in Buchanan, if you buy it in Dickenson or Bland or Roanoke or anywhere, you get the same quality. That's the important element and that is the sum total of my effort.

     F.   So when you were on the board, you and Justice Powell worked for a uniformly good public school system. Of course, you sought an increase in funds.

     D.   That was essential along with the qualification of teachers and paying attention to the offerings of the teachers' colleges.

     F.   We were talking about governors calling on former governors; of course, Godwin called on you and Albertis Harrison to work on the Commission to Revise the Virginia Constitution in 1969. That's a good example of Virginia governors' turning to one another for help. It's a companionable sort of club atmosphere.

     D.   That's right, because if that atmosphere didn't exist, you wouldn't do it. The club was the old Democratic outfit that ran the state. Not all the Democrats were in that, because others, trying to get in and take charge, were good Democrats. There isn't any question about their party loyalty, but the members in the Byrd crowd were all clubby and cozy with each other and then they'd reach out into the opposition from time to time and—

     F.   —pull somebody in.

     D.   Yes.

     F.   Who promised to give them trouble.

     D.   Maybe so, or who was thought to be capable of helping them.

     F.   Sort of like China absorbing invaders.

     D.   Very much like China's absorbing invaders.

     F.   But it runs counter to the popular view of political theories about Virginia: that Byrd's Organization was reactionary and nothing good could come from it. It runs counter to the feelings of some younger Virginians who came along after the Organization had passed its prime.

D. That's right and when really it was fighting for survival, trying to repel assaults on its flanks. In 1954 the Young Turks were good, solid party people with progressive ideas, but they were a little too forward of the old Organization, and in that contest the old Organization was wrong and the Young Turks were right. Of course the Old Guard should have taken them in and would have—because the lines would have given away—but for the coming of Massive Resistance.

F. That was really a death rattle though because—

D. That's all in God's world it was! It was a death rattle, rather long continued, but that's what it was. It was a frenzied dance of death.

F. And, if the Organization had taken in these young people, it would have taken a new lease on life.

D. It would have been renewing, but organizations don't renew in exactly that way. They change. These young fellows would inevitably have altered it, and the change would have been acceptable to the people of Virginia because it would have been a change for the better and would have continued the forward momentum.

F. To get back to education, the final effort was the Commission to Revise the Virginia Constitution.

D. I worked on the commission's subcommittee on education with Pat Paschal, former state superintendent of public instruction and president of the College of William and Mary. Pat and I saw eye to eye on what needed to be done, as did the other members of the constitutional commission. It was a fine group, and one of the most rewarding efforts in which I was ever involved.

F. The commission's recommendations, adopted by the General Assembly, nailed into the State Constitution the guarantee to every child the opportunity for a sound education.

D. That's exactly it. That is the essential, big solid accomplishment. That, I would say, was worth every minute of a lifetime of effort, moving toward the objective of being able to say to a child, "When you come out of our schools you are prepared for a life in a competitive society."

F. You inserted the guarantees in two ways. You gathered Jefferson's remarks on education from throughout the constitution and put them in the Declaration of Rights. And then to bolster that right, the commission recommended that the General Assembly see to it that an educational program of high quality is maintained continually. The State Board of Education determines the standards of quality, subject to revision only by the General Assembly. And, finally, the General Assembly provided that if a locality doesn't meet the standards of quality, the attorney general has to bring suit against the locality. And I would guess that even if the attorney general didn't bring suit, the parents could.

D.   Yes, I think so.

F.   So it is right there. Virginia may not always have uniformly good education, but the means is there to get it. The constitutional revisions for education were directly in line with Jefferson's bill for the general diffusion of knowledge. The bill failed to pass, but he had planted the idea.

Isn't it interesting that Jefferson was so bent on devising a public school system, extending through a university, in a day when a formal education was uncommon. In that pioneer society if a youth tired of schooling, he simply headed for the frontier. Jefferson was advocating what amounted in his time to universal education.

D.   Jefferson realized that if people were going to try to govern themselves, which is an extremely difficult task, they had to be educated. Wasn't any escape from that. Many people in the colonies shared that view. He certainly was the leader in the Virginia movement, but thoughtful people who have looked at self-government—which rests on self-discipline, and self-discipline isn't easy to come by—have realized that the people must be educated if they are to have any chance in managing their affairs successfully. If Jefferson realized that in a world far less complicated than is this world, it ought to be easier to understand now than it was in his day.

F.   And yet, despite his example and all of his power—I don't guess anybody has ever been any stronger politically in Virginia than Jefferson—

D.   Oh, no. We talk about Virginia organizations of one kind or another; nobody ever had a more complete political organization than Jefferson had. All the management that they have talked about during my lifetime pales into insignificance compared with Jefferson's management. His ally was Judge Spencer Roane of the Supreme Court of Appeals of Virginia. If you had anything like that relationship now between the court and a political leader, the people would yell to high heaven. He and Roane and Madison, and others sitting around ran it. But the main fellow who ran it was Jefferson.

F.   What is the chief distinction between Jefferson's machine and the machines that are so criticized today?

D.   There is not a great difference insofar as the attention to organization. You don't operate a machine or an organization or whatever you call it unless you work at it pretty much full time. The marked difference was that you had there at the head of it a great speculative thinker who was shaping it. The distinguishing mark about Jefferson, in my opinion, is his insatiable intellectual curiosity. You do not get an individual like that but now and then in a century or so.

F.   In his *Notes on Virginia* he said he had a canine appetite for learning.

D.   That's true. But, of course, he wasn't always right. For instance, Jefferson's idea about the Kentucky Resolution was just as dangerous as it could be. Had he succeeded in the resolution, he would have disestablished the Union in fifteen years.

F.   But even that was a reaction to another excess, the Alien and Sedition laws.

D.   Jefferson got off base because he hadn't talked to Madison. Madison straightened it out, you know. He got himself elected to the General Assembly and succeeded in having a resolution adopted that put the theory on sound constitutional ground: namely, that the states could change the Constitution but a single state could not disobey it. That was a far departure from Jefferson's idea that if a state didn't like what was going on, it could strike out on its own. Calhoun and his crowd in South Carolina were preaching the unmodified Jeffersonian doctrine when they decided they were going to set aside the federal tariff, and Andrew Jackson told them if they did he was going to hang them. He was going to settle it very simply, and would have done it, tough as he was. The Kentucky Resolution continues to throw its shadow across Virginia history. It reappeared as interposition during the feverish days of Massive Resistance. It was just as unsound then as it was in Calhoun's day.

But basically what distinguishes Jefferson's organization is the great intellectual equipment of the leader.

F.   How do you square his insistence on integrity with this powerful organization?

D.   I don't believe that there was any charge of corruption against Jefferson's organization. His idea was to collect those people who thought as he thought and to get them out and make their will felt.

F.   But today we would regard the dabbling of a Virginia chief justice in politics in itself a—

D.   We would. That's quite true. But that's a change of time and custom.

F.   How was it that with all of his power Jefferson was not able to get his education bill through the General Assembly?

D.   He was not able to do it for one very simple reason, which is not alien to these times. The landowners who controlled the General Assembly of Virginia looked at the bill and realized that Jefferson's system was going to cost them a very great deal of money and they were able to restrain their enthusiasm for his plan without any difficulty. He ran into the same opposition in building the University of Virginia much later on. It was only the work of Joseph Cabell and others in the Assembly that finally got together for him the modest sum to start the university.

When you think of a man going up there on a red clay farm in Albemarle County and laying out a beautiful building, adapted, of course, from some architecture that was quite ancient but very commanding, how he could ever get any money from them for that—it just boggles the imagination! Only an enormously powerful organization could have done it.

F.   So in a way you and others picked up Jefferson's work and carried it forward.

D.   Yes, and for my part the beginning goes back to the struggle in 1932 when Jack Eggleston and I tried to halt the closing of schools in some localities because the money had run out.

I'll tell you an instructive experience that fortified my desire to see a constitutional guarantee that the children in the poorer communities would have as good an opportunity as any in the state. While I was governor, I was being driven from Lexington to Hot

Springs for a meeting. I'd fallen asleep in the back seat as we were pulling up a mountain and the car stopped and I woke up. I looked to see what had happened, and we were waiting behind a school bus. Out of the bus hopped a little boy in overalls, neatly turned out. He scrambled up the side of the road cut into the flank of the mountain and ran up a path just like a little rabbit, not over forty yards in all, to a cabin which had never known paint. He darted through the front door and was gone.

I realized that what that door opened on was not the interior of a cabin. Thanks to the schoolhouse he had just left, it opened on tomorrow. You couldn't guarantee him success, but you could guarantee him a chance at it.

If he was ambitious and he wanted to learn and the state did its part you gave him his chance. You gave him what Napoleon used to say belonged to his troops. He said each of them carried a marshal's baton in his knapsack. You gave the child the marshal's baton when you gave him a public school education. When that little fellow went bouncing up the hill with his lunch pail, he carried the future right with him.

      F. He had the baton in his pail, didn't he?

      D. Yes, he had it right there. And nobody could take it away from him.

GOVERNMENT—
MASTER OR SERVANT?

F. The revision of the Virginia Constitution—recommended by the commission in 1969 and adopted by the General Assembly and approved by the people in 1970—achieved many substantive reforms.

D. Yes, it did, and one of our liveliest discussions within the commission dealt with the obligations resting upon a citizen in a society such as we hoped Virginia would enjoy. It centered on a proposition to amend Article I, Section 15 of George Mason's Declaration of Rights by adding that a duty rested on everybody to obey the law. The first time it came up for a vote, it carried sizably; but Albertis, our chairman, said he wanted us to be unanimous on the subject. Several of us said we were never going to be unanimous because we were not going along with the notion that to be a good citizen a person must do whatever the government tells him to do.

The division was along Jeffersonian versus Federalist lines in political thinking. If you pick out exponents of the two lines, one could be "Lighthorse Harry" Lee, General Lee's father and a very stout spokesman on behalf of the Federalist view. On the other hand, there could be Jefferson, whose view is embodied in his remark that a little revolution serves a very good purpose, and that, consequently, you ought to have the means of revising a constitution periodically.

There was no difference of opinion among the members of our commission that the General Assembly's enactments were entitled to the greatest respect. However, it has always been my view that in a matter of conscience an individual could refuse to obey the laws and accept the consequences. Others on the commission also took that view. We felt that right should not be impaired under any circumstances and a fellow should be permitted to dissent and to appeal to others to agree with him and pay the penalty of a violation of a state law that he chose to challenge. In the end, the language that presently appears seems well suited to satisfy the two groups: the little revolution group versus those who believe it unwise to question the authority of the state.

F. As the section emerged from the commission, it's innocuous enough. To George Mason's observation that no free government can be preserved except by adhering to justice, moderation, temperance, frugality, and virtue and by frequent recurrence to fundamental principles, the 1969 amendment added: "and by the recognition by all citizens that they have duties as well as rights, and that such rights cannot be enjoyed save in a society where law is respected and due process is observed."

D. It is important enough, and I think its supporters are sound in their position that it grows out of a climate that differs from that of George Mason's day. The Founders saw in front of them almost limitless opportunity, and it was hard for them to believe that the government would not, with the opportunities in front of it, be well received by the people. But when we met in 1969, the country was wracked by bitter dissent, by almost revolution, in fact, and consequently our commission thought it important to call attention to the fact that government not only provides benefits but imposes obligations.

F. I'm glad you diluted the original proposal put forth in the commission's meetings that every man had to obey the law—

D. There is no question that you cannot put in such a rigid provision without ultimately encountering great trouble. A subtle difference marks the two statements. The statement as it reads in George Mason's Declaration of Rights, the bill of rights at the beginning of the State Constitution, suggests that the government is the servant of the people. The addition to this section, as originally proposed in the commission's meeting, seemed to suggest that the government is master of the people. This impression all of us wished to avoid.

F. To argue, because the country was having demonstrations, that everybody had to obey the law was, it seems to me, a mistaken viewpoint. I don't think that the diluted version makes any difference except that it clutters up George Mason's Declaration.

D. It does not clutter it up; it points out something that was not readily apparent to the people of Mason's day, but the turbulence of our day brings it home. The support for the first reading arose out of the fact that the easy answer would be, if people obeyed the law, you wouldn't have any trouble. Of course, you can have a great deal of trouble even if people obey the law. There is no question that slavery was legal in the United States and other parts of the world for a very long time, but it was wrong.

F. As finally adopted the amendment seems to say it would be nice if everybody obeyed the law.

D. Well, it is more than nice. There is a presumption in favor of the law, but only that. What you have to be careful to safeguard is the right of dissent. The gagging of dissent in the Alien-Sedition Acts was what caused so much trouble in Jefferson's time. Many prominent Virginians favored them. Lighthorse Harry Lee went to Baltimore and got into a demonstration on behalf of the acts and the rioters fell on him and beat him nearly to death.

F. So you are saying that the commission's original proposal in 1969—

D. The original proposal's difficulty was that it was simply too rigid.

F. Another implication is troubling in the commission's original proposition, and that is the assumption that rights automatically bring on responsibilities. A person's right is a right. It just seems—and I'm speaking now of the original proposal—prim and privileged and aristocratic in the sense of wealth and station, not Jefferson's meritocracy, to be saying, "Yes, you have these rights, but you also must remember that you must do certain things to deserve them." It runs counter to the view of Jefferson, Madison, and Mason that we want the least government possible.

D. Well, now, is it possible to have self-government by people unless you have people who take an interest and participate in the government?

F. No, sir, you can't have self-government if people don't participate in it, but I don't think that individuals can be required to take an interest.

D. Does that individual who does absolutely nothing have the right to enjoy the benefits coming from the labors of others?

F.   To enjoy what are naturally his rights, yes. The fact that he doesn't vote or exercise free speech doesn't mean that he should be denied those rights.

D.   Yes, but if he does not do it, this whole structure that we are trying to maintain falters and fails.

F.   No, sir, I don't think it does, because not many would be minded that way.

D.   Now wait a minute! I would agree that many people would not be of that mind, but the reason is they understand that without participation the system fails.

F.   Yes, sir, but it has to be left to an individual to decide whether or not he is going to exercise those rights. I fear that if the government begins to draw up lists of duties that it will begin to nibble at the rights.

D.   Certainly it will begin to nibble, because that goes back to the basic theory that underlies my whole thinking. Mind you, I'm not talking about duties imposed by the government. I'm talking about those duties which are an inescapable part of the system of self-government and without which the entire effort will fail. If you don't assume the duties, you don't have government because it won't function.

I used to get in a wrangle around the University of Virginia with faculty members. One fellow thought that the enlargement of the government and the entrusting of the affairs of men to the government was all on the positive side.

When I would say to him, "My theory is that all government tends to tyranny and will end there unless you watch it like a hawk," he'd just about have a stroke.

He also was a great federal consultant. I had to watch several of that sort to keep them from rigging up their classes so that they could teach at their convenience and shoot up to Washington and get fifty to a hundred dollars a day consulting with the federal government.

The federal government's theory is quite simple. Up there they believe that a janitorship in Washington is the equivalent to any position in the provinces—or the states, as we call them. Consequently, they believe that any time you can offer a person in the provinces a job he ought to drop whatever he is doing and come rushing to Washington and get his fee on consulting. I worked out a simple rule: "If you want to work with the federal government, you do that, and then take up teaching again at some time in the future."

"Will you give us leave?" they asked.

"No," I said. "I'm not going to leave you on tenure at the University of Virginia and place you in front of other faculty members and maintain your position while you're hopping and skipping around the world with the federal government, and then have you several years from now say that you have decided to come back to Charlottesville."

But going back to the question of rights. I don't believe you can separate freedom from obligation.

F.   Ideally every person should wish to exercise his rights.

D.   Yes, but you are not living in an ideally organized world. Why isn't it reasonable to point out that the operation of our system entails some work on the part of those people who are part of it?

F.   To me there's an implication that it is more than a pointing out, that it is a laying on, an imposing of terms on rights that are naturally yours, God-given, Jefferson said.

D.   I see your point. I'm not quarreling with that, except that you are setting up a system that is utterly unworkable. What about Mason's provision in the Declaration that you should have a virtuous, frugal government? Suppose the Watergaters got in charge? Doesn't Mason impose there an obligation in order for the government, as he sees it, to succeed? Doesn't it have to be directed by men who are frugal and virtuous?

F.   Yes, I think it does for long periods of time, certainly. I think that it can stand the other for a while—

D.   Not for long.

F.   No, not for long. And, furthermore, the Watergaters were breaking the law.

D.   You go back to the thrust of the commission's original version that you have to obey the law. You can't permit a person not to obey the law. The other side of that is the statement that you've got to obey the law.

F.   Yes, but there are laws—slavery, as you pointed out—that if you feel run counter to natural rights, you may choose to disobey and accept the consequences. But as the commission's proposition was originally framed, there was no such open door. It was simply slammed shut: "Every citizen shall obey the law."

    D.   Yes, and that was its weakness.

    F.   Which is why you were wise to draw its teeth.

    D.   The thing that did it was Albertis, sitting there quietly, saying he didn't want any dissent in the report. Four or five of us said, "Well, you are going to get some dissents, because we are going to set about writing them."

It did surprise me that we were overcome in opposing the first proposal and mowed right down. But we popped up quickly and pointed to illustrations in history of the necessity of dissent. I think we called John Milton as a witness, and I know we called Socrates because Hardy Dillard never gets in any argument that he doesn't repair at once to Socrates and is able to have his way because his listeners know little of Socrates.

Hardy would jump back to Socrates at once and achieve an impregnable position. He couldn't even be appraised by his allies, much less assaulted by his opponents!

We called up some powerful people. I reminded them of the only important thing we college presidents ever did in the Association of American Universities. At the beginning of the unrest in the 1950s over the Supreme Court's desegregation decisions, we issued a declaration supporting the right of dissent, which was doggone good, tell you the truth. Now lost in the mists of time.

So we returned to the attack the next day under the leadership of Hardy and Socrates. I don't believe there is any question that my general observation has much to recommend it. All government does tend to tyranny, and it's going to end there unless you watch it like a hawk. Always! Take your eye off it and it's on the road to a blackjack and a gun.

VOICES OF THE OPPOSITION

F. Republican Linwood Holton used to say that everybody had a governor and his governor was Governor Darden. When did that relationship begin?

D. He came by my office during the campaign for governor in 1969. In the course of a friendly chat, I told him I was a lifelong Democrat and party man, but if he was elected and wanted me to help him I'd be glad to try. During his term he called me about one thing and another. Once we were discussing some knotty problem, and I told him, "Don't be discouraged; be of good cheer, but I'm glad that you're there and I'm here!" That became a sort of byword between us. He conferred with a great many people around the state. He didn't go off half-cocked.

F. What were his strengths as governor?

D. He was of an inquiring mind and much more attached to the future than to the old order. Holton was a courageous experimenter. His policy on patronage drew criticism from some Republicans, but to get anything done he had to deal with a Democratic legislature.

F. Also, he was determined to appoint individuals of merit without regard to race, age, or sex. To fill many offices he looked outside the state.

D. Yes, and found good, solid persons.

F. What was his administration's high point?

D. That came in the selection of schools for his children. The Richmond School Board had told the Holtons that because they lived on state property, they could send their children to any public school they pleased. Instead of choosing a lightly integrated public school or a private school, they let their three children attend the heavily integrated schools to which they were assigned.

They made their decision when agitation over busing was at its height. On the morning after schools opened, the front pages of newspapers throughout the country carried a picture of Holton walking beside his daughter Tayloe into a public high school that was 92 percent black. Fifty years from now, when somebody writes the story after the passions have cooled, that picture of Holton walking with Tayloe is what they will center on.

F.   He got along well with the General Assembly.

D.   I think the legislators felt that he had dealt fairly with them and they tried to deal fairly with him.

F.   Not long after he took office he told me that what elated him was that State Senator M. M. Long of Wise, one of the oldest Democrats, had come to see him about a matter. The legislators were so accustomed to going to the governor that some of them just automatically came to him without distinguishing that he was a Republican or a Democrat, like an old horse that knows a certain way to go and continues on that route no matter who's in the seat.

D.   Well, it's more than that. Long is a fine example of it. He went because it was the center of power. He knew that and he made up his mind he was going to deal—it was the only place for him to deal, really, in matters that he wanted. And then, too, it can be fairly said that he and Holton had a lot in common. They both were Southwest Virginians, and they were strong partisans, one on one side and one on the other. That gave them something in common and also gave them a sense of the necessity of working together.

F.   He enjoyed being governor, didn't he?

D.   Yes, even as much as Bill Tuck.

F.   Holton seemed to enjoy the problems.

D.   Yes, he did, but he also enjoyed the power. That never affected Bill because he was so much a part of the ruling hierarchy, it never occurred to him there'd be any question about authority. Now with Holton it was like diving into a big comber coming into the beach and being able to swim through it and get on the other side all right. After all, he was Virginia's first Republican governor in this century.

F.   He wondered how he would be accepted?

D.   It was not so much a question in his mind about how he would be accepted as it was the question of how the thing ran, what went on, and whether or not there would be any partisan infighting.

F.   So there was a sort of exhilaration when it began to work?

D.   I think so; he enjoyed the fray. He enjoyed the slashing and fighting and head cracking.

F.   You know he had to be shown the way to the governor's office when he went in after his election.

D.   I'm not at all sure that wasn't put on. That's like Ted Dalton talking about "Kain-tucky," lapsing into those various little western Virginia expressions.

F.   Ted Dalton shaped the modern Republican party. When he ran for governor against Tom Stanley in 1953, he was one of only three Republicans in the State Senate. After his defeat, when the 1954 General Assembly convened and Dalton strode into the Senate chamber to take his seat, all the other senators arose and gave him an ovation.

D.   He deserved it.

F.   The Democrats feared Dalton's popularity. After his close race against Stanley in 1953, the Republicans were bent on nominating him again in 1957; but Dalton had voted against the Massive Resistance bills in the 1956 General Assembly, and he knew those votes would be used against him in a campaign for governor. While he was trying to make up his mind about whether to run, the Democrats held their Jefferson-Jackson Day Dinner in the John Marshall Hotel in Richmond. Byrd was the center of attention in the throng in the lobby, and Democrats kept pushing up to Byrd to tell him they thought that Dalton would run, and Byrd kept saying, "Get him to run! Get him to run! Get him to run!"

D.   He did, really?

F.   Yes, Byrd felt that the Democrats could beat Dalton on that issue and thereby remove a powerful opponent. Dalton told a meeting of the Republican State Central Committee that if he did run, it would be on the basis of saving the public schools from the fund-cutoff laws of Massive Resistance. Well, he went into that campaign against Lindsay Almond knowing, of course, that the odds were heavily against his winning.

D.   I'm not sure he did, because they were very uneasy times. I just don't know.

F.   The only debate between Dalton and Almond was at a high school in Roanoke. Dalton drew an ovation when he said there was no sense in talking about closing schools to save education from integration. In the General Assembly and in campaigns, Dalton never wavered on the issues.

D.   He is a very fine person and deserves the esteem in which he's held. There's nothing narrow about Ted Dalton, nothing that you'd expect in a political partisan. He's broad-gauged.

F.   Another great voice in the General Assembly was that of Robert Whitehead of Lovingston.

D.   An interesting thing about Whitehead is that his father was one of the stoutest of the Organization people in the old days.

F.   Whitehead first fell out with them in a dispute with the State Compensation Board over his salary as commonwealth's attorney of Nelson County in 1934. A breakaway was almost inevitable because Whitehead was at his best as an opponent.

D.   Much. And he was useful to the state in that. He'd come on the Assembly floor knowing what not three or four people knew in the state, and that is the budget.

F.   He knew as much as Budget Director J. H. Bradford. When word went around that Whitehead had the center aisle in the House of Delegates, you could see people running into the Capitol from all around the square. It was as if an alarm bell had rung. They wanted to hear him expound on the budget.

D.   I used to talk to him and he would say of a bill that had come up time and again, "That's nothing but the same old coon with another ring around its tail!"

F.   One time Byrd made an extreme statement on an issue, and Whitehead, when he was asked for reaction, said, "Senator Byrd ought to put some poplar leaves in his hat before he goes out in the sun."

D.   I didn't remember that. That's perfect!

F.   Another time, not long after Whitehead's first wife died, Delegate Frank Richeson of Richmond attacked a proposition of Whitehead's. I called Whitehead for comment, and he said he would defer extended rebuttal while he was in mourning and then he proceeded to blister Richeson in two or three sentences. When I read Whitehead's comment to Richeson and asked if he wished to reply, there was a long silence and then Richeson said, "God help us when he comes out of mourning!"

The Organization leaders feared that Whitehead was going to run for governor, but he just couldn't bring himself to make that sacrificial effort. He wanted to run and yet he wanted to do it only under the very best circumstances. Francis Pickens Miller was aggrieved that Whitehead wouldn't carry on the cause.

D. Yes, but Miller had more of a commitment to the abstract cause than Whitehead had. Or rather, I think Whitehead could weigh with greater precision the pros and cons. And another thing, Whitehead had a very valuable place in the General Assembly which he didn't want to sacrifice.

F. He was really the voice of opposition in the House. As long as he could run for governor they had to treat him with a great deal of care.

D. I think so. Probably more. They adopted the run-off primary to check him out.

F. And he called it the fraidy cat bill.

D. Robert had a wicked tongue, but there's been nobody in my lifetime that had the deadly voice of old man Glass. That rasping voice of his was just like a summons to eternity, ringing out across the land.

F. One of Whitehead's most persistent battles was for the abolition of the automatic tax credit act.

D. In my opinion, that was the most wasteful piece of legislation that was ever put on the books in Virginia.

F. That act was sending money back to the taxpayers when the schools and mental hospitals needed funds sorely.

D. The worst part was that it went back in the days of the federal excess profit tax, which meant that more than 70 percent of it ended up in the federal treasury.

F. The waste enraged Whitehead. He'd get up and flail his right arm like a pump handle and tell them of the folly. He's best of anybody I ever knew at taking an abstruse fiscal issue and infusing emotion into it.

D. And also really explaining it. So few people can do it because so very few understand it.

F. The minute the budget came out he'd head for his room in the Hotel Richmond, lugging a bulging briefcase. I wish he had run just once for governor so we could have heard him tear into the majority.

D. Robert was a loner. I used to tell him this story. If you sat him down and said, "Now, Robert, I've got a deal. This thing is perfect. We are all going to heaven on a rug. We are not going to have to die and endure what people ordinarily go through. We are just going to be taken up on a rug."

He would be very enthusiastic about it, and the next day he'd want to know more about the details. And you'd say, "Well, we're going up on a Persian, the last word in rugs, and we're going to have six seats: two, two, and two."

He'd be very much interested and then the next morning he'd come back and say, "I've been giving it some thought. I don't want to go on a Persian rug. I think we ought to have an American rug."

You'd wrestle around about that and finally agree to the substitute only to have him come back next day and say, "I've been thinking about this thing. I don't think we ought to sit two, two, and two on that rug. I believe we ought to be three and three." And that would go on indefinitely until you gave up from sheer exhaustion. There wasn't any way anybody in the world could team up with him. He wasn't a team man.

F. One time he teamed up was with the Young Turks in their rebellion in 1954. He was their elder statesman. They consulted with him about strategy at his desk on the floor of the House and he purposely didn't enter into the debate. As much as he enjoyed the give and take of a debate, he stayed in the background. Armistead Boothe was another of the older Young Turks.

In 1950 Boothe introduced bills to abolish segregation on common carriers. The previous year, studying the Supreme Court's decisions on civil rights for an article in the *Virginia Law Review*, Boothe recognized that their tenor for fifteen years anticipated a ruling against segregation and that Virginia better get ready by eliminating segregation laws where it could. He had you come down from the University of Virginia and testify before the General Assembly in behalf of the bills.

D.   Yes, I told them there was no question about the advisability of integrating streetcars, buses, and trains. It was simply nonsense to require the blacks to fight their way through crowded cars to the rear. The thing to do, I said, was to legalize what was already happening and accept it.

F.   In so many ways the Young Turks were on the side of the future when they rebelled in 1954.

D.   That was, I think, a turning point in Virginia. Putting them down was when the Virginia Organization moved over to a defense of place rather than to the projection of ideas.

F.   What has been the impact of Henry Howell's three campaigns for governor?

D.   He stirred Virginia politics only like dynamite could have done in a pond. Howell gave greater impetus to mass voting in Virginia and stirred people more than anybody in my lifetime. He was not unlike William Mahone.

The interesting thing we've seen in politics in recent years is the narrowing too much of the base of support. We saw that with the Republicans in Goldwater's bid for the presidency and then in McGovern's bid with the Democrats. Both pulled away from what I've always believed is the element that can win, and that is moderation—plodding along in center.

Now in Virginia, Howell vacated that position to the Republicans. He narrowed the Democratic strength. He concentrated on the labor-black vote, which interacts in Virginia because of the large number of blacks who are big earners in stevedoring and government work. My guess is that the Democratic leadership is coming to rest in the hands of the moderates.

F.   Was it so much Howell's policies as it was the way he presented them?

D.   It was both. Certainly there is nothing new in politicians overclaiming. They've done that from time immemorial. You pick up statements now and then about Howell's claim of saving $75 million or $150 million. But what happened is the utilities would ask for substantial rate increases which would be granted only in part by the Corporation Commission. Many people protested the proposed increases. The United States government, for instance, was very restive under the big bills it was paying for its establishments. Howell, who had been one of the contestants, would claim credit for the whole thing.

The Corporation Commission has suffered from the malady found so frequently in the federal regulatory commissions. They all tend to become captives of the industries they are regulating. Notwithstanding this tendency, the State Corporation Commission has done well protecting the people's interests. For Howell to claim credit for all those decisions is so patently wrong that it alienated a lot of people.

F. Virginians not only like moderate issues, they want them presented moderately.

D. Yes. They like the moderate stand and the moderate presentation.

F. The Democratic party seemed embarked on a moderate course in the mid-1960s. Lieutenant Governor J. Sergeant Reynolds had endorsements for governor from labor and the blacks as well as the backing of conservative Democrats. Then Reynolds died, and that left the way open for a lurch to the left.

D. It opened wide the gate. Whether the extremists who dominate the party are willing to permit it to come back or want another fight on the ground that they'll ultimately win, remains to be seen. In my opinion they'll never win on their present course.

F. Much of Howell's strength lay with the young people attracted by his phrasemaking, his espousing of minorities, and his challenge to the establishment.

D. Yes, they liked his adventurous spirit.

F. John Dalton made a good start after the election in saying he was going to bring Lieutenant Governor Robb into the government.

D. Oh, I think so, too. Ted Dalton guided him there. I ran into John Dalton during the campaign and I told him: "If you win this election you have a simpler undertaking than any man I know. You have right there in the house the best possible adviser. Talk with him an hour or two once a month and then do what he says, and you'll have a very successful administration."

I say that the move to include Robb comes out of Ted. I don't mean that he told John last week. But what Ted had counseled him about has always been to try to bring discordant elements together.

F.   Governor, why did you support Howell?

D.   In the Democratic primary when I was campaigning for Andy Miller, many of us said we would support the
nominee. Of course, I was expecting that Andy would be our nominee. I didn't want to see a repeat of what happened in 1969 when the
Howell followers deserted wholesale after he lost in the primary. We
were fortunate then in that we ended up with a good governor in Linwood Holton, but it was death to our party effort.

I don't think I'm ever going into another Democratic primary.
This one convinced me that we have to revamp the party machinery
if we are to have any chance of success.

My brother, who was a Dalton man in the general election, had
great difficulty explaining my position. He finally hit upon a very
simple explanation. One night they got after him so hard that at
last he said, "Well, I'll tell you. I hate to say this, and it's just in the
family, but you know Colgate is right much older than I am, and
he's really a little senile."

He said that stopped the whole argument in its tracks. People
looked at him in sympathy and they turned to another subject.

We lost the primary to Howell because of overconfidence. And
certainly that included me. I had told Pickens that Andy would
win, and then after he lost, I said, "You know, he has plenty of
time."

Pickens said, "He may have, but I haven't."

Andy would have made a splendid governor.

F.   He enjoys work as much as anybody I've ever
seen.

D.   And he has the capacity for it. I hope he continues his interest in public life. His withdrawal would be a great loss
to all of us.   .

The Miller campaign had a top organization but apparently it
didn't reach sufficiently to the grass roots.

F.   Much of Dalton's expenditures in the campaign
against Howell was in phone banks through which his workers
touched the individual voter much as Byrd used to do through his
courthouse organization.

D.   I'm sure the phones helped, but many voters
marched to the polls for John Dalton because of his father, Ted.

It wasn't just a sentimental journey. They knew that with Ted to advise him he wouldn't go wrong.

F. Mills Godwin, first a Democratic and then a Republican governor, has been a pivotal figure. How do you assess his career in the light of his complete reversal of views on some major issues—his change, for instance, from a state senator dedicated to Massive Resistance to a progressive governor who boosted education?

D. One thing that runs through it is an aptitude for appraising public sentiment in Virginia. That explains his course starting with Massive Resistance. I don't know that he's ever changed his views in reference to school integration. I haven't talked to him about it. The issue had receded and did not play much part in the 1977 campaign.

F. It was brought to bear to an extent in that the office for civil rights in HEW had asked Virginia to do more to remove the vestiges of a segregated system in higher education. And Godwin, in his last days in office, insisted that HEW's so-called goals were quotas. Could that bout with HEW be considered, in a mild way, a return full circle to a kind of massive resistance?

D. I don't think so. Godwin's position seemed to be an acceptance of integration in good faith, but not an altering of the quality of higher education. As I understand it, his position was, and it's a tenable position, that where students are qualified to do the work, they should be admitted. That is not full circle to Massive Resistance.

F. I just wonder if he looked enough into whether we have improved black colleges to the extent we should, whether we have explored sufficiently exchanges of students between, say, Old Dominion University and Norfolk State College.

D. You've touched on a sensitive point there. It's something that we must continue to work on. In my working with Norfolk State, and with Virginia State College in Petersburg, one thing that struck me especially was the blacks' fierce pride in their own institutions. I believe that might take a long time to emerge again if Norfolk State and Old Dominion were put together, and, further, education would suffer if the two were put together forcibly by law.

F. I was thinking of persuading rather than

coercing. For instance, already all the social work studies in Hampton Roads are at Norfolk State College.

D. Yes, several years ago we pushed to organize that offering at Norfolk State.

F. In an interview with Bob Mason, editor of the *Virginian-Pilot,* an official of HEW said that the department wished to have no part in assigning students and that even if the state fails to meet goals, as long as it demonstrates good faith, that will be acceptable. That may indicate that if the governor and his education aides show interest in improving conditions that we might avoid an impasse. It may be the first test of Governor Dalton.

D. In what I've read, Dalton seems to be working to satisfy himself that the state is not backward. I think Godwin believes that the state is offering the opportunity.

F. Yes, Godwin's statements indicate that he believes no further efforts are required. I wonder if Dalton will look at it on its merits.

D. My guess is he will, and, moreover, he can avail himself of the judgment of his father, who I believe would view that subject with as much wisdom as anybody in the state.

F. As a state senator in the late 1950s Godwin led the Massives and in 1960 he opposed vehemently the sales tax that would have funded Governor Almond's advances, and yet when Godwin became governor in 1966 he led the way for the sales tax. In a short time he had made a complete switch.

D. He certainly did.

F. In his first term he certainly had an excellent administration. It even earned the endorsement of his old foes, notably Armistead Boothe, who had opposed him for lieutenant governor in 1961 and said later he had educated him in that campaign. Godwin's first administration caught up with a great many—

D. It moved very substantially toward catching up. But would not that lead you to believe, his having been the guiding light or captain in that endeavor, that his position in the dispute with HEW was based on broader ground than his old Massive Resistance experience might suggest? And that when he says he fears quotas that that is just what he does fear. How you arrange to overcome the lag in educating our Negro population is another matter.

F. It is a terribly complex problem because many blacks seem reluctant to integrate in colleges. We are, as you suggest, really having to overcome the disadvantages of three centuries in many respects. I wonder whether Godwin looked at the challenge with a sufficiently open mind. You think he did because of his progressive administration. I question whether he might have been influenced by his Massive Resistance background.

D. That is the issue.

F. Another aspect interests me. Godwin contributed to the stalemate in the late '50s and in 1960 that resulted in the state's having pent-up needs. Yet when the logjam broke, he rode the wave.

D. Yes, no question about that.

F. In assessing his record should you consider the fact that he had contributed to the very problem that he worked to solve?

D. If I understand it, the point you make is whether it was a fundamental conversion, Saul on the road to Damascus, or political opportunism.

F. Yes, that interests me.

D. I don't believe any of us can dope that out. The answer lies with time.

To go back to the observation about Godwin's being so susceptible to mass sentiment, what is representative government but that?

F. On occasion, when a legislator knows that the sentiment is wrong, should he try to educate people and change it?

D. Certainly he should. Sam Houston did just that when he opposed secession and was dismissed as the governor of Texas. That doesn't happen as often as people think. But there are times that a stand must be made if you are really going to try to advance the general welfare. That doesn't mean that you won't be swept right out.

I think Godwin is sincere in his belief that the problems are met if the colleges are good and opened to all.

F. The next step, in the light of our record of discrimination, is whether we ought to make extra exertions to encourage the blacks and to help their institutions and to facilitate transfers between black and white colleges.

D. Of course, we must do that, and it will take time and money and it will not be done overnight, so we must be about it.

THE SERVANT OF
THE HOUSE

F. Did many former members of the House of Representatives return this May for the 1975 reunion on Capitol Hill?

D. About 120 of the old boys came back, and a fair number of the present House members attended.

F. How did your speech go?

D. You know, nothing brings back the old House to you better than an experience like that. You start talking and then an argument breaks out among members over in a corner of the House. Don't pay a damn bit of attention to what you are talking about. And the Speaker gavels them down and quiets them and you go along, and then it busts out in another section in a free-for-all and gradually builds up to where you can't hear your own voice it's so noisy, and then it dies away.

But I declare I enjoyed the day immensely and I had dreaded going up there. It was a nice gathering. I enjoyed seeing Speaker Carl Albert. The Speaker now presides over our hearings. I presided over the first meeting of the association when we organized five years ago, but since that time they have stepped it up to quite a dignified occasion.

The greatest place in the world to learn to speak is the House of Representatives, because if you can speak there, you can speak anywhere. You can walk into the most tumultuous gathering and fire off your piece and go on, because that's the way the House behaves ordinarily. In the old days, a fellow would go down there in the well of the House and start making a speech. Some other fellow would come in and open up the New York *Times,* great big, bulky paper. He'd sit on the second row and start reading something, folding the paper around trying to find out where the article continued, creating God knows how much noise, not paying the slightest bit of attention to the fellow up there trying to speak.

And some other member would come in and see a friend of his over the way, and he'd wave to him, go over, and sit down by him and start talking about business or telling a joke, and the House would grind on and on. After you learn to speak under those circumstances, you can go right down to the railroad station at rush hour and open up with no difficulty at all.

Now occasionally someone would address the members and win absolute attention. Jim Wadsworth of New York could do that. He'd been in the Senate, been defeated on the wet issue, and then he had come over to the House. Jim would go down and start talking to them and the House would clam up and listen. And when the Speaker would get out of his chair and come down to harangue them about something he wanted them to do, they'd grow quiet, but by and large the ordinary member speaking got no more attention than a rabbit at a convention on morality.

Huey Long used to come over from the Senate from time to time and hold a meeting of the Louisiana delegation right in our midst. Instead of taking his followers back to the telephone rooms behind the rail, he'd hold a meeting in the back part of the chamber on the House floor. He wouldn't sit down in the seats with them; he'd sit up on the arm of a seat and have his loyal supporters gather around. He'd be holding the caucus, addressing them, not dropping his voice at all, while we were trying to transact the business of the House. The Speaker finally would hammer down and say, "A little order in this room!" Huey'd drop his voice and go on with the caucus, pay no more attention to us than if we were meeting in China. He'd come over from the Senate and call them back there and give them hell, tell them this and that, with utter disregard of the rest of us.

The former members did not seem to have changed, except this: there was a soberness about them that was quite noticeable, and it may be because they were older. John Bricker of Ohio was there. Remember him in the Senate and the Bricker Amendment? Then there was Stubby Cole of New York who was on the Naval Committee with me.

I saw Wilbur Mills sitting in the Speaker's lobby, and he said he'd heard me speak and asked me how I was getting along.

I told him I was doing reasonably well, but that my eyes had failed to such an extent that I was hobbled. "The truth is, Wilbur," I said, "I'm just getting old, and I've got a lot of trouble."

"Hell," he said, "you don't know what trouble is."

You know, the truth is nobody in the House ever worked harder than did Wilbur.

Many were younger people, but they were all friendly to us older ones, and the older ones enjoyed it. You could see that they were having a good time, really kind of getting back home. The highlight was when President Ford had us to the White House. There is nothing in the world that a member of Congress likes so much as a free meal, especially at the White House. That's true of the former members, too.

The president received us in the East Room. He was in fine spirits. You could just see he was relaxed. He was surrounded by congenial company. He knew most of the members. Nobody was going to edge up to him and ask him about Joe Doaks or what he was going to do about the damn strip mining bill or about the Middle East or the Laotian situation.

"You people are the most fortunate people in the world," he said. "You don't have anything to worry about. You go home, and you sleep the whole night. You get up late the next morning, and then you go down for breakfast. And then you get the newspaper and you sit around and read that for about an hour. Finally you lay it aside and you say to your wife, 'You reckon there is anybody in the world who is ever going to get that mess down in Washington straightened out?' "

That just took them by storm. That tickled them to death. "Now," he said, "let's step down the hall for some refreshments." You never saw such a layout, and we held forth there an hour or two.

I certainly did enjoy it, and afterward I enjoyed talking to Howard Smith. Porter Hardy and I slipped over to Alexandria to see him, and the three of us talked and laughed about old times. In the few times Howard spoke to the House, you never got the ranting and carrying on that you usually get in the House. And he never talked for long. But every time it was like firing a rifle. Every time he opened his mouth, he tapped them. He had a superb mind, and he organized his affairs. He was another who could quiet the House.

F. Do you remember when President Kennedy's backers broke Smith's control over the Rules Committee in 1963? I covered that fight. And after it was over Smith got up to make a little speech. "All right," he said, "you want these bills to come out, they are going to come out, and some of you are going to be sorry."

Later on he told me that a member would come to him privately and say, "Now this is my bill, but I want your committee to hold it." Then the member would go out in his district and blame Howard Smith for killing the bill.

D. That's right. Howard was their great protector, and that's why he came close in 1963 to beating Kennedy, Sam Rayburn, and all of them put together. The House had members say to him time after time, "For God's sake don't let that thing get out. Because I'm on a narrow margin and if it gets out, I'm a goner!"

Howard and the other members of the Rules Committee really did what the House wanted done and took the rap for it. As a matter of fact, the House always had the power to relieve the committee if it wanted to do it. The idea of talking about Howard choking the House to death is a lot of nonsense.

F. Judge Smith said that Franklin Roosevelt established the idea that a legislative body was like a football team. When the president called the signals, you couldn't stop and argue in the middle of the play; you had to do what the quarterback told you to do. But the judge said the pleas for him to kill legislation in committee came mostly from the members of the team, not from the conservatives, who knew how he was going to vote anyway.

D. The hardboiledness that they attributed to Howard was really their own responsibility. They were shirking, you see? And he was perfectly willing to do it because he had plenty of courage, and in addition he knew most of it was bad legislation and he wanted to stop it anyway. The rest of them were scared to take any stand like that; and they'd just leave him there open to the fire.

F. The final fight, though, was fought on such a lofty constitutional plane that nobody pointed out how he had served them.

D. That's right. If ever a person was the servant of the House, Howard was. He'd stand there and knock the bills down and the rest of them would cheer him, stick their heads up out of the holes, and bellow at the top of their voices, "For God's sake don't let them through!" And then pull back down in the holes and leave him to take the bullets.

He didn't lack courage, and he didn't deviate from principle either. His old friend, Judge Albert Bryan, Sr., described him perfectly as "old wishy-washy, always so smooth and flexible, just like granite."

Pat Drewry dubbed him "the terrapin" because, he said, "anytime the judge doesn't want to say anything, he pulls his head down in those stiff wing collars like he's drawing into a shell." All of us in the delegation called him the terrapin, but not one of us ever called him that to his face.

F. Once I compared him, tall, wavering, and bushy-browed, to a praying mantis, and the next time we met he grumbled he'd heard I'd described him as some sort of bug. Anyway, he lived to see a turnabout in the rhetoric on spending.

D. Yes, and it's significant in that it represents a feedback from the people themselves. Most of the American people work hard and are constantly on guard not to let their families exceed their budgets. It's becoming increasingly difficult to convince them that you can run the country by simply printing money beyond what you're willing to raise by taxation. They don't believe it, and more and more they are beginning to say it. Unless they prevail, this form of government is going to change radically.

Government cannot exist unless you can have in the electorate reasonable restraint. Now that does not mean great wisdom necessarily; but it means a willingness to avoid a recurrence of excesses such as we are having. The great development of my lifetime has been recognition of the added responsibilities of government toward the individual. Coupled with that there has to be a due regard for the financial ability of the country to meet those social responsibilities. The burden has to be sustained by taxation or the vehicle breaks down.

Since the sixties it would appear that the government has decided it isn't going to balance the budget. In my little talk to the old boys I drew on figures compiled by George Mahon of Texas, chairman of the House Appropriations Committee. In the last ten years we have doubled the debt of the United States. It took 189 years to build the first half, and we've built the second half in 10 years.

Now here is the fatal defect. We have candidates who can't get elected unless they promise to do more for the people than the person in the office. They promise, but they don't promise to tax for it. When the time comes to pay, instead of imposing the taxes they print the money. That string has about run out with us in the United States. We have done that to a point where as we print, money sinks and prices rise and that printed money is the great engine of inflation. It has been all through history. If the people would say to their representatives: You can enact any social program you please if you will impose the taxes to meet the costs, that would reinstitute the tax system as a counterbalance to spending. That doesn't mean that you are not willing to spend money for social services. It simply means that you recognize that social services must be paid for by the productive capacity of the nation and not by the printing presses.

THE EXERCISE OF POWER

F. People marvel that so small an episode as the Watergate break-in brought down the Nixon White House, but it was part of a pattern, was it not?

D. Yes, and the origin of the deception is covered in Theodore White's book, *Breach of Faith*. White said that Nixon was a product of Republicanism in California that was fighting to maintain the control that Hiram Johnson had achieved by cleaning up the California government. When the dust bowl and the depression set off an invasion of newcomers into California, the Republicans devised a system of campaigning wherein they created the image that they knew would appeal to the voters and then brought in a candidate to fit it. The fabricating had little relationship to the fellow who happened to be running. When they advertised for a candidate for Congress, White said, the screening committee listened to five or six and decided that Nixon was the most suitable. And in the brutal assault that Nixon made on Jerry Voorhis, he gave evidence of what was being created.

Voorhis was as innocent a fellow as you could imagine. I served with him. He came into the House of Representatives confident that he could remake the world for the better. No more Communist than the man in the moon or any of the rest of us sitting around there. Around the House the story was that his father, a man of means, had wanted him to go into the family business, but the boy wanted to be a public servant and play a part in the regeneration of the nation. When they assaulted Jerry Voorhis, they pictured him as the greatest rascal that ever lived. They accused him of being a fellow traveler bent on the destruction of the people of California. They frightened the voters and beat him. This success convinced them that they were effective in shaping public opinion, and they enlarged on the operation and Nixon went on to become a national figure.

G.   The lies disillusioned young people. They are really going to have to build their own ideals.

D.   The question is whether or not they can do it. That's really the danger that hangs over us. The effectiveness of the deception was frightening.

F.   We should have expected it from the record.

D.   You may be right, but although I was not a Nixon supporter, I didn't believe that the charges against him, when they were first made, were true; I did not think that the scheming was anything like as deep and dangerous as the tapes finally revealed. You saw my letter to Sterling Cole who sought expressions from former House members. I thought the House Judiciary Committee should condemn Nixon's conduct as reprehensible, but I did not think he ought to be tried by the Senate. I didn't think he'd be convicted, and I thought then that a trial would tear the country to pieces; but when the final tapes burst on the people, they showed that not only had there been falsification of the record but he had been the leader.

I never supported Nixon. I had never been part of the Virginia Creepers, that branch of the national organization, the Committee to Re-elect the President. But until the tapes surfaced I didn't have any idea that he was really the danger that he was. I believed that he had been the victim of deceptive schemes for which he was not responsible. Now I did feel that his insistence upon the rights of the presidency were extreme, but I did not realize that he was insisting on them to cover up misdeeds.

F.   Throughout his career there is a vein. So often he used the phrase that an opponent was soft on Communism and this and that issue. You couldn't disagree with the hard line of Nixon without being an alien.

D.   That's true.

F.   A part of this country's strength has been the ability of people to dissent—

D.   Yes, and keep going—

F.   —and maintain self-respect and the respect of their neighbors. His attitude of knowing what was best was almost the divine right of kings.

D.   Yes, it was. He ferociously opposed anything that might divulge his own wrongdoing. He's bound to have known that what he was doing was wrong, but he was fiercely determined not to let it be disclosed to the American people, because they would never follow him down that road.

But I'll tell you big government is just dangerous. When I was on the review committee of the CIA no end of matters were "top secret." They put us under all kinds of oaths not to reveal these secrets that were at the very heart of America's security. But I saw papers stamped top secret that didn't amount to a hoorah. It would be like stamping top secret a remark by a member of the commission that he was going out to get a cup of coffee and would be back in a minute. The bureaucrats just stamped everything in sight. They didn't want anybody looking at anything. They just didn't want to be bothered. And that was one of the things that contributed to the difficulty that finally came to a head in Watergate.

G.   Did you see the TV documentary on the CIA? I had no idea how huge it is.

D.   Oh, it's tremendous, requiring gigantic sums of money! Congress would say it wanted to look at the records, and Allen Dulles would reply that if we opened the files to congressional investigation, we might as well shut down the CIA because we couldn't get agents around the world. Their names would become public and their lives put in jeopardy.

F.   Watergate was exposed, the courts went to work, and the system purified itself of these people. I hope hereafter more newspapers will be alert.

D.   Many newspapers did not feel that this terrible thing could happen.

F.   And newspapers ought to feel that anything can happen.

You know, Nixon just didn't seem to like people. The ordinary politician, whatever his shortcomings, feels that he can persuade and consult with them.

D.   But Nixon was a cool calculator against them, really. I'm not sure that if that crowd had stayed in, they wouldn't have tried to seize the United States government before they were through.

G.   They had gone far.

D.   And certainly beyond anything that I dreamed of. It never occurred to me that we had at the head of our government people who held in utter contempt our constitutional limitations.

G. What do you think they hoped to gain from all that—the power?

D. Yes, I think so.

G. What about the income tax evasions? They involved a lot of money.

D. Yes, Nixon was in real estating, too. They were not even money-honest, to use an old expression. I'm convinced that we were dealing with a group of people that would have swept aside the government as we have known it and set up a ruling machinery of their own that they controlled through television and other ways.

G. I think happiness really comes from how much effort you put in trying to do right. There's a certain contentment even if you are—

D. You mean inner contentment? I agree with you in that.

G. I've watched people who have really just labored, making things do and telling their children to do right. Some of the black parents of my schoolchildren have been treated miserably, but because they are honest and hardworking and haven't succumbed to violence or meanness, they seem to be as happy as anybody I see with a million dollars.

D. Or happier.

G. There's something about individuals like that. They have serenity.

D. I think that is based on the fact—and I believe it's quite true—that the struggle of life is won or lost within yourself. I mean, that's where the victory is achieved or the defeat is endured.

F. Some people, though, are adept at rationalizing and smoothing over with themselves the moral shortcuts.

D. Yes, I'll have to agree with you on that.

F. But you do meet individuals who have that serenity. Most people recognize it particularly if the person is in a position of leadership.

G. I never saw Dag Hammarskjöld, but it seems

to me that he was honestly trying to do the right thing, insomuch as I could follow his life.

F. I'm just skeptical enough about politicians—and that's what he was—but, no, I just wouldn't know. I haven't read enough about him.

D. I'm not sure. He was in the UN when I was there. I'd always felt about Hammarskjöld—and I've got no real reason to say this because I never knew him well, but I worked with him—that he was one of those individuals who was able to believe that because he thought it was right, it was, in truth, right. That what he wanted to do was in the best interest of the world, whether it was or not.

F. There was something of the zealot about him.

D. There was a good deal of the zealot about him.

G. Well, the only hero I found that you two have happens to be one that I think was rather self-indulgent—Mr. Jefferson!

D. Well, he was a little self-indulgent, but he had every right to be. I think this, I think he was extraordinary—

G. But he loved his comforts, he loved—

D. Oh, he did—

G. He went off and left his wife months and months. She was pathetic to me. And his gardens with all that flurry with all those slaves. And he had musicales and he did just what he enjoyed doing and when things got rough in Washington, he would come back to that mountain.

D. The one great thing in understanding Jefferson is to remember that he had Madison. Without Madison as a balance, Jefferson would have jumped the track. But Jefferson was a fearfully interesting person, and his great distinguishing mark, not that he was right in every instance, was that he had insatiable intellectual curiosity, and that's what we need.

If you want an illustration of it, get Jefferson's letter to his brother about how to run his farm. It's one of the most interesting and complicated documents you've ever read. He just lays it out in various sections, how to rotate crops and how to do that and this and the other. Now I expect his brother parked the letter in the wastebasket, because he was a much better farmer anyway.

The difference between Jefferson and John Marshall is most interesting. Marshall was superb in the simple knowledge that something had to work. You had to get the Union to a point where somebody would pay attention to it, and he thought that Jefferson was a visionary sort of fellow and he could not stand him because he regarded him as totally impractical. Now Marshall was very practical. They talk about the extension of the power of the Supreme Court. Nobody extended the court's power like Marshall did. All these latter-day fellows that have scared everybody to death are children stacked up against Marshall. But it so happens that he extended it in the right way. He had the native wit and intelligence to make it an instrument in the development of this country that has been without equal; and without it the country would have failed. It couldn't have made the grade. The real difference between Jefferson and Marshall is that Jefferson said it ought to be better and Marshall said it must work.

G.   I was fascinated by the biography of Marshall. One thing that interested me was that Marshall really never showed off with a house or anything of that sort.

D.   A touching aspect of Marshall was his deep attachment to his wife, who was an invalid many years. He looked after her with the utmost tenderness.

G.   I just wondered why the country has hailed Jefferson so much above Marshall.

D.   Now I don't know that it has!

G.   If you asked anybody to pick one person, don't you think he'd pick Jefferson?

D.   Yes, he would, but he certainly would not throw Marshall in the discard—

F.   No, people simply think of him second. He did a particular work. Jefferson ranged over everything.

D.   Yes, he doped out more things. As Randolph of Roanoke said, he built a plow that wouldn't work. Randolph, his distant relative and severe critic, took the view that if you listened to Jefferson, he'd have all the farms in the country growing weeds.

G.   I just don't want you all to leave Marshall too far out of the picture.

D. I've got him right up in the forefront, but you know for the first time in my life, I fear that this system of ours may not work; and it's so utterly unnecessary because when you consider the enormous resources of the American people, all they need is faith in themselves. If you could bind us together, what we could accomplish is beyond calculation.

ROME AND AMERICA

F. Governor, how do you feel about the disclosure that Henry Kissinger approved wiretapping as chief of the National Security Council?

D. I thought that the United States had a duty to tap to prevent disclosure of national secrets touching its security; but apparently this safeguard was embarrassing to Kissinger. I've always thought that his testimony before the Senate committee lacked frankness. This conclusion was reenforced by the memorandum found in J. Edgar Hoover's papers indicating that Kissinger wanted the checks made.

F. Commentators keep comparing him to Metternich.

D. That's partly self-promoted though, isn't it? Didn't he put the word out that he was Metternich's spiritual heir?

F. Is it fair to say that problems in Metternich's time lent themselves more readily to solutions because there was no threat of nuclear war?

D. Probably so. Not only that, there were not so many people to contend with nor so many widely scattered centers of power. But even at that, the Russian emperor's plan for restoring the ruling houses failed.

It's very interesting and very human. We always seek to reestablish the past, and, of course, in a fluid, moving society, even a slow-moving one such as was true in that day, you can't recreate the past with any degree of success. You are able to do better with the future if you know the past reasonably well, but most of such efforts founder because they are journeys into nostalgia. It's really a retreat into something that's thought to be known as against the unknown.

F. Artists deal with the past and when they recreate it, much of it is fantasy.

D. And when politicians do it, it's still fantasy. There's no better example than the volumes that have been written concerning the Roman Empire which followed the Roman Republic. So many people assume, and probably correctly, that the Roman Empire was a retrogression; but I'm not at all certain but that the Republic had reached a point where it couldn't be governed. Sentimentally, I share Cicero's views in the defense of the republic; but Rome's conquests and resulting expansion were made in large part under the republic. Rome the Republic destroyed Etruria after almost two hundred years of war, invaded England, stretched the frontiers toward the Tigris and Euphrates, and pushed them north beyond the Danube and the Rhine.

Emperor Trajan pushed the frontiers to the extreme limits in the hope of making the empire more stable and defensible; Hadrian, who followed him, determined to shorten the Roman lines to an area more easily defended.

Just as Rome found it difficult to function in the vast area it had won by arms, I am not sure that the United States, with its increasing centralization, can overcome the formidable obstacles it is beginning to encounter. However we have advantages that the Romans lacked. Most important, our basic freedoms have not eroded. We have uniformity of language, rapid transportation, almost instant communication with all parts of our holdings, and also a more secure position behind these great oceans. Maybe we can pull it off.

Rome extended ran up against bitter enemies. I don't think the republic that Cicero dreamed of and defended so eloquently and finally with his life was equal to the administrative burdens.

F. What was the essence of Cicero's republic? How do you define it?

D. The ancient lines of authority of the senate.

F. Cicero's republic, you said, was as he dreamed it.

D. He dreamed it as it was. I didn't mean that it was a creation of his own imagination to be superimposed upon the Roman people. Cicero saw the great days of Rome and the contributions made by individuals of rare worth and ability in administration. You take the Romans and their protection of the rights of married women and the protection of slaves. In a way it was an enlightened society. The Romans weren't the Greeks' equal in the arts, but when it came to government they were superior.

Cicero's idea was to continue a very fine system; but Rome had grown tired. Its citizens were disillusioned and suspicious, torn by internal war with factions fighting over the spoils of office and beset with official corruption, and exhausted by foreign conquest. Notwithstanding Cicero's admiration of republican institutions, the material with which he worked was not equal to the task. The great foundations put in place in stone could not be held together by putty.

F.   Didn't later events demonstrate that representative government would have done better against the forces attacking Rome than the imperial government did?

D.   That's a question that I don't think you can answer. The imperial system faltered, as it so often falters, because of corruption and inability at the top. If a greater number of the emperors had been of the caliber of Augustus, Trajan, and Hadrian, the empire would have fared better.

F.   Wasn't the loss of individual rights a calamity?

D.   Yes, the tragedy is that the loss was an abandonment by the citizens themselves. Life in the early republic was a far simpler, harder, more virtuous life than that which took its place in the later days of the republic. In the later days, the senate had grown rich and servile. Small farmers had disappeared in front of the great landowners who cultivated their properties with slaves imported from conquered countries. The structure had weakened within.

F.   Did the mistake lie in the republic's pushing its boundaries too far?

D.   Nobody knows. Certainly pushing the boundaries and including the conquered races made the problems of government much more difficult. Somewhat the same situation obtains with us. It's not as apparent, but the forces are at work. We have reached the point in the extension of power, affluence, and the bidding for various sectors of our people by use of public revenues that is not unlike the situation the Romans faced at the close of the republic. However, we have come on this not by conquest. Of course, the opening of the frontier was in part conquest. Witness the lands taken from the Indians, Mexico, and Spain.

F.   We are pulling back now.

D.   What you are witnessing is the retreat of the white race around the globe. The great voyages of Henry the Navigator and the Portuguese began the outward push that continued four hundred years until the early part of this century. The First World War marked the turning point in Western power, and the journey has been downhill ever since. Nobody knows where we will reach a point of stability.

F.   That mere size and numbers could defeat us is hard to accept. The representative government envisioned by the founders has procedures to correct itself as it goes wrong.

D.   That's a valid argument, and our children and grandchildren will see that answered. The corrective measures are beginning to work with us, but the violations had gone very deep in American society when you look at what happened to the presidency and some of the nation's top officers. The corrective machinery ought to have worked earlier. The idea of the imperial presidency is dangerous nonsense. It was appealing in a way to the American people because the Congress had just dillydallied so much that the average fellow in the street said if we were ever going to get anything done, the president had to do it. The desire to make the government more efficient was responsible in part for the concentration of power in the presidency. I don't know whether when this is over there will be a residue of virtue in our people sufficient to sustain representative government. Because representative government depends in the long run upon self-restraint and also upon a dedicated and virtuous citizenry.

F.   And upon a free, vigorous press. Much of the press is in danger of losing power through not using it.

D.   But after all, when we compare the press with what we've had in the past it looks pretty good. When you look at progress being made in many fields, there is not any reason to be too discouraged. The question is whether we have the wisdom to guard ourselves against the demagogues who, under the guise of helping the people, really undertake to help themselves.

F.   You were wondering whether there was a residue of virtue in the citizenry, saying that in the end any country's survival rests on the character of the individual citizen.

D.   In sum.

F.   What prompts you to wonder that?

D.   I don't know that I'd go so far as to say there's a loss of virtue. The public reaction to Watergate would indicate a very deep attachment to ancient virtues.

F.   Does sheer affluence engender corruption in a population as it does sometimes in an individual?

D.   I just don't know. The affluence is the outward sign of the rising standard of living which certainly you would wish for a people.

F.   We hear of Americans being soft, but many seem almost consumed by work.

D.   I don't think it's very widespread.

F.   Many in public service, for instance, put in long hours, and others who are just working for their livelihoods often are doing two jobs. The question of the affluent society, how hard we work, how we play, how much we consume—I wonder how much that contributes to a softness—

D.   I'm not sure that that has contributed to the softness. I am certain that the softness has occurred. For instance, let's go to Vietnam. It may be that the misstatements by the highest officials in the United States government have done more damage internally in the United States than the loss of Vietnam itself. It shook the confidence of millions of people.

F.   In college education, for instance, students, once they get in—that's difficult—may choose courses with far greater flexibility than we had.

D.   In that way they come out with a less good grounding than we did. The more effective illustration is in the public school system.

F.   It's hard for me to reconcile the hardness and easiness of schools because some college students today produce papers that would have been beyond most students in my generation. You hear that the courses are easier, and yet you see evidences of extremely persistent application.

D.   That's the encouraging part because if you can train even a limited number of very good minds you can push this system along.

F.   You mentioned the public school system. There

again I see evidence both ways. You know the Supreme Court has ruled that children have rights.

    D. I think the Supreme Court has gone a very long way toward making the public schools unmanageable.

    F. I'm not speaking of busing. The thrust of this age has been for "everybody doing his own thing." Well, of course, everybody can't do his own thing all the time.

    D. And live in an ordered society.

    F. Certainly can't do it to the exclusion of somebody else's rights; but the awakening to women's rights and to those of children and blacks and other minorities shows that the system is working and improving opportunities.

    D. I hope you're right, but I'll have to see much more evidence to be convinced that we can achieve the stability a society must have to function.

An interesting point in thinking about government is the restrictions on the rights of the individual. Many are necessary in providing for the general welfare. We have reached the point where life is going to be so circumscribed that the ordinary fellow walking around won't have any rights, really, except the right to have somebody in government decide whether he can do something or not. Unless we are careful, we are going to have an ordered society that's going to bear an alarming resemblance to a prison.

WOMEN'S RIGHTS

F.   Governor, what's your feeling about the Equal
Rights Amendment that equality of rights under the law should not
be abridged on account of sex?

D.   There isn't any question about the justice of
that. Moreover, the broadening interest of women in public life,
as well as other endeavors, will alter our civilization profoundly
within a generation or two.

I see two problems. First, their joining the work force has kept
them from being in the home where they're desperately needed.
The absence of parents is responsible in large part for the difficulties
encountered by children in recent years. That has to be mended, or
we are going to move into state-controlled centers for rearing children, which is not good because it makes for uniformity of thought
handed down from on high. However much money you spend on
day-care centers, I don't believe they can replace a mother. We must
set up, through subsidies where they're needed, the means to enable
the mother to remain with the children through their tender years.
We cannot turn the children over to the state without, in the end,
creating a society that would be unendurable.

The next objection is that the Equal Rights Amendment would
permit the government to use women in combat. When I look back
on that bloodbath at Verdun, I'm unwilling to leave any door open
that might lead to the induction of women into combat units.

F.   There's no intention they would be put in
combat. Most of the men inducted serve behind the lines, and, anyway, the next war might be so unconventional that everybody would
be in a combat zone.

D.   That's very likely. We probably have seen the
end of the mass armies moving across the world. I think it's going to
be struggles between populations and women would suffer dread-
fully just as they did in the bombing of London.

F.   From the age of five a child is in school much of the day, anyway, and many women put off working outside the home until their children enter school. A way could be found to care for some of them an additional two or three hours a day after school to free their mothers, where necessary.

D.   I don't believe that's something that's beyond our reach at all, and you will bring into the work force an influence that's going to improve American life. To do it will take a generation or two, but it will happen because in sheer wisdom women are the superior. They simply have more sense than do men. That's the reason that the henpecked men get along so well, if you look around. Most of the husbands in Virginia are henpecked, and the state's better off by reason of it!

Women are more deliberate in another way, too. They have had to fight from a weak vantage point through life. Their struggle has been against great odds. Consequently they have had to use their minds more than do men, who use brawn and rudeness and kick people out of the way and keep going. Women deploy their strengths more effectively than do men. A society led by women would in the long run, I believe, be a better one than that which we have had over the centuries. There's no question but that their full participation would be beneficial. You talk about arms limitation agreements, the present conversations with Russia would pale into insignificance compared with what would be brought about by women were they in charge of the governments of the world. You'd find far less jumping to a gun than you find with men.

An outstanding example occurred at the war conference called by the Persians after they had overrun Athens and the Athenians had fallen back on their fleet. The only one of Xerxes' captains to object to an attack on the fleet as being too dangerous was a woman, Artemisia, the queen of one of the tribes associated with the Persians. Leave them alone, she advised. They overrode her counsel, attacked them, and lost.

F.   In nature the male has been the more aggressive, the hunter, while the female rears the young. Does that contradict your view of what we should do as human beings?

D.   No, it does not for the reason that in the human race you have a higher level of intelligence. The bodily strength, the brawn and muscle mankind needed over the centuries are now not so much needed as are the brains to operate the machines that we have created. You don't need the hunter in the sense that the Eskimo or the Indian has been the hunter. What you need is an order of intelligence high enough to utilize our best resources and in that the women are certainly the equal and in many cases the superior of men.

In these years that we have lived through, women have built a power base. You are going to see their increasing influence on public and private affairs in a way that we wouldn't have dreamed even a few years ago.

F.   The women members in the General Assembly seem to vote more on the merits of issues than do the men.

D.   The constitutional guarantee that they shall stand equal is absolutely sound and will result in an improved society. It also will prevent any state's denying them rights to which they are entitled.

When I grew up on a farm in Southampton County and went to public school, I assumed that the laws were immutable and mankind was on a set, steady course with a fair wind and it was simply moving on. Of course, that attitude reflected my lack of knowledge, and as I've grown older, I've come to realize that we are a part of eternal ferment and that's what makes life. It is perpetual change. It's not only change for progress, it's a change to escape boredom that the human race struggles with. Something different . . . something else. It's the constant struggle for change and for betterment that sweeps this current of humanity on around the world.

In later years I've seen so much of it that I know now that change—not serenity and peace and quiet—is the constant in human affairs. Change is the constant, and if you are prepared for that, you are not so shocked by the changes that don't go to suit you.

I remember an incident that offended me so deeply, and yet it didn't shock me because I had come to accept change. Do you recall when several University of Virginia students carried the North Vietnamese flag marching in an antiwar demonstration in Richmond? I don't know anything that irked me more than that; and yet it was not unexpected. It did not surprise me, because I had long before come to understand—at least I think I understand—that change is the normal state.

Not all change is good. Change that comes as a revolt against boredom may not be for the good. The idea of change and progress always being the same is one of the great illusions of mankind. Often they are not the same at all.

One of the most enlightening comments on people's attitude toward change came from Imogene Coca many years ago on a radio program. Some learned people were expounding about the great improvement that time and change had wrought, and the announcer said, "Miss Coca, what do you think about change?"

"I'm agin it even if it's for the better!" she said.

F. Most of the fears the opponents raise about the Equal Rights Amendment seem groundless. Common sense says that you are not going to have joint restrooms. That doesn't lie in the law; that lies in the customs of society.

D. I'm such an advocate of the guarantees that women want that it pains me that I'm not able to overcome one objection. I simply would not permit any government, if I had a hand in it, to be able to commit women to combat. It simply would be a downgrading of civilization.

F. They might argue that if they are going to have access and influence in all other aspects of human endeavor that they also should take part in the one that is the last stronghold of barbarism.

D. I think theoretically you are right. But those who'd be the foot soldiers and who would be slaughtered are not going to make policies. We are putting women in a position to make policy. I want to say to the government: Give women all the rights that you give men. You can do everything in the world for them, but you are not going to commit them to combat and you are not going to do it because they are women. That's my song, as the fellow says, and that's what I'd stand or fall on.

After all, you can't fail to realize that women are now exerting an increasingly broad influence on American affairs, and that's going to continue to increase and it's going to improve conditions.

F. As their influence becomes more pervasive, it doesn't make any difference what we say anyway about the amendment, because they soon will have the strength to get what they want.

D. I quite agree with that. That's the reason the amendment probably isn't really of any great consequence. You are developing a political system in which within a few years they will stand superior to the men. You think of their influence on business and the social structure of this country. They are going to alter it tremendously in the next fifty years.

F.   Wonder how long it will be before there's a woman president?

D.   Oh, I think in fifty years.

F.   I think it will be before that.

D.   Might easily be. Might be in the next twenty-five years.

F.   I was thinking we might see one in the next ten or fifteen.

D.   I would guess not likely. You will see it as soon as the parties feel that they can rally around one that they can elect.

F.   You might see one become vice-president and then succeed to the presidency.

D.   Oh, I hadn't thought about that. That might well happen any time.

F.   And when you think back on some of the presidents we've had, there's no doubt but what countless women would have been far better.

D.   There's no doubt about that. An example is one of our most popular presidents. Mrs. Roosevelt would have made a far abler president than Franklin Roosevelt when it came down to sheer ability and stability. But you don't have to go that far afield. Think of the secretaries whom you encounter who are sharper and more decisive than the men for whom they work. Over forty years' association with my secretary, Sue Whetstone, has convinced me of that.

F.   Governor, the women themselves are divided over ERA. Some think that you shouldn't send women into combat; but others believe they should have the amendment without reservation, just as there are no exceptions in the amendment guaranteeing free speech. That comes along in court interpretations. They say they are as durable and patriotic as men and therefore—

D.   No question about their being as patriotic as men. It's my belief that war is a fearfully brutalizing influence, and I would discriminate for that reason and for the welfare of the race regardless of how much hell they raised about it or anything else.

I'd simply say no government's going to commit them, if I can help it. Now, of course, if there was a mass move and they voted overwhelmingly to have it, they'd sweep the opposition aside, but I'm not going to make it easier for them. I'm opposed to it, absolutely opposed to it, because I think we'd be striking down a civilizing influence in our society that's worth far more than the simple statement that women have the right to bear arms and fight. Does that make my point clear? I'm talking about the fact that they're not going to be lined up in a killing operation and turned loose on each other, if I can help it.

ROOTS

F. Governor, *Roots*—the book and television show—has had considerable impact.

D. I didn't read the book or see the show. In the first place I can't read so much now, and in the next place slavery to me just is an unalloyed evil. That's all there is to it and to tie it down to any point in man's history is nonsense. It is an evil that is as old as the human race.

The first assignment given me at the United Nations was to sit in a group investigating the charges of slavery against the Arabs trading down the east coast of Africa where they had dealt in slaves for centuries. The African chiefs would round these people up and sell them, perhaps because they weren't able to feed them. Information indicated that they were well treated in Arab homes—if anybody who is in bondage can be well treated.

F. I didn't read *Roots* or see the show either, but I have been reading narratives by ex-slaves in Virginia, *Weevils in the Wheat.* In 1937 the WPA sent interviewers to talk with former slaves. Their direct testimony is gripping. Slaves, of course, couldn't leave the plantations without passes from their masters. Patrollers rode around the countryside at night, and if they caught a black without a pass, they gave him "thirty and nine" lashes.

D. There also was harsh legislation against teaching slaves. Here the Founders were carrying on the educational plans that were to shape the world and cutting out a whole race of people from taking part in the government!

In Southampton County after all these years there is feeling against a native son, General George Thomas, who fought with the Union. You get little ripple effects of it. One thing that they say accounts for Thomas's failure to join the Confederacy was that as a boy he taught slaves at a little school on his father's farm.

F. You'd think that feeling would have faded by this time.

D. It really gives you an idea of how enduring has been the prejudice.

F. The beatings were terrible. Some owners, for instance, took turns whipping a runaway all day and then threw him over in blackberry vines and when his people reached him he was dead. There are stories of black men having to stand to one side while the overseer or the master abused their wives.

D. These are evidences of the unspeakable outrages of human slavery. I remember my father saying to me, "You ought never to forget that the War Between the States set free more white people than it did blacks." The more I've thought about it, the surer I am he was right; actually there aren't any free people in a slave society. Neither master nor slave is free.

F. Slavery was a terrible penalty in so many ways. Some of these accounts make Greek tragedy seem pale. So often a person can recognize rationally that slavery is cruel, but only when he learns the details does he get the full impact. That may account for the intense reaction to *Roots*.

D. Maybe so, maybe so. How do you account for slavery's existing so long before it reached a boiling point that brought a war? Slavery was just as objectionable in 1810 and 1815 and 1820. Why did it take until 1860 for it to break out into war?

F. Didn't the resistance to it after a period begin to intensify steadily?

D. Certainly that was true in Virginia. Think of what could have happened in the development of this country if the first slaves hadn't been landed here. Europeans who were good farmers would have gone into the southern territories where the land was well suited for agriculture instead of moving along in the West and in the colder sections of the North.

F. Even though the Europeans did not come into the South, had the slaves been able to start as indentured servants—

D. —as many whites did

F. —they could have made their own way and contributed a great deal.

D. They could have made their own way and also

they could have made their way into other sections of the country when living conditions in one section weren't good.

Few of my friends agree, but I believe that Nat Turner's insurrection—even though a limited number of people were killed—was infinitely more far-reaching than has ever been thought. Had it not occurred, the War Between the States might have been avoided. The high tide of opposition in Virginia to slavery came in the 1830s with Governor Floyd. He had stated in his diary that he intended to set Virginia on a course of the prohibition of slavery. In the General Assembly the antislave forces were led by Thomas Jefferson Randolph, Jefferson's grandson.

When the 1831 Assembly was elected, a tremendous movement against slavery was underway. There were more societies against slavery in Virginia than in any other state. When you think about it, you see the reason. Virginia was the largest state; it swept to the Ohio River. Once you passed the Blue Ridge and got in the Alleghenies and went west, animosity toward the slaveholding east in Virginia was very deep. All that area was fertile ground for organizations condemning slavery, not only because many people out there disapproved of slavery but also because an even larger number believed that it had been used as a weapon to hold them in captivity politically.

The Convention of 1829–30, probably the ablest political crowd ever gathered in Virginia, had allowed the east to count three-fifths of the slave population in making up the total as a basis for representation. The west bitterly opposed it. They wanted manhood suffrage without any slave representation. When the constitution was submitted for ratification, it was overwhelmingly defeated in the west but was adopted by the support in the east. So that coming along after the Virginia Constitutional Convention, the legislators assembled for the 1831 General Assembly with a majority against slavery; but then Nat Turner's insurrection broke in fury over Southampton County and shocked the South. All the slave states had become uneasy about revolt among their slaves. Even little fights were magnified and thought to be incipient revolution. They were scared to death, as all people are of those whom they hold in slavery.

Well, that storm broke, and despite that Thomas Jefferson Randolph came within a few votes in getting through the Assembly a bill which would have set in motion the liquidation of slavery and the withdrawal of Virginia from the slave states. Now had Randolph won, the determination to have done with the institution would have put Virginia in position where it would not have thrown its weight with the seceding states thirty years later. I don't believe anybody could have pulled it over there, and I don't think that Lincoln would have been pushed to call for troops to put down secession because Virginia could have done for the Union what it did in 1832 when South Carolina was threatening nullification against the imposition of unfair tariffs. Virginia sent a delegation to South Carolina and said, "We love you dearly, but we are not going to leave the Union. We are willing to use our influence and do whatever we can to get an amelioration of the tariff." The northern forces conceded.

Now that would have happened in 1861, in my opinion. And you'd have had a resolution of the problem. Just think! My God! You could have bought and freed the slaves at a fraction of what the war cost. Now I'm not talking about the incalculable losses of the killed and the wounded, orphaned and widowed. I'm simply talking about what it cost in money to carry on the grim and terrible fight.

F. Had Virginia eliminated slavery, it would have done in the nineteenth century as great a service as the founders did in the eighteenth century.

D. Certainly as great because slavery was the Achilles heel of the American venture.

F. Even had there been a war, had Virginia been on the side of the Union, with Robert E. Lee and Lincoln working together—

D. It wouldn't have lasted two weeks!

F. Of course, even if Randolph's basic motivation was humanitarian, politically he was wise in emphasizing the economic aspect. I don't think he would have made as much ground appealing solely to humanitarian feelings.

D. No, I don't think so either; but then also, he was an intelligent, well-educated man. He had an overview of American institutions. It was so apparent that the miserable venture was a failure. Only a few people were slaveholders in Virginia anyway. The great mass of whites was as poorly treated by the institution almost as the slaves themselves.

F. But many plantation owners were profiting through breeding slaves. We had become a breeding state.

D. There again, that was not consequential measured against the economy of the entire state. The slaves were concentrated in the east. That was the basis of the bitter hostility of the west. Left unsettled, that might well have caused a civil war in Virginia itself.

F. Even more basic than the system's inefficiency was that it was just inhuman.

D. No question about that, but it didn't take the North to bring that home. That was known in Virginia.

F. It was known, but apparently it wasn't felt to the extent that it led people to throw it off. I know we came close with Thomas Jefferson Randolph. And perhaps the humanitarian motive was the basic drive with him, as it was with Jefferson.

D. I don't believe there is any doubt that is true; but the humanitarian aspect was reenforced by the recognition that slavery was a fiercely wasting thing in the economic life of the state.

F. The effect of Nat Turner's rebellion raises an interesting question. Rebellion against tyranny was Jefferson's chief vow. Yet in his own state a people were absolutely tyrannized. A few rebelled and it cost them their lives and perhaps cost their people additional years in servitude. Should they not have rebelled? Was Nat Turner wrong in principle, as well as tactics as it turned out?

D. I don't know that he was wrong in principle because you can certainly make a case for rebellion against any terrible injustice such as that, but certainly in tactics he was mistaken. Had the insurrection not taken place, Virginia would have set out on the course of the gradual liquidation of slavery.

F. I have read that some blacks feel defensive about their ancestors' remaining in captivity with few efforts to rebel.

D. That is nothing for their descendants to be ashamed of. The Negro people had hardly any opportunity to rebel.

Going back to your question about the tactics, I think the insurrection was as costly as the launching of the British Light Brigade in the Crimea at Balaklava against the Russians straight into those guns massed against them. It was a magnificent example of courage. Certainly nothing else can be said for it.

F. Of course, Turner was launching his assault against the entire white population.

D. And not only that, the white population of Virginia and the other southern states was on guard constantly against a revolt.

F. The individual resistance blacks put up all over the South, the indignities they bore, and the bravery they showed are as heroic a chronicle of human endurance as we will ever see.

D. I think so too.

F. It was just impossible to organize a successful rebellion. They couldn't read, couldn't write, had no way of communicating from plantation to plantation, much less from one state to another. I don't think that any race in such bondage could have started a successful revolt.

D. Nor do I.

F. The revolution in 1776 was based so much on communication, wasn't it? Writing and speaking?

D. Yes.

F. And very little fighting.

D. Not much, no. But let me tell you. When you look at this thing and see it going back to the distinction, which isn't a great one, between the economic pressure and the humanitarian pressure, bear this in mind—the humanitarian pressure was there from the beginning when the framers of the Constitution banned the importation of slaves after twenty years. Humanitarian pressure brought that about, and yet war didn't break out until over half a century later. So humanitarian reasons alone didn't bring about the fighting in 1861. The desire of the northern states, expanding westward, to break the political grip of the slave states had much to do with it. If the humanitarian urge had been as powerful as it is often claimed, the war would have come much earlier, probably at the time of the Missouri Compromise in 1820. It was when the two came together that you got the explosion.

F. Suppose the war had come in 1820?

D. The South would have won it—which would have been a tragedy. For one thing, we would have been gobbled up by a foreign power within a few years.

F. The reason that the humanitarian motive wasn't stronger may have been because relatively so little was known throughout the country and even within the South as to what was happening to the slaves.

D.   That's probable, but I'm not sure that there was as little known as you seem to think. There was a good deal of transfer of information. And yet the statutes penalizing those who wanted to teach the blacks indicated that the South was desperately afraid of their being able to read and write.

F.   To pick up a book was almost the worst sin a black could commit.

D.   Yes, and the worst a white could do was try to teach him to read.

F.   In this book are stories about white parents discovering their children teaching their black playmates to read, and the parents whipping both the white and the black children. So the whites knew the danger of the blacks' learning to communicate.

D.   Communicate! No question about that.

F.   I don't believe that there was communication enough among the whites themselves, not only in the North but in the South as well, for many to comprehend fully the barbarities practiced on some plantations.

Slavery should have weighed as heavily on the conscience of the South as we expected concentration camps to trouble Germany and Russia. The general population was not forced to think about slavery. It could look away.

D.   I don't believe that the general population could look away from it. I think it knew far more about slavery than the Germans and Russians knew about slave camps. But it all goes back to the time fuse that ends in slavery's ultimate destruction, and that is, the institution itself is bitterly wrong. That's what destroyed it, and I don't believe that's necessarily a part of Christianity either. I think that men knew long before the birth of Christ that slavery was wrong and they wanted to end it because they saw what happened to themselves and their families and others.

F.   A friend of mine, a decent person who likes order, is outraged at the television portrayal of slavery in *Roots*. No good purpose is served in telling people in detail what went on in that time, he contends. All it does is stir unrest among the blacks. That sort of thing is best put behind us, he says.

D.   It may well be that it is best put behind us, but

certainly I would not say that it is wise that we not know it. There you come face to face with a fundamental issue about people trying to manage their own affairs. How do they do it unless they know what has happened?

F.   A few years ago a former legislator was engaged in a project to help the blacks in Norfolk, going to meeting after meeting. He complained that they couldn't settle down to resolve their present plight until they had told him everything that had happened to them since 1619.

The more you reflect on it, the more understandable it is that they wished to show what they had endured and why they are in a dilemma.

D.   That certainly is understandable. However, our sympathy must not be permitted to obscure the need for rigorous training and imaginative education so that they may share in our industrial society.

F.   Some years ago a black militant demanded that the government make reparations to the black race for its years of deprivation. Now that seemed exaggerated to me, unnecessarily inflammatory; but when I read of what they went through, the idea has a practical aspect. There are reparations among nations for war. So here within our own nation was a massive population that—

D.   Yes, but what we have been doing for some time is paying a tremendous reparation in our efforts to educate and help move the blacks forward. Also, remember that the start of this institution, as far as we are concerned, was a joint undertaking between the tribal leaders and the merchants and captains who sold them into slavery, so that the whites were by no means entirely responsible for the difficulties the blacks encountered.

F.   We shouldn't feel guilty personally about something in which we had no hand. It simply is a matter of recognizing the injustice of what was done here. Whether or not it started with connivance of blacks in Africa, it continued on plantations in Virginia.

D.   That's right, but a fabulous amount has been done in the last one hundred years, and more especially in the last fifty years, to rectify that.

F.   But it is infinitesimal compared to the wrongs done them and the remedies that need to be done. Furthermore, much of the reform within the past twenty-five years has been ordered by the federal courts. It was not done out of any matter of conscience by most of the states.

D. That's certainly true.

F. As I look back there was more logic in what that black fellow said than I was prepared to see, although his scheme, of course, wasn't workable. Not enough white people are willing to recognize the enormity of the abuse, like my friend who wants to forget it all.

D. Yes, but forgetting doesn't solve the problem. I don't think the militant's plan is workable, nor do I think it reasonable. It does not balance out all of the inequities, by any means, if in truth there can be any balancing out of inequities in slavery.

Going back to your friend saying that all that has to be forgotten, you don't just forget it and move along because you come face to face with a group of people who haven't a bit of knowledge of what olden times were and who create a picture of the past that never existed. The important thing is to understand the difficulties through which the human race has passed, and you don't understand them unless you know the past, because you wouldn't paint them in their true somber color. They always want to talk about the good old times.

F. Everybody sitting around picking a banjo and eating a watermelon. That's their view of it.

D. That's exactly right! Hell, there's nothing you can do with people like that!

F. Slavery to them was a benign institution.

D. Best thing that ever happened. Just so long as they didn't happen to be a slave.

My father wasn't opposed to educating colored people, but he said, "These people running around talking about educating the black people and holding them in subjection just don't know what they are talking about." And that's absolutely true.

F. That was it. The blacks understood intuitively that books were the—

D. Key!

ALMOST A GOLDEN AGE

D.   The country is at a perilous place today, and it has been brought to that point in part by a deep desire to improve the lot of the human race. That desire has led us at times to attempt what is beyond our capacity. That, combined with the fact that we have fallen prey occasionally to demagogues who have used that worthy objective for their own selfish purposes. These dangerous individuals are explained by something I read many years ago; that all dictatorship stems either from a person who proclaims himself the defender of the common man or one who calls himself the vicar of God Almighty. In those two categories are found all the oppressors of mankind. But that does not mean that the yearning to benefit the human race is not sound and desirable and isn't based on sentiments that are altogether good. It's important that we bear in mind that this worthy sentiment is not infrequently abused.

F.   And they pick for their vehicles—

D.   The two impulses that most appeal to the human race: the love of God and the love of their fellow human beings.

Our present difficulties—and certainly there never have been people more generous than are the American people—come from a miscalculation of our resources. We have in recent years undertaken to do things beyond our capacity in a desire to create almost a golden age on earth. That doesn't come quickly, if in truth it ever comes.

F.   Governor, don't you think that for a long time we believed literally there was nothing we couldn't do?

D.   No question about that. Only in the last few years, and more especially with the stunning defeat in Vietnam, have we come to a realization that there are commitments beyond our grasp and power.

F.   Don't you also believe that seeing what we had done and being mortal and prone to error, we had fairly good cause to think that we could do anything we wanted to do?

D.   No, I don't think so. We were reading it wrong, and we were doing so because we wanted to believe it, not because anything in history undergirded the thought, because nothing in history does support it.

F.   Considering that we had—as many Americans interpreted it—saved Europe in the First World War, and then we had gone back during the lifetime of many of our people and had done as much in World War II, or more, because then we had defeated Japan, too, many Americans, I guess, thought that nothing was beyond us.

D.   Yes, but that was a great miscalculation. It's true that in the First World War we threw the balance of American power with the Allies when they were exhausted, as was Germany. That balance turned the tide, but we didn't begin to make the sacrifices that the French and the English and, for that matter, the Russians had made. Technically we tipped the balance, but it's not fair to say that we won the war. The manpower and industrial might of the United States, thrown into the balance, brought the First World War to a successful conclusion. Again in the Second World War, the enormous resources of the United States made the difference; but we gathered from that the impression of unilateral power which never really existed.

I remember talking to one of the top commanders in the air force after the Second World War. He said, "I'm retiring. I don't want to live through another war because we are not going to win the next one. We can't do it."

That seemed so forbidding at the time that I found it hard to believe, but I am inclined to think that fellow was more nearly right than I realized.

F.   I don't think any nation has had any more reason to think it was invincible than we did.

D.   That may be true, but it was a dreadful mistake. It grew not out of selfishness, but from a reckless overconfidence. We were never able to comprehend how very great had been the contribution of those with whom we allied ourselves.

F.   Because of the part we played we just assumed

that in a clutch we could throw ourselves into any situation and resolve it. I think we could have done it in Vietnam had we cared to pay the price to risk what would follow. And it seems to me that what has changed the game, so to speak, is atomic power. We no longer can engage in a major war with any assurance of containing it.

         D.   Yes, that's true; but I would agree with you on Vietnam in one way only. I think we could have won easily in Vietnam had we been willing to resort in the beginning to the drastic and brutal measures necessary to wipe out Hanoi and Haiphong without regard to their civilian population. We would have achieved immediate victory; whether it would have lasted or not is another question, but our idea of waging war within limits was tactically wrong.

The old German generals probably were correct in their theory that once you resort to war you must use all the power at your disposal to win and win quickly. That was the basis in the Second World War of the panzer drive that crushed France in 1940. Maybe we were right in not utilizing our full power, which means we shouldn't have been there in the first place.

That was what the French realized when they liquidated their commitments there and in North Africa. It was cold realism. The French were good soldiers. There were never any better soldiers than the French in the First World War. I never have seen anything to equal the bravery of the French troops at Verdun. I saw them die there. We hauled them back from the lines by the hundreds. The commonest wound was a bullet through the stomach that the doctors then couldn't deal with. I never heard one of the French wounded whimper during the slaughter that went on there.

But going back to Vietnam, we believed that the air force with intensive bombing could bring the enemy to their knees, but we never were willing to move against the cities and bomb the vital places. And that was where, in the end, we lost. And then, too, the dependence on very sophisticated weapons broke down with us just as it broke down with the French. Did you ever read Bernard Fall's *Hell in a Very Small Place?*

It is beautifully written. The theory of the concentration of French troops at Dien Bien Phu was based on the thought that with modern weapons they could destroy the hordes moving against them. Also, that the terrain was so bad that the Communists would never be able to haul heavy guns across the mountains and bring them to bear on the French troops in the plain. The encampment there was envisioned as a bait for the Vietnam armies; it proved to be a trap for the French. Many French officers opposed the strategy, but they were overruled and the ruse was tried. The man who commanded the French artillery killed himself after he saw that his calculation was not working and that the Vietcong not only were able to pull their large guns over the mountains but could not be destroyed by the French artillery when they moved out into the plains. That kind of perseverance, which comes from a race of people who are convinced that they are being oppressed by another race, is universal.

The most damaging aspect of the Vietnamese War lies in another direction. Many believe that we witnessed in the Vietnam venture a coalition between certain military and political leaders to deceive the American people. It wasn't just the fighting, it was the conviction of the people themselves that they had been deeply deceived that was devastating. We have to be sure that we or our children and grandchildren don't fall victim to that again because it might come at a time when we won't get out of the trap. The preposterous reports of the body counts supported the people's distrust. There never was any challenge of the authority of the civil government by the military establishment, but there was a terrifying willingness of some of the military to collaborate with some in the civil government in deceiving the American people.

The deception shattered—to a degree that few understand—the confidence of the ordinary fellow on the street in the government of the United States and in the high command of the military. Our basic illness is the people's deep distrust of our political system, and to this Vietnam made a deadly contribution.

F. You could take another view: because the deception had been uncovered and because to a degree, after a long time, the system had worked and purged itself, we realize, as you said, we have to be careful. We are in a healthier state than we have been in a long time. I see it more as an awakening to realities. That we must be vigilant.

D. It goes back to an ancient saying that you heard as a schoolboy, that eternal vigilance is the price of liberty.

The fifteen or twenty years around the Vietnamese War demonstrated that beyond a doubt.

Now you didn't have that in the Second World War. It grew out of the Vietnamese struggle which at the outset seemed rather simple and easy, given the enormous power of the United States. When things started to go against us, our leaders simply were not willing to face up to the necessity of telling the people.

F.   So there was the long deception and then the exposure that reached right up to the White House.

D.   It had to reach to the top or it couldn't have occurred. But I do agree that we are in a healthier state, much healthier than we have been in some time. The question is whether or not, with all of that information, we are able to get back on firm ground. One factor that makes it very difficult is that the American people, while they love to talk of sacrifices, have rarely been forced to make them. And they are not given to them. Many regard going without a cup of coffee in the morning for a day or two as being a great sacrifice. It is something more than that—much more than that.

What we must do is to assume the increasing social responsibilities of society and be willing to pay for them. Otherwise, the whole structure falls apart. Our political institutions will be destroyed, and what follows will be an authoritarianism that is awfully rugged and selfish. Does that get into your noggin?

F.   I like that. It goes back to what I've noticed. You persist in trying to reshape and reform conditions, all the time professing to be skeptical of the results.

D.   Well, that's true. I am skeptical of our ability to achieve the goal, but I have faith in mankind's ability to do it.

F.   I just never knew anybody before to labor as hard at remedying wrongs while having so little expectation that the remedies will work.

D.   That may be true, but that is the fact of the case. The odds are great against us, but remember that mankind, in its present form, has been on the earth some millions of years. If you draw on the wall behind you a long line to represent that span, and place the 5,000 or 10,000 years for which we have some record at the end of the line, it would be a pencil point.

Now suppose our efforts don't succeed fully. Man up to now has not shown evidence of being able to govern himself for long sustained periods. The Greeks, who were as shrewd and capable a race as we have seen, were not able to do it. That does not mean that long before the heat gives out and the earth is a drifting cinder man will not have achieved a plan that will work.

Isn't it much better to work to that end than to sit and just grouch and growl and do nothing? That's the choice. Either you are going to try to make it go along or you are going to say it can't be done and give up. And, of course, the temptation in old age, especially when you get arthritis as I have now, is to say to yourself, "Hell, I'm tired. I'm tired of it."

But the truth is that is not the answer. You have to keep up the struggle, because somewhere down the line, maybe a very long way down the line—the two hundred years that we are celebrating now are inconsequential in the long sweep of history—mankind is going to put together a civilization that's going to work. Wouldn't you agree to that?

    F. Yes, sir. I agree.

    D. All right. Well, let's write that down, close our book, and call it a day.

Index

INDEX

Southwest Virginia, 117–18, 122, 144
Soviet Union, 138, 140, 141
Spong, William B., Jr., 59–60, 149
Sports, 16
Stanley, Thomas, 67, 75, 134, 150, 157, 158, 161, 162, 165, 197
Steel, Anthony, 136
Steel, Mrs. Anthony (Aileen), 136
Stephens, A. E. S., 68
Stevenson-Sparkman campaign, 45
Stuart, Henry Carter, 151
Submarine warfare, 90
Sullivan, Neil, 177
Supreme Court, 218, 225; *Brown* v. *Board of Education*, 157, 162, 163, 164; *Plessy* v. *Ferguson*, 157
Swanson, Claude, 61, 78

Talbot, Ralph, 26–27, 29
Taxation, 40–42, 47, 211–12
Tax credit act, 199
Thomas, George, 232
Thomas Jefferson Award, 127
Thompson, William, Sr., 117
Trajan, 221, 222
Trinkle, E. Lee, 53
Truman, Harry, 93–95, 140–42, 146–47
Truxton, Walke, 61
Tuck, William, 62–65, 67, 74, 77, 111, 124, 168, 169, 196
Tucker, Ellis, 18
Tucker, St. George, 78
Tuition grants, 157, 158, 162
Tumulty, Joseph, 53
Turner, Nat, 164, 234, 236, 237

Underwood, Cecil, 147
United Nations, 20, 137–42, 144
United States Navy, 71–72
University of North Carolina, 104
University of Virginia, 95–96, 187; administration, 106–8; admissions policy, 110–11, 114–15; building program, 124; classical languages, 17; Copeley Hill village, 107; enrollment, 106; extension courses, 117, 118; fraternities, 16, 111–13;

landscaping, 125–26; law school, 115; public schools and, 104, 110–11, 114; School of Business Administration, 125–27; science education, 17–18; sports, 16; student government, 108, student life, 15–19; student union (Newcomb Hall), 109, 111, 112; veterans at, 106–7; Whipple expulsion, 81–82; women students, 114–15
Urbanization, 171, 172
Utility rates, 201–2

Vandenberg, Arthur, 52
Vanden Heuvel, William J., 176, 177
Verdun, 22–24, 243
Veterans Act, 30
Veterans' bonus, 53, 58
Vietnam, 142, 224, 241, 243–45
Vinogradoff, Sir Paul, 32
Vinson, Carl, 59
Vinson, Fred M., 52
Virginia: Corporation Commission, 81, 201–2; debt policy, 46–48, 96, 97; Department of Education, 90; governorship, 64–68; "pay-as-you-go" policy, 46, 47, 48; Probation and Parole Board, 91; public policy, 40–41; redistricting, 50; State Board of Education, 180, 185; state government reorganization, 170; tolls, 46, 48; university system, 95; urban vs. rural power base, 170–71
Virginia Advisory Legislative Council, 91
Virginia Beach, 171
Virginia Constitution, 46–47, 86–88, 104, 117, 183–85, 189–90
Virginia Manufacturers Association, 170
Virginians, 46, 48, 90, 94, 164, 173, 202
Virginia Organization, 10, 37–49, 61, 64–70, 73, 77–80, 82–85, 88, 149, 153–54, 164, 167–70, 181, 183, 184
Virginia State College, 95
Voorhis, Jerry, 213